SHONEN JUMP MANGA

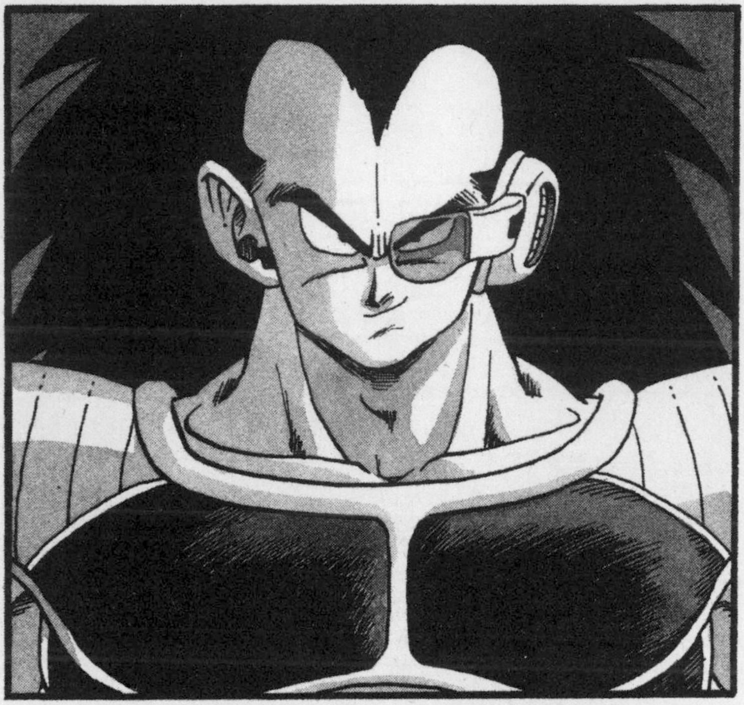

DRAGON BALL Z

Vol. 1

DB: 17 of 42

STORY AND ART BY
AKIRA TORIYAMA

Piccolo

Goku's arch-enemy, Piccolo *Daimaô* ("Piccolo the Great Demon King") once tried to become ruler of the world. Finally the score was settled at the Tenka'ichi Budôkai, the world fighting tournament, where Goku fought Piccolo five years before this story begins.

Raditz

This mysterious warrior is the most powerful foe Goku—or *anyone* on Earth—has ever encountered.

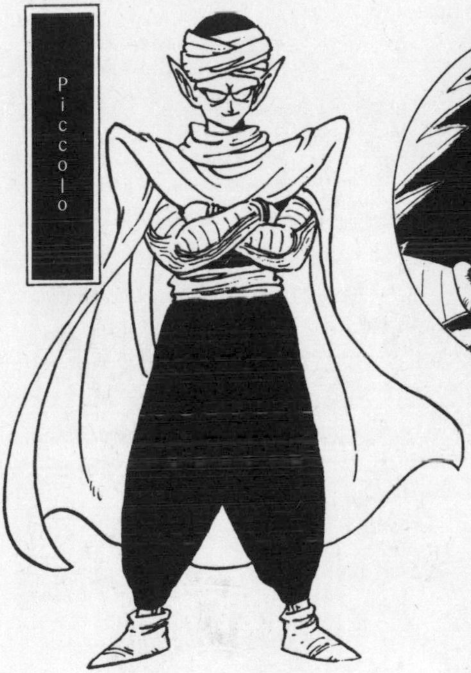

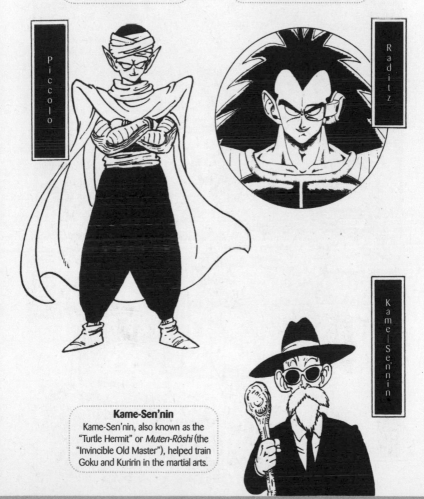

Piccolo

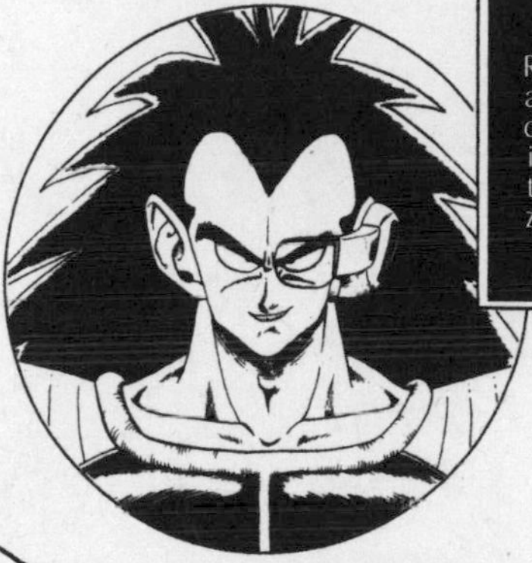

Raditz

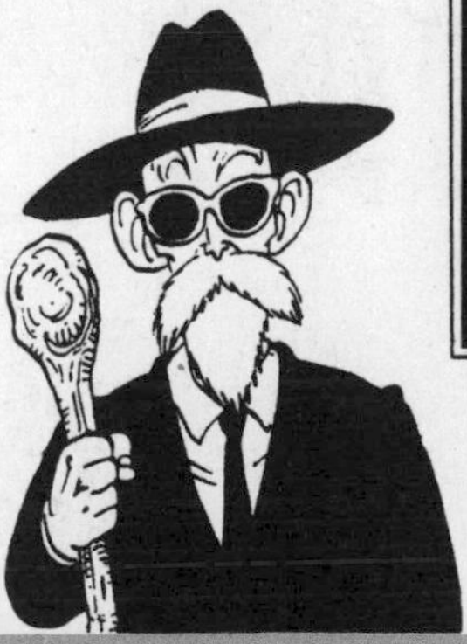

Kame-Sen'nin

Kame-Sen'nin

Kame-Sen'nin, also known as the "Turtle Hermit" or *Muten-Rôshi* (the "Invincible Old Master"), helped train Goku and Kuririn in the martial arts.

THE MAIN CHARACTERS

Son Goku
The greatest martial artist the world has ever known. Goku can produce the energy blast called the *Kamehameha*, and rides a flying cloud called the *Kinto'un*, a gift from Kame-Sen'nin. When he was younger, he used to have a tail like a monkey's. Five years ago, he married Chi-Chi and had a son.

Son Gohan
Goku's four-year-old son with his wife Chi-Chi (not pictured).

Bulma
A friend who has known Goku longer than anybody. Bulma is the daughter of a great inventor and is a mechanical genius who met Goku while on a quest for the seven magical Dragon Balls. For a while she was dating Yamcha (not pictured).

Kuririn
Goku's former martial arts schoolmate under Kame-Sen'nin.

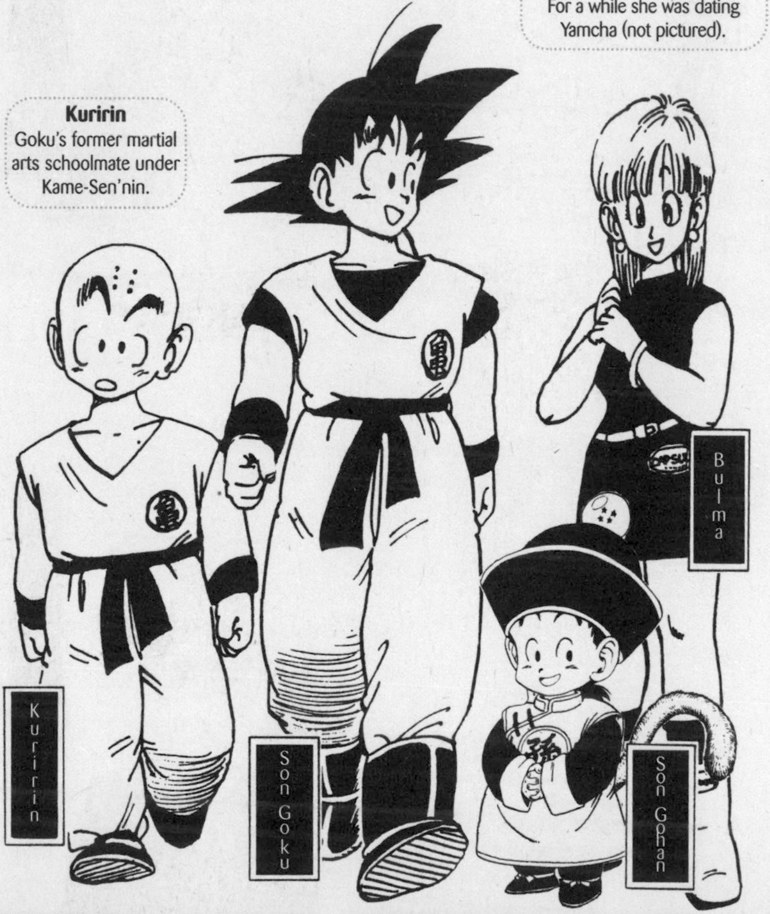
Bulma
Son Gohan
Son Goku
Kuririn

DRAGON BALL Z 1

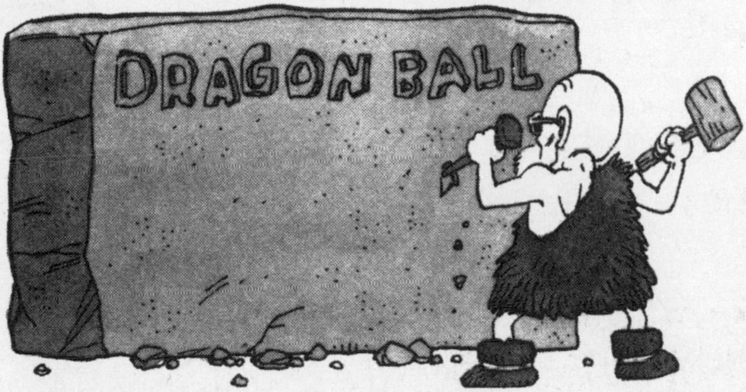
DRAGON BALL

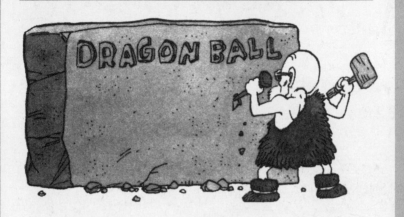

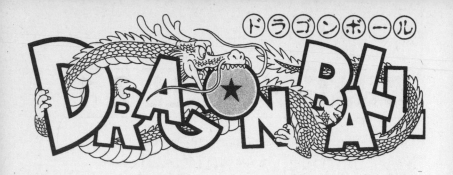

ドラゴンボール

DRAGON BALL

Five Years Later, A New Shadow is Cast
DBZ:01 • The Mysterious Warrior from Space

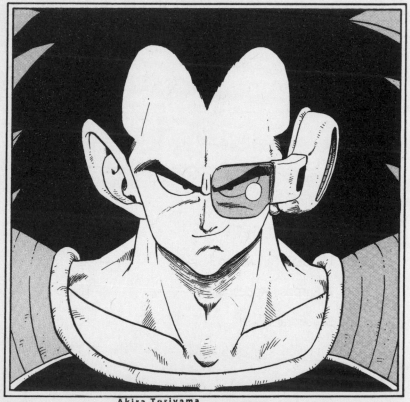

Akira Toriyama
鳥山明 BIRD STUDIO

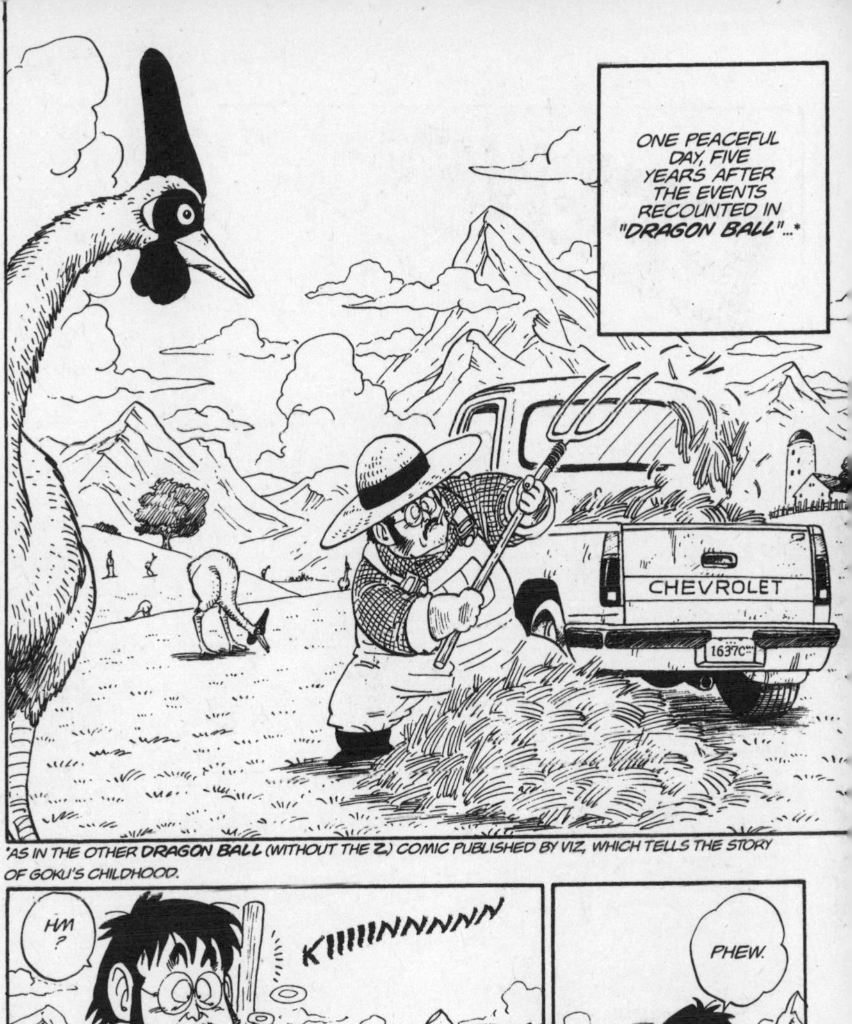
ONE PEACEFUL DAY, FIVE YEARS AFTER THE EVENTS RECOUNTED IN "DRAGON BALL"...*
CHEVROLET
1637C

*AS IN THE OTHER **DRAGON BALL** (WITHOUT THE Z) COMIC PUBLISHED BY VIZ, WHICH TELLS THE STORY OF GOKU'S CHILDHOOD.

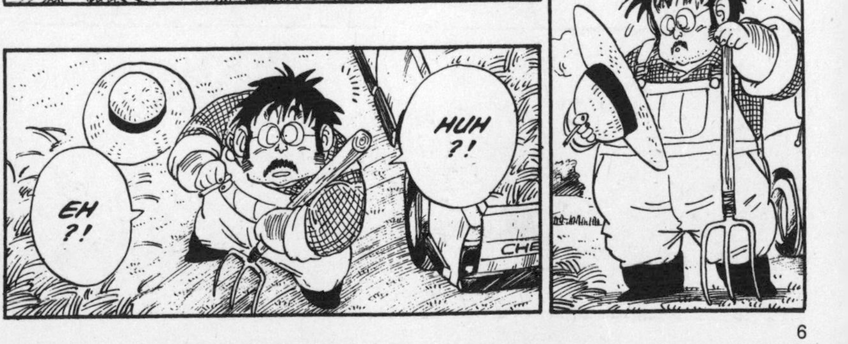
PHEW.
HM ?
KIIIINNNNN
HUH ?!
EH ?!
CHE

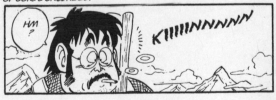

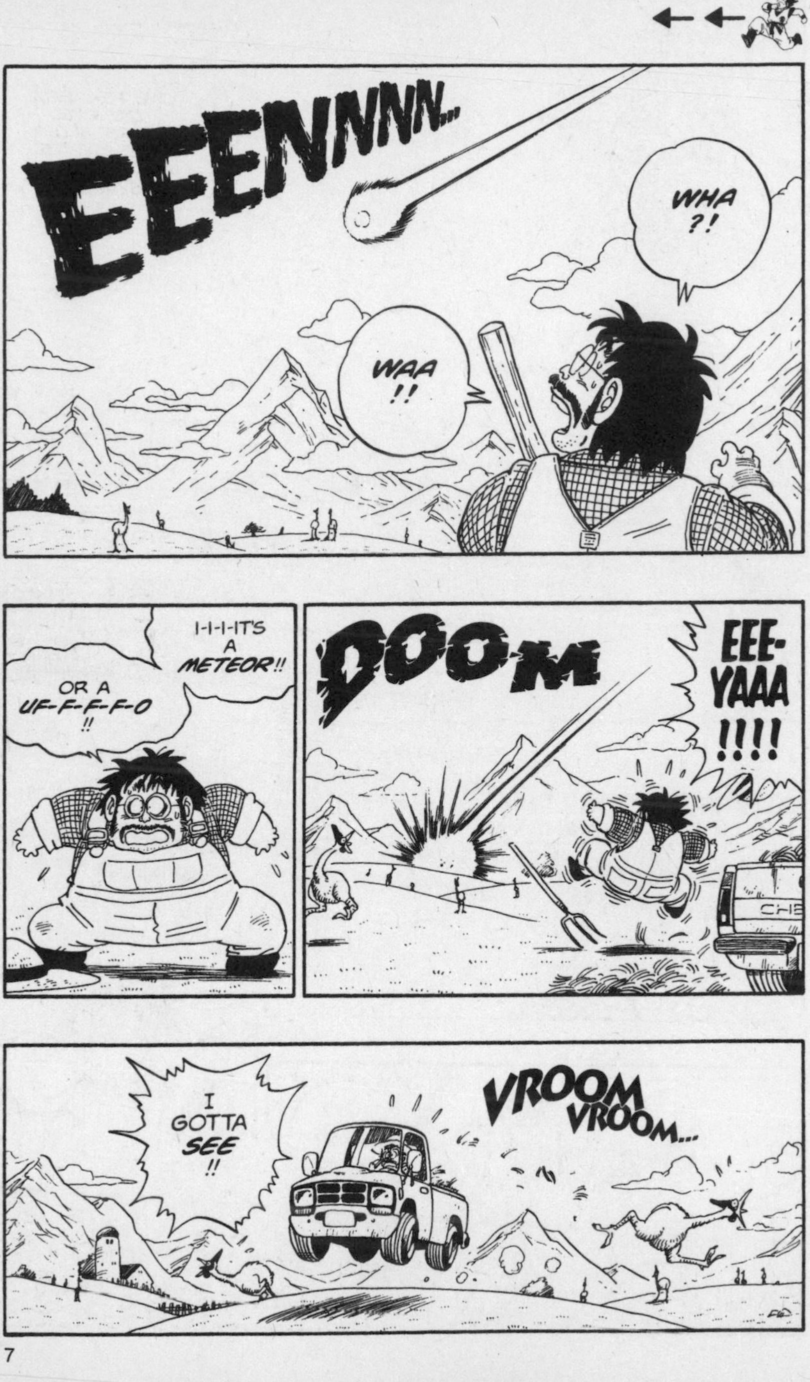
EEENNNN...
WHA ?!
WAA !!
DOOM
EEE-YAAA !!!!
I-I-I-IT'S A METEOR!!
OR A UF-F-F-F-O !!
VROOM VROOM...
I GOTTA SEE !!

SSHHH
SSHHH
IT'S... IT'S INCREDIBLE...
.....
N-NOT A METEOR...
KREEEN...
EEEE!!

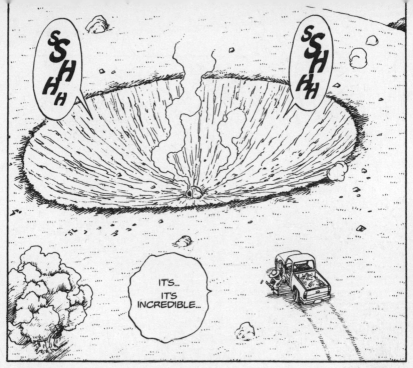

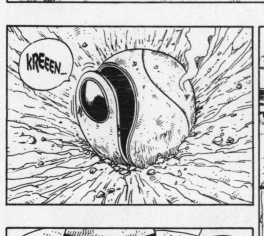

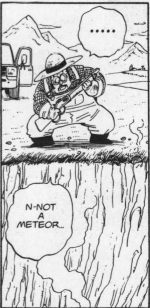

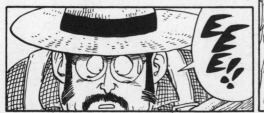

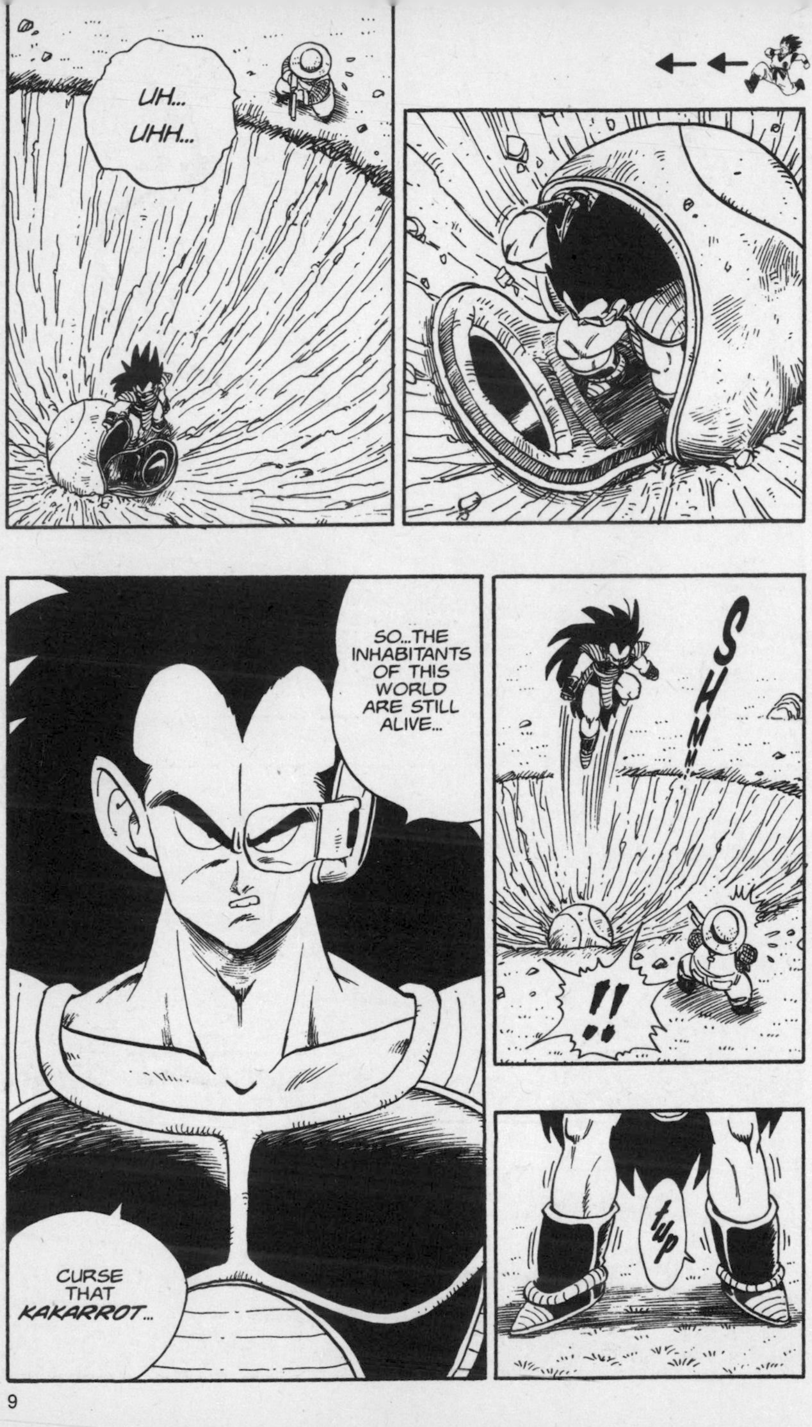
UH... UHH...
SHM
!!
tup
SO...THE INHABITANTS OF THIS WORLD ARE STILL ALIVE...
CURSE THAT KAKARROT...

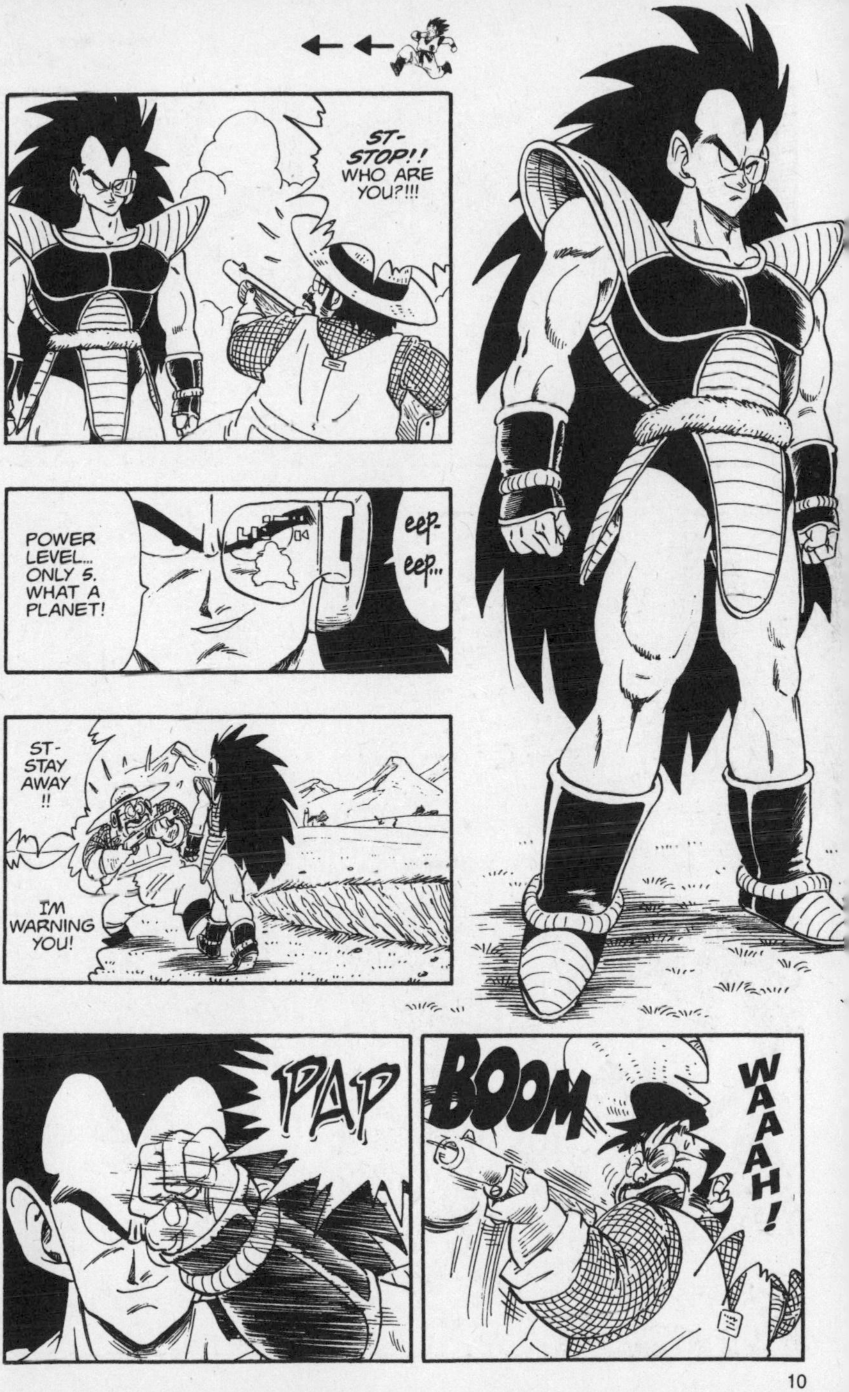
ST-STOP!! WHO ARE YOU?!!!
eep-eep...
POWER LEVEL... ONLY 5. WHAT A PLANET!
ST-STAY AWAY!!
I'M WARNING YOU!
BOOM
WAAAH!
PAP

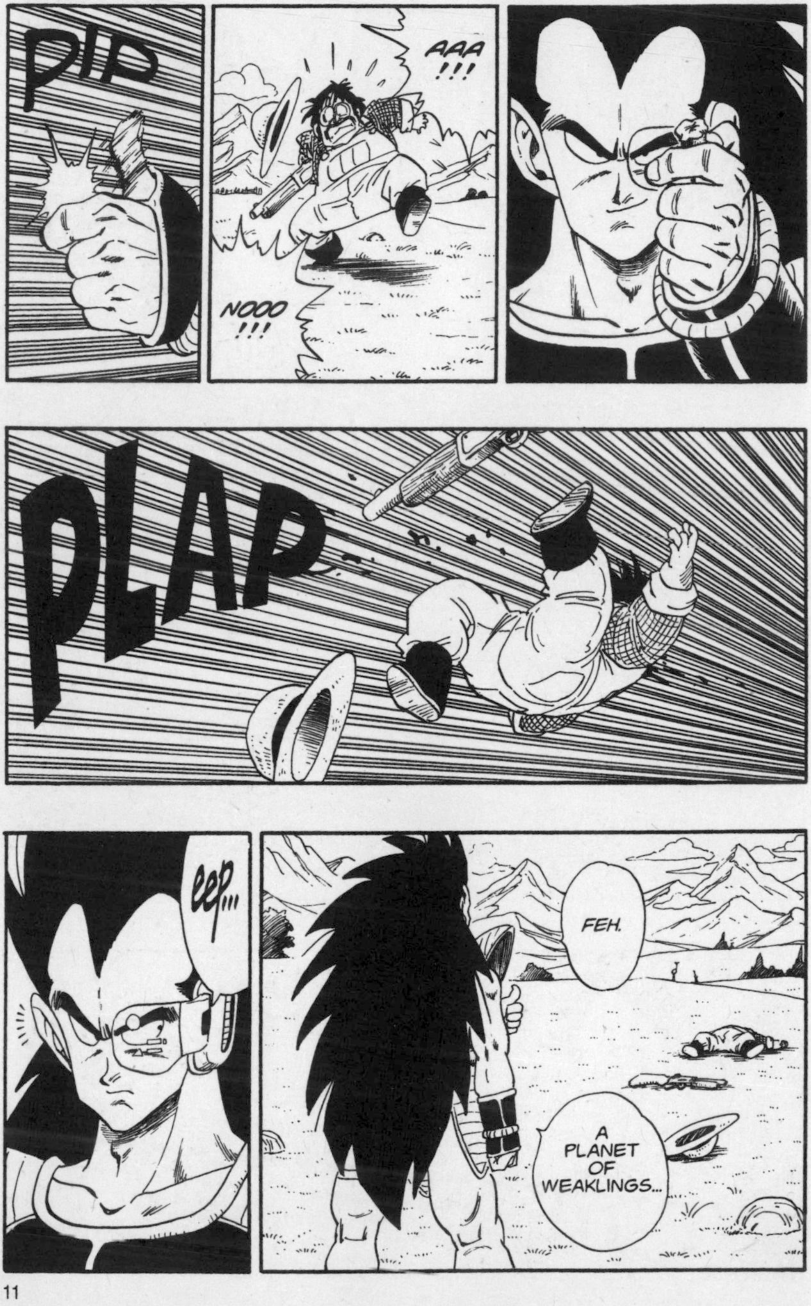
PIP
AAA!!!
NOOO!!!
PLAP
eep...
FEH.
A PLANET OF WEAKLINGS...

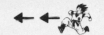

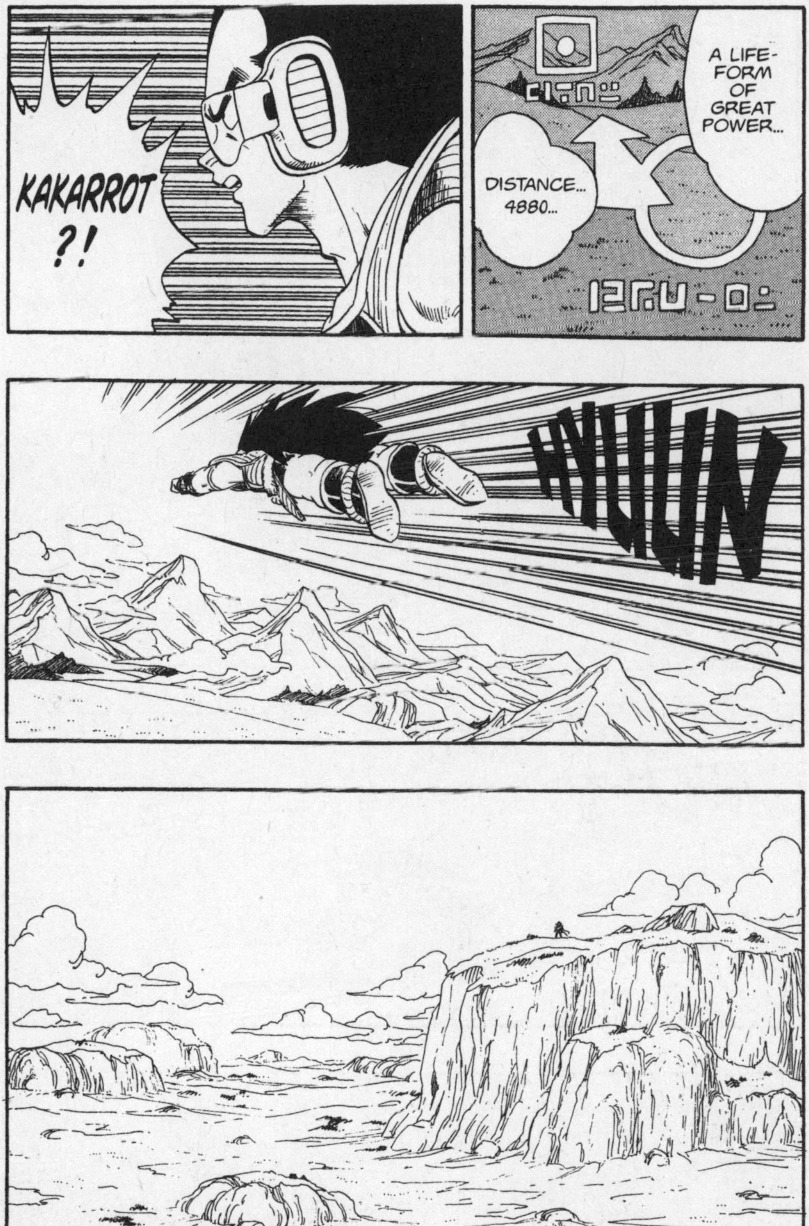
A LIFE-FORM OF GREAT POWER...
DISTANCE... 4880...
KAKARROT ?!
HYUUN

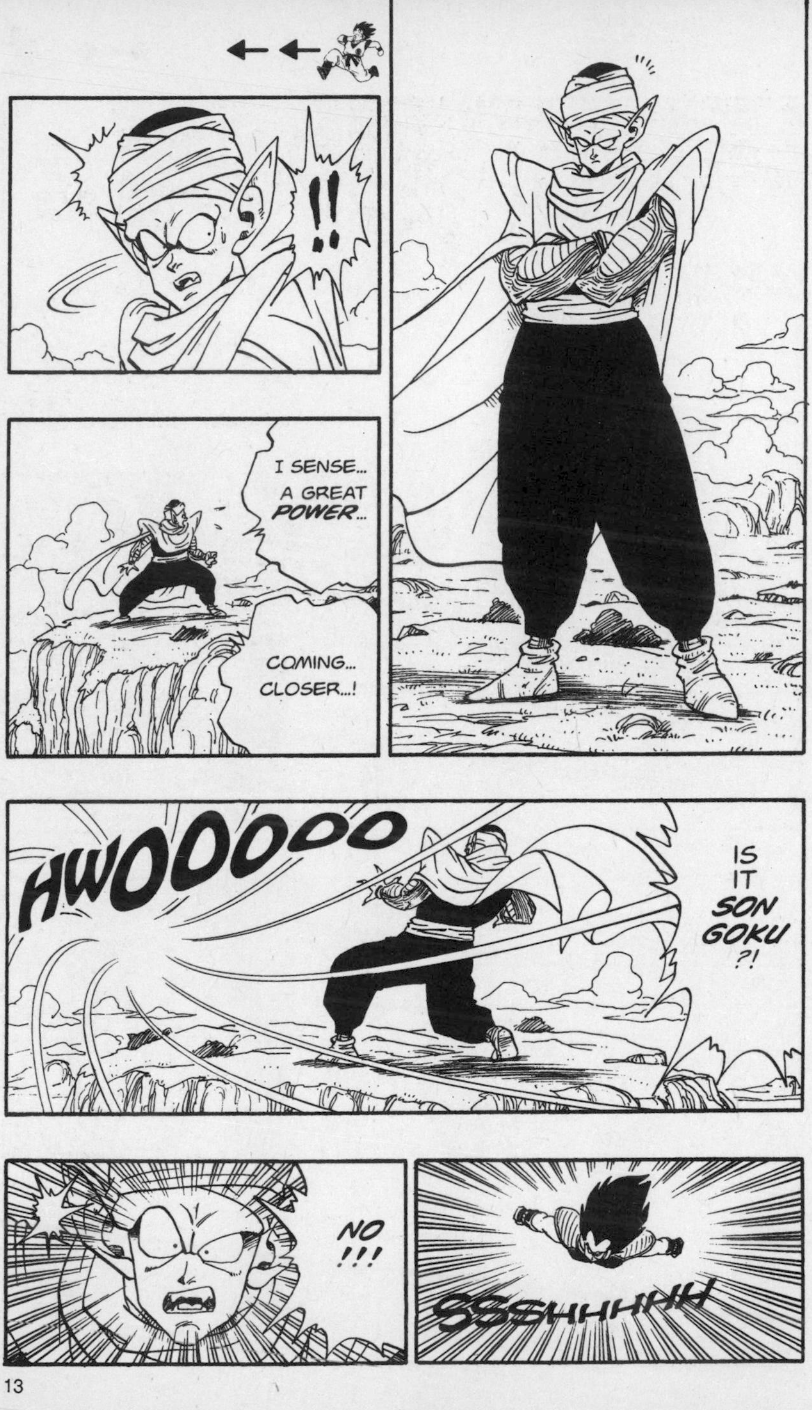
!!
I SENSE... A GREAT POWER...
COMING... CLOSER...!
IS IT SON GOKU ?!
HWOOOOO
SSSHHHHH
NO !!!

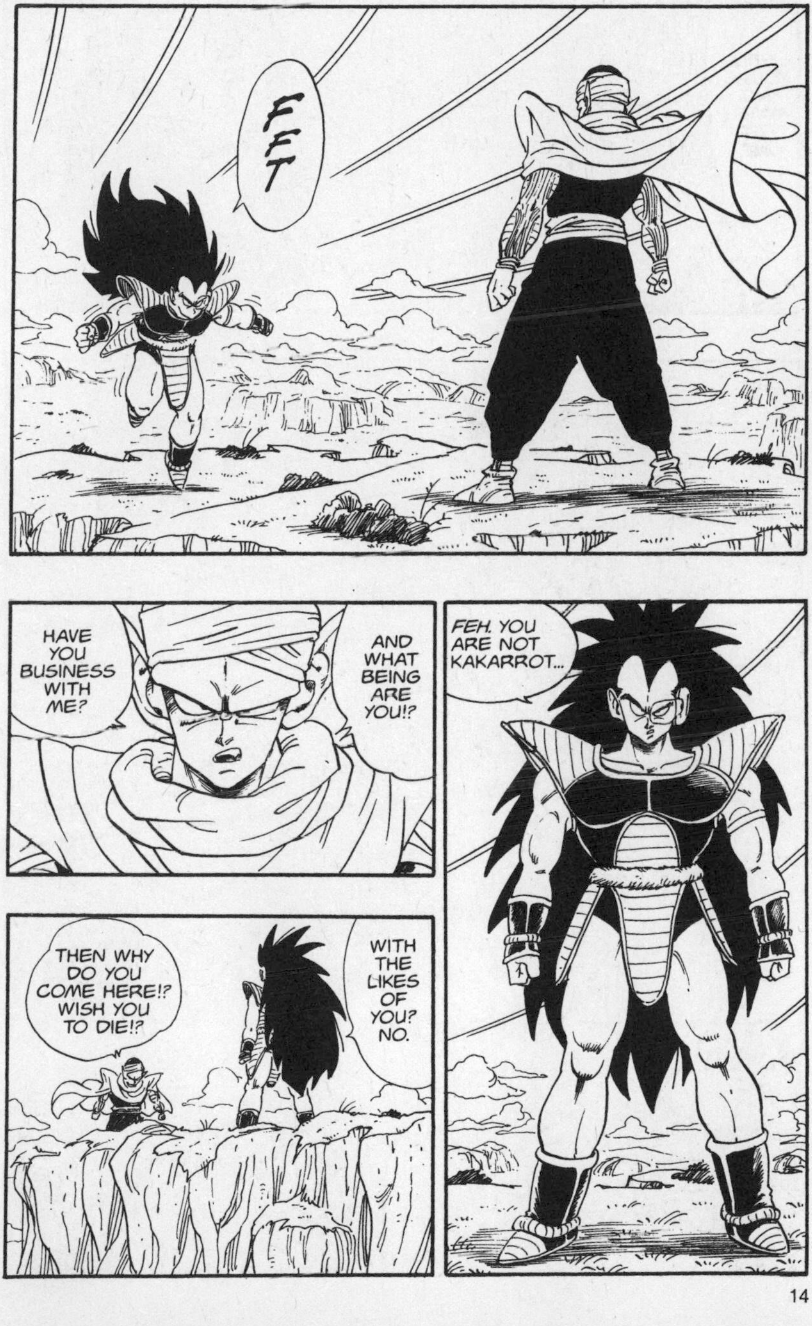
FFT
FEH. YOU ARE NOT KAKARROT...
AND WHAT BEING ARE YOU!?
HAVE YOU BUSINESS WITH ME?
WITH THE LIKES OF YOU? NO.
THEN WHY DO YOU COME HERE!? WISH YOU TO DIE!?

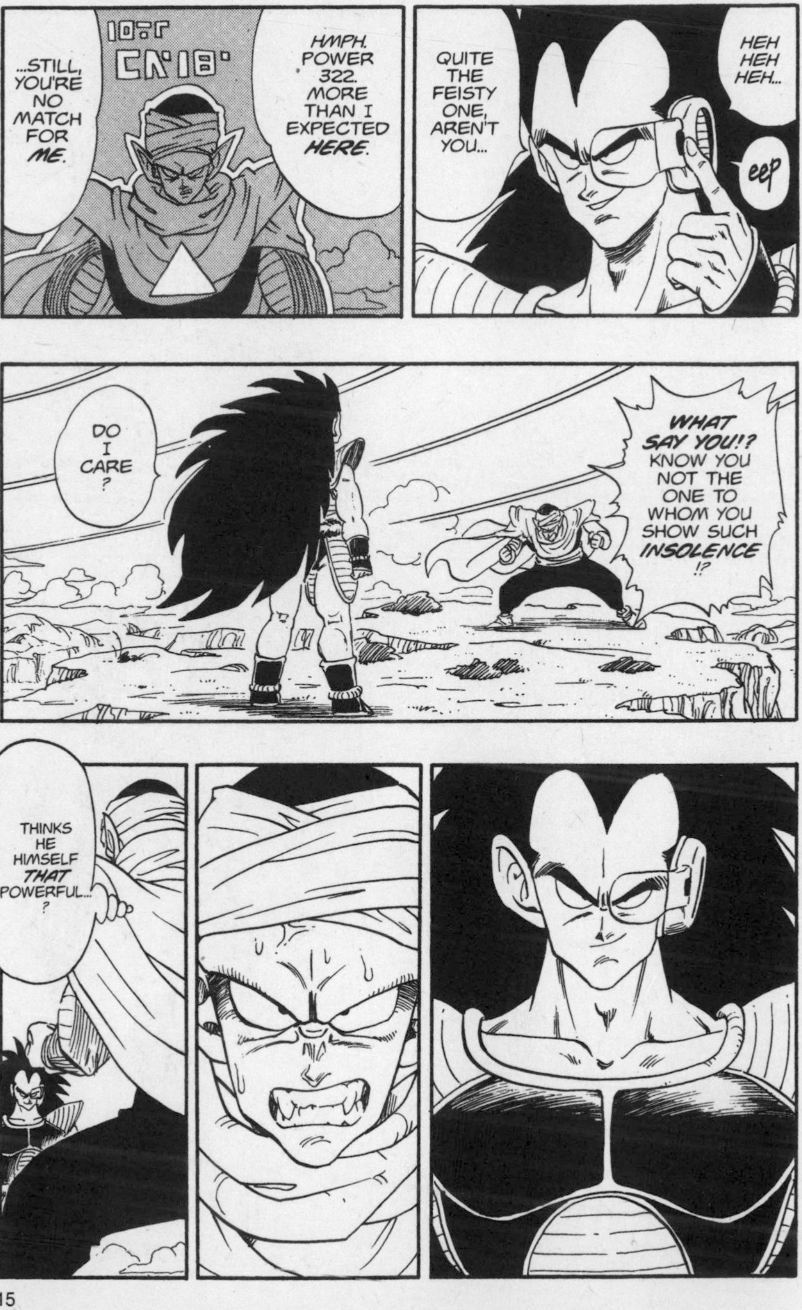
HEH HEH HEH...
eep
QUITE THE FEISTY ONE, AREN'T YOU...
HMPH. POWER 322. MORE THAN I EXPECTED *HERE*.
...STILL, YOU'RE NO MATCH FOR *ME*.
WHAT SAY YOU!? KNOW YOU NOT THE ONE TO WHOM YOU SHOW SUCH *INSOLENCE* !?
DO I CARE ?
THINKS HE HIMSELF *THAT* POWERFUL... ?

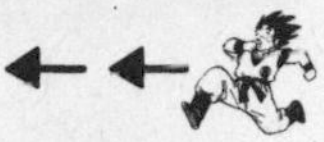

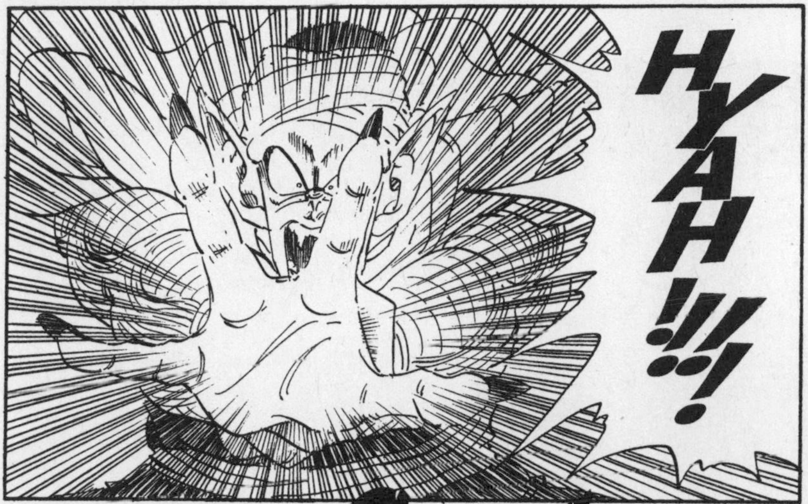
HYAH!!!!

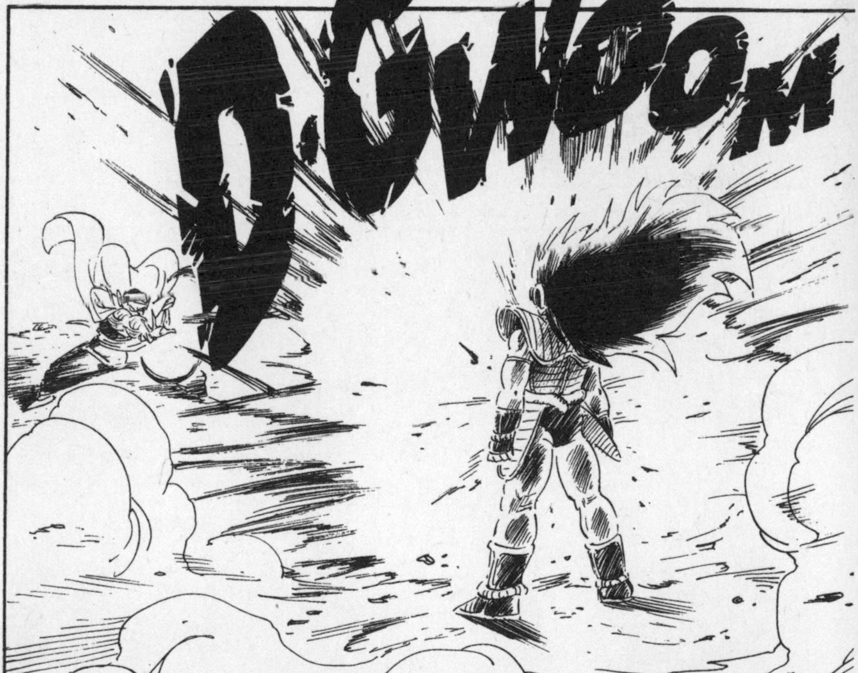
D-GWOOM

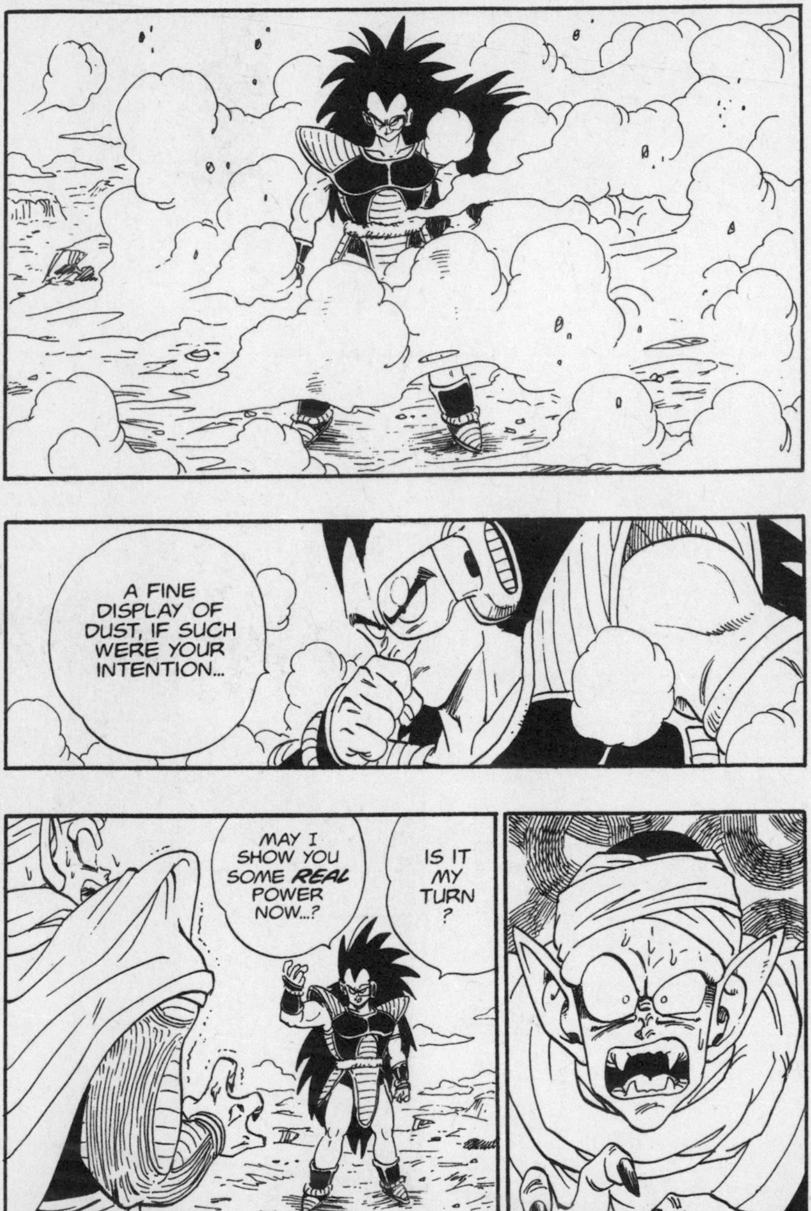
A FINE DISPLAY OF DUST, IF SUCH WERE YOUR INTENTION...
IS IT MY TURN ?
MAY I SHOW YOU SOME REAL POWER NOW...?

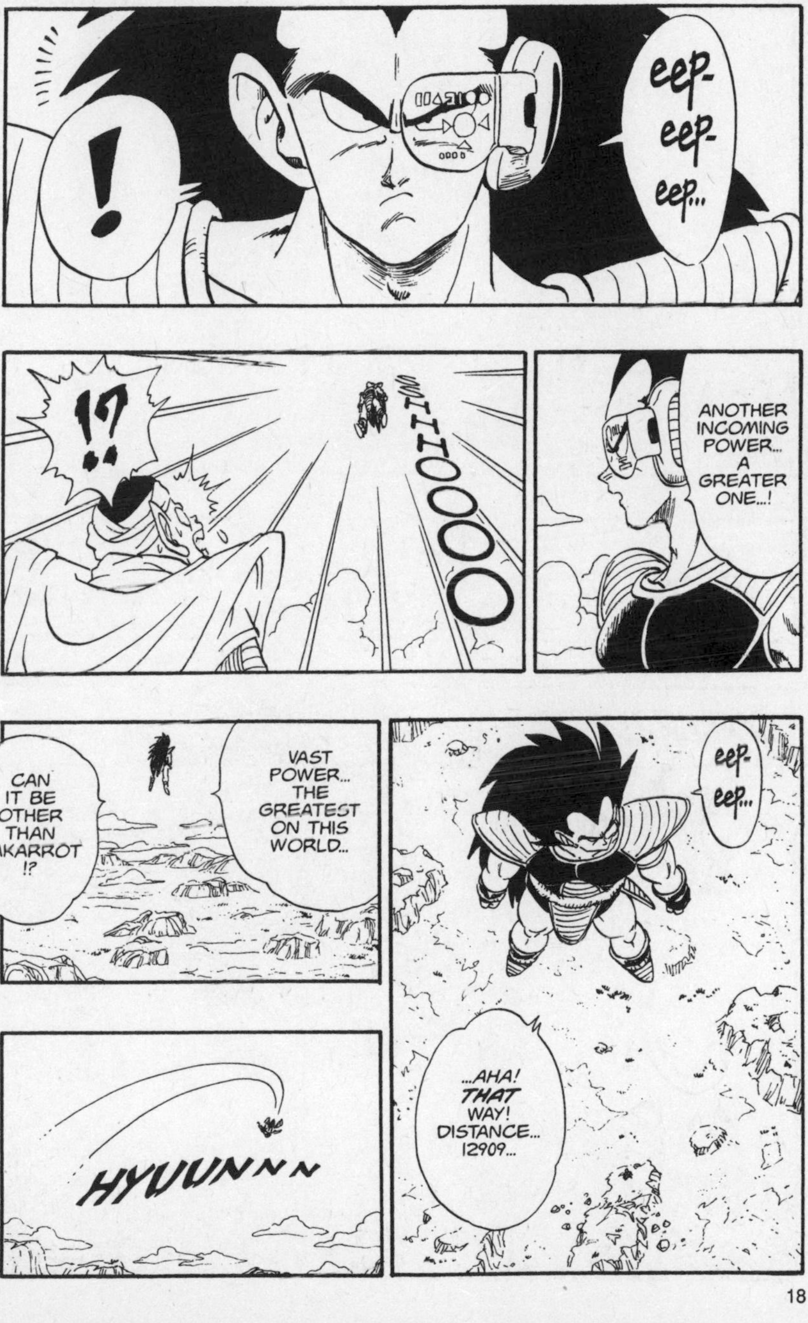
eep-eep-eep...
!
ANOTHER INCOMING POWER... A GREATER ONE...!
!?
SHHOOOOO
eep-eep...
...AHA! THAT WAY! DISTANCE... 12909...
VAST POWER... THE GREATEST ON THIS WORLD...
CAN IT BE OTHER THAN KAKARROT !?
HYUUNNN

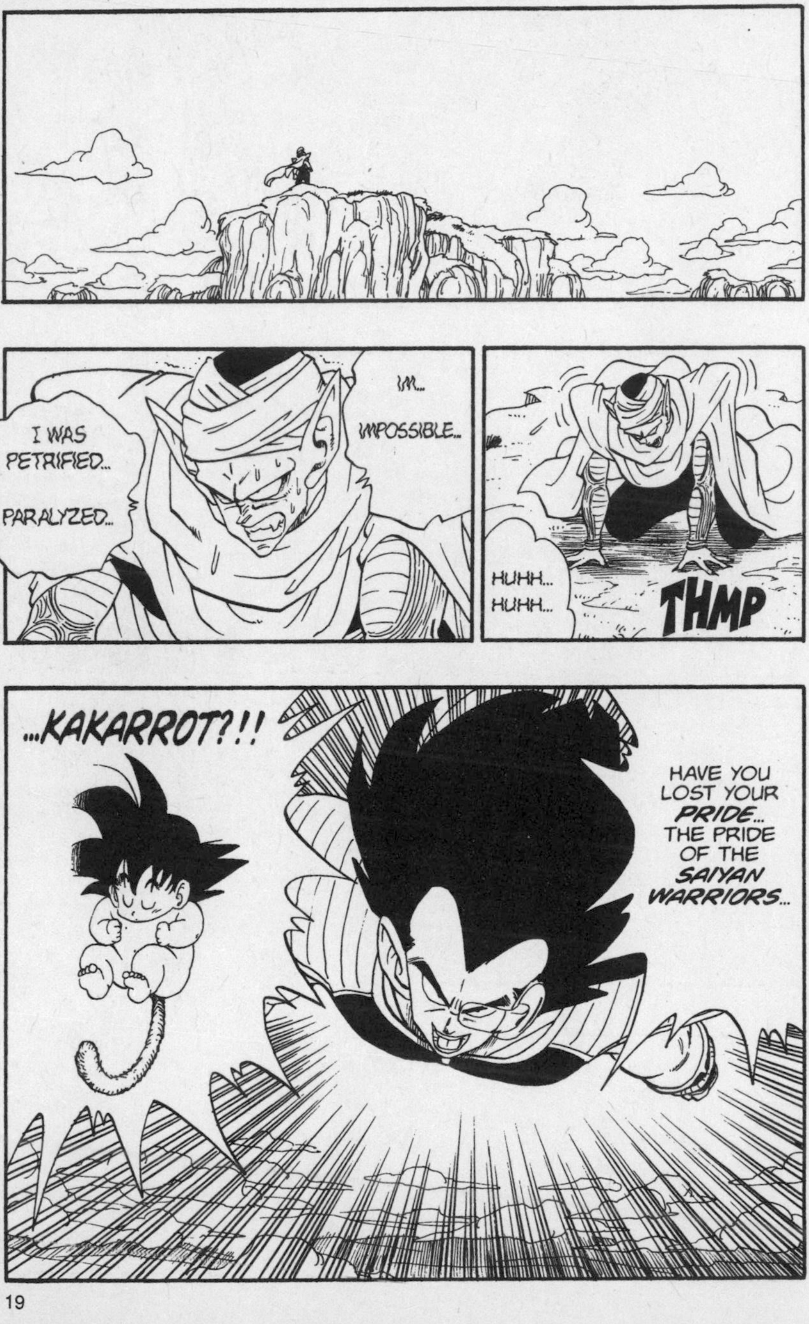
HUHH... HUHH...
THMP
IM... IMPOSSIBLE...
I WAS PETRIFIED... PARALYZED...
HAVE YOU LOST YOUR PRIDE... THE PRIDE OF THE SAIYAN WARRIORS...
...KAKARROT?!!

DRAGON BALL

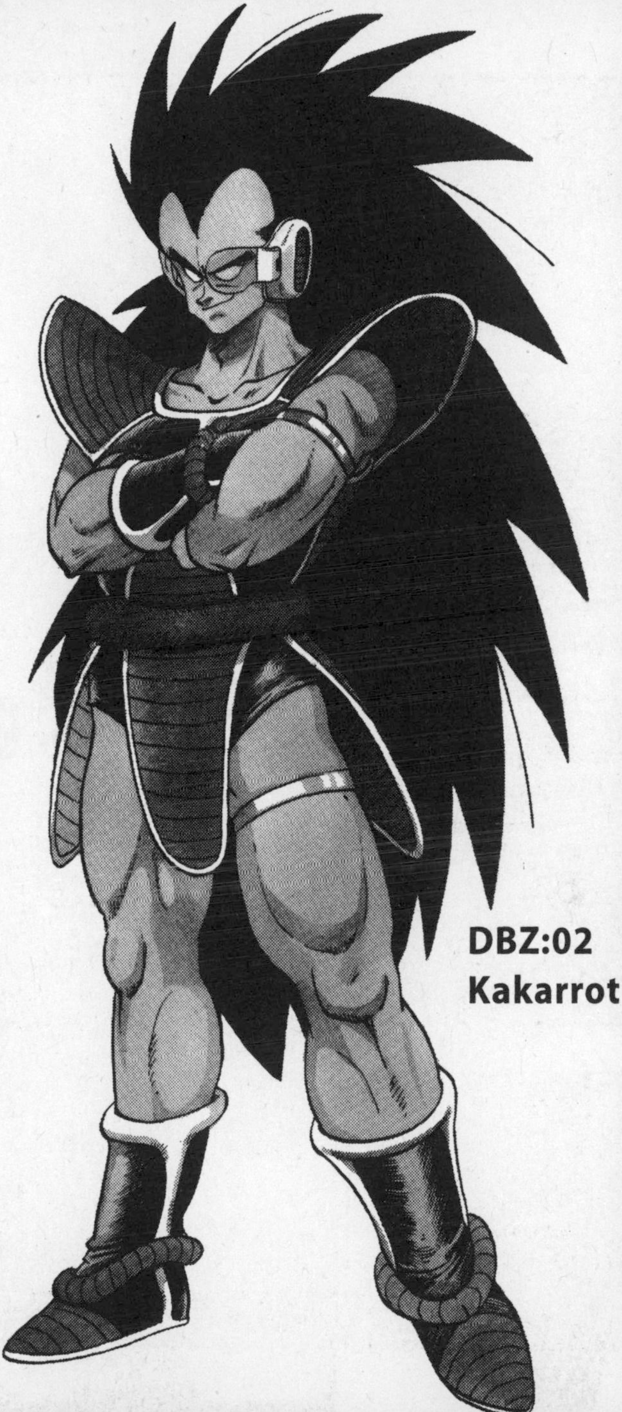

DBZ:02
Kakarrot

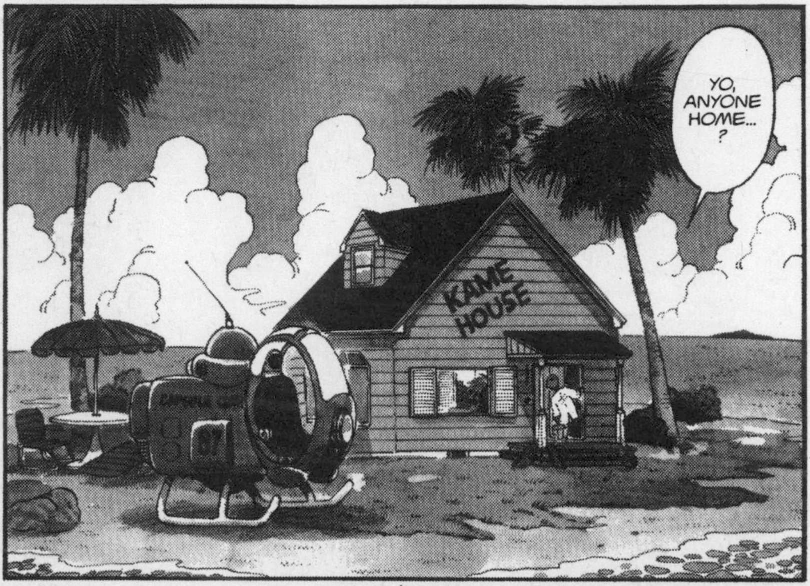
YO, ANYONE HOME...?
KAME HOUSE

*KAME (PRONOUNCED "KAHMEH") IS THE JAPANESE WORD FOR "TURTLE," AS IN KAME-SEN'NIN, THE "TURTLE HERMIT."

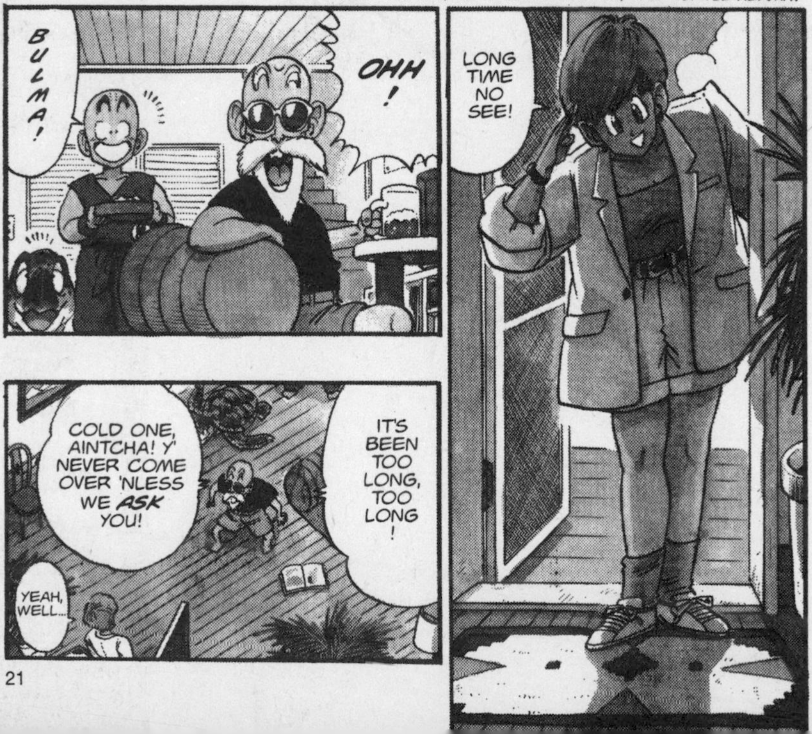
LONG TIME NO SEE!
OHH!
BULMA!
IT'S BEEN TOO LONG, TOO LONG!
COLD ONE, AINTCHA! Y' NEVER COME OVER 'NLESS WE *ASK* YOU!
YEAH, WELL...

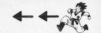

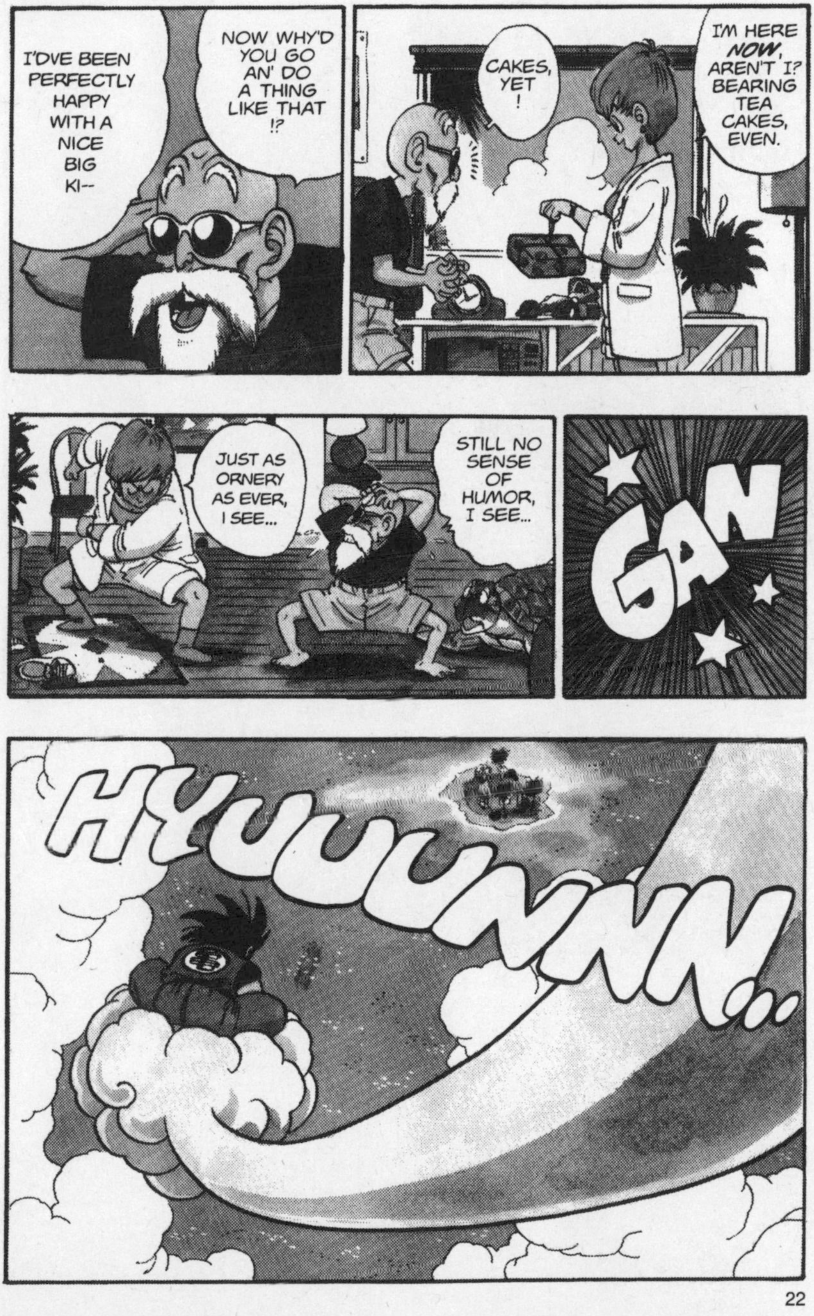
I'M HERE NOW, AREN'T I? BEARING TEA CAKES, EVEN.
CAKES, YET!
NOW WHY'D YOU GO AN' DO A THING LIKE THAT!?
I'DVE BEEN PERFECTLY HAPPY WITH A NICE BIG KI--
GAN
STILL NO SENSE OF HUMOR, I SEE...
JUST AS ORNERY AS EVER, I SEE...
HYUUUNNN...

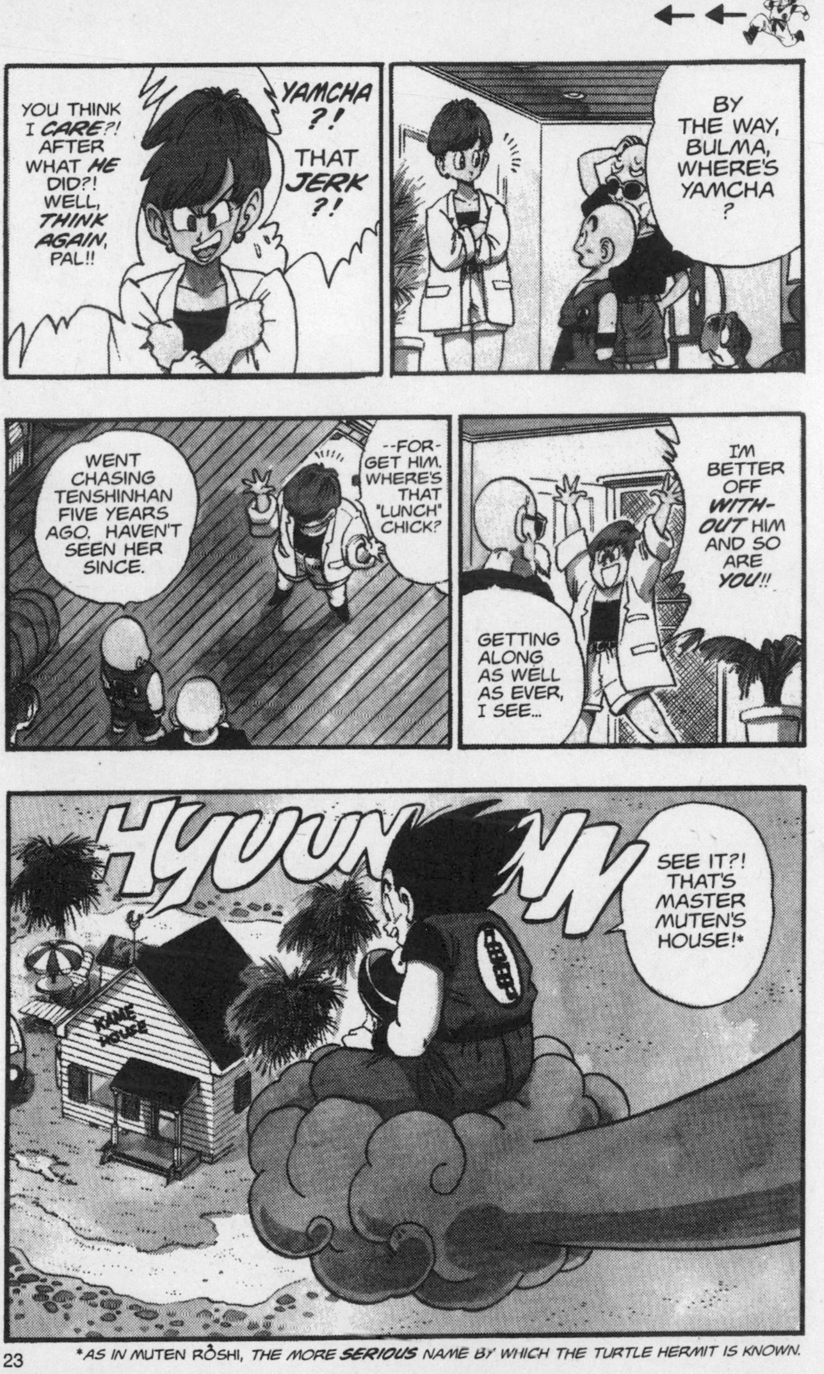
BY THE WAY, BULMA, WHERE'S YAMCHA?
YAMCHA?!
THAT JERK?!
YOU THINK I CARE?! AFTER WHAT HE DID?! WELL, THINK AGAIN, PAL!!
I'M BETTER OFF WITHOUT HIM AND SO ARE YOU!!
GETTING ALONG AS WELL AS EVER, I SEE...
--FORGET HIM. WHERE'S THAT "LUNCH" CHICK?
WENT CHASING TENSHINHAN FIVE YEARS AGO. HAVEN'T SEEN HER SINCE.
HYUUUNNN
SEE IT?! THAT'S MASTER MUTEN'S HOUSE!*
KAME HOUSE

*AS IN MUTEN RŌSHI, THE MORE **SERIOUS** NAME BY WHICH THE TURTLE HERMIT IS KNOWN.

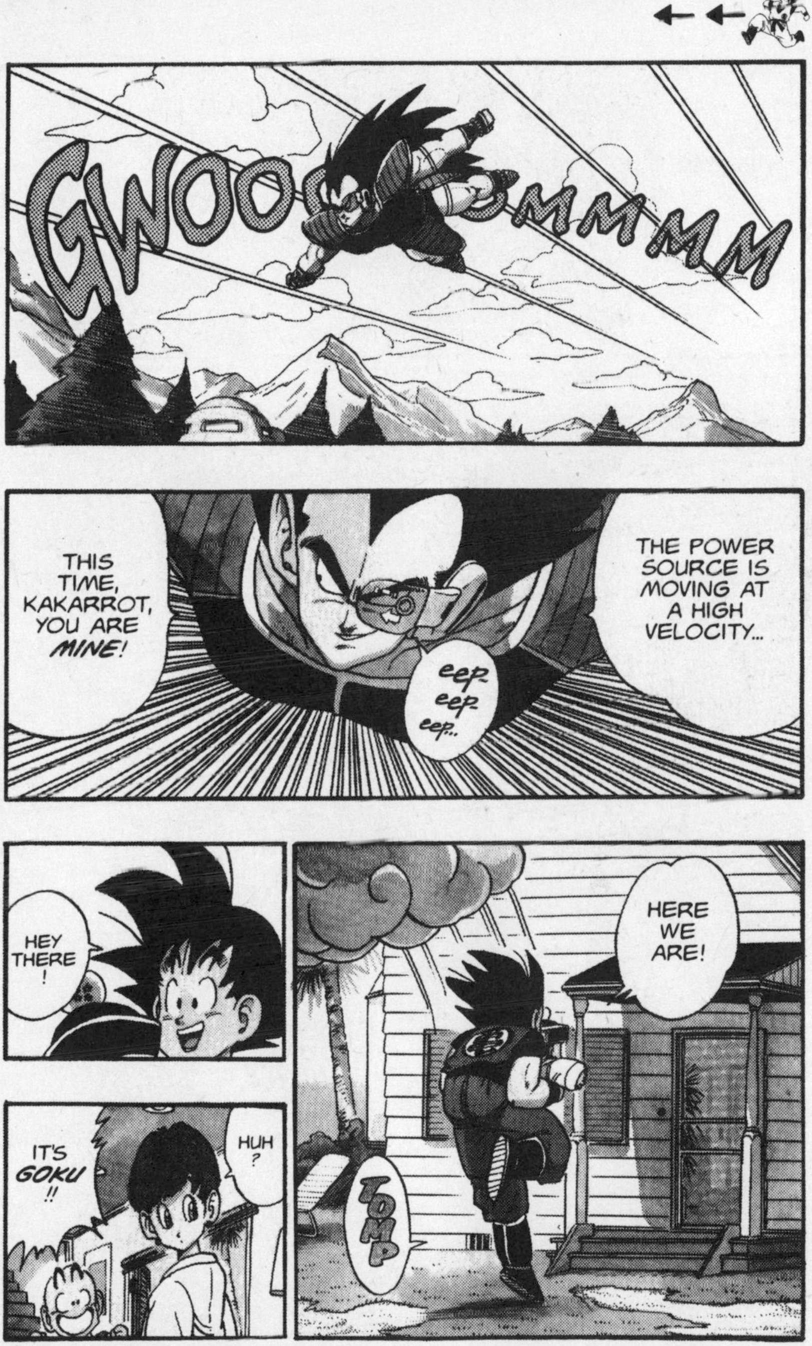
GWOOOMMMMMM
THE POWER SOURCE IS MOVING AT A HIGH VELOCITY...
eep eep eep...
THIS TIME, KAKARROT, YOU ARE *MINE*!
HERE WE ARE!
TOMP
HEY THERE!
HUH?
IT'S *GOKU*!!

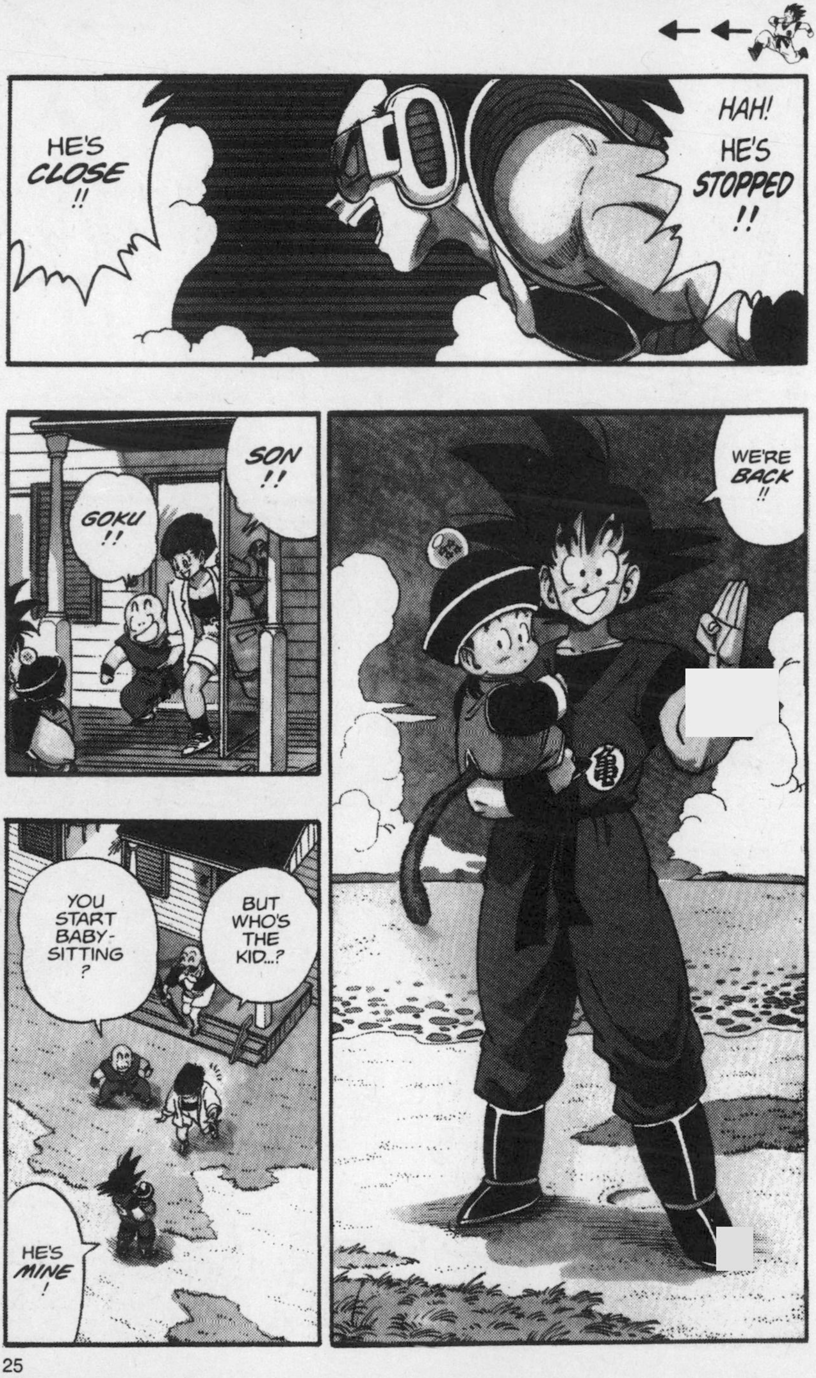
HAH! HE'S STOPPED!!
HE'S CLOSE!!
WE'RE BACK!!
SON!!
GOKU!!
BUT WHO'S THE KID...?
YOU START BABY-SITTING?
HE'S MINE!

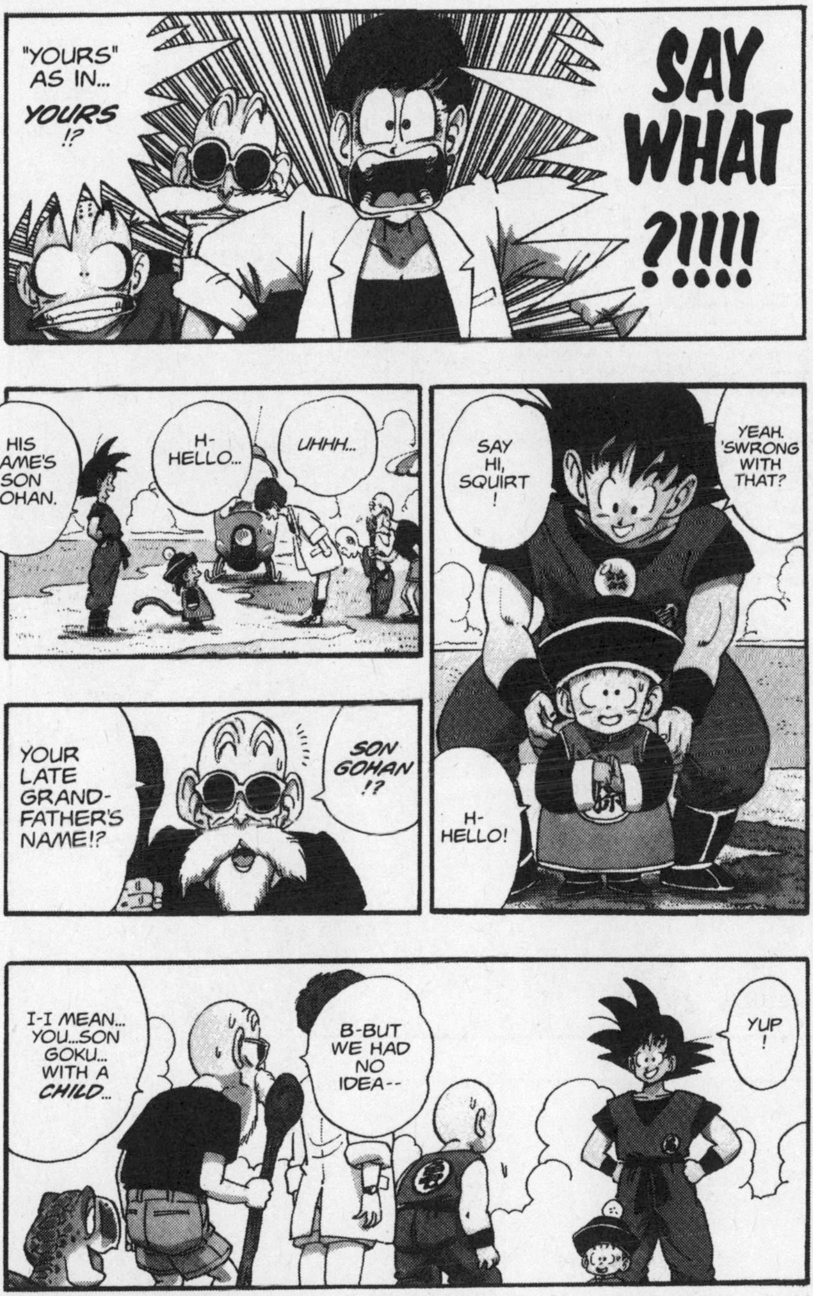
SAY WHAT ?!!!!
"YOURS" AS IN... YOURS !?
YEAH. 'SWRONG WITH THAT?
SAY HI, SQUIRT !
H-HELLO!
UHHH...
H-HELLO...
HIS NAME'S SON GOHAN.
SON GOHAN !?
YOUR LATE GRAND-FATHER'S NAME!?
YUP !
B-BUT WE HAD NO IDEA--
I-I MEAN... YOU...SON GOKU... WITH A CHILD...

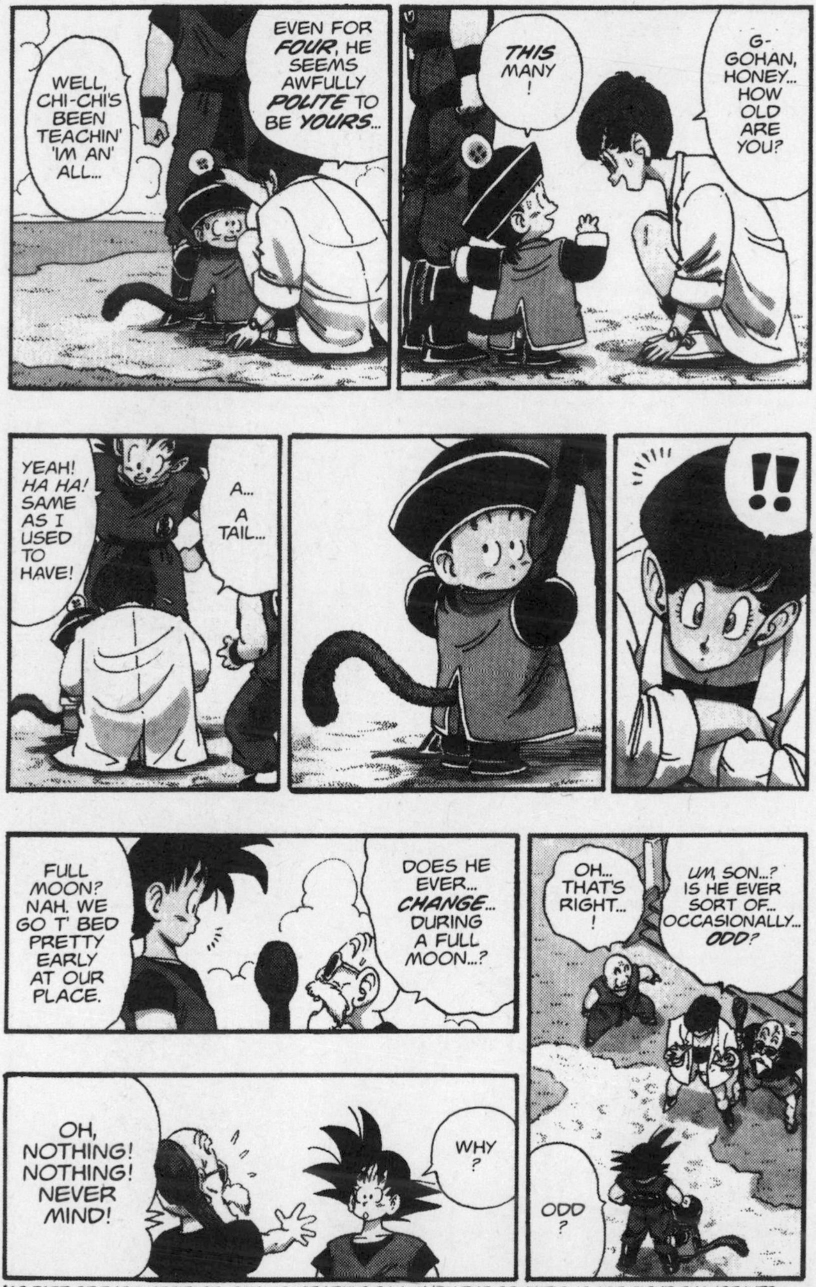
G-GOHAN, HONEY... HOW OLD ARE YOU?
THIS MANY!
EVEN FOR FOUR, HE SEEMS AWFULLY POLITE TO BE YOURS...
WELL, CHI-CHI'S BEEN TEACHIN' 'IM AN' ALL...
!!
A... A TAIL...
YEAH! HA HA! SAME AS I USED TO HAVE!
UM, SON...? IS HE EVER SORT OF... OCCASIONALLY... ODD?
OH... THAT'S RIGHT...!
ODD?
DOES HE EVER... CHANGE... DURING A FULL MOON...?
FULL MOON? NAH. WE GO T' BED PRETTY EARLY AT OUR PLACE.
WHY?
OH, NOTHING! NOTHING! NEVER MIND!

*AS PART OF THEIR HERITAGE, SAIYANS WITH TAILS CAN, WHEN THE CONDITIONS ARE RIGHT, CHANGE INTO GIANT MONKEY-APES! FOR MORE INFO, SEE THE EARLY TV SERIES OR **DRAGON BALL** VOL. 2.

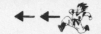

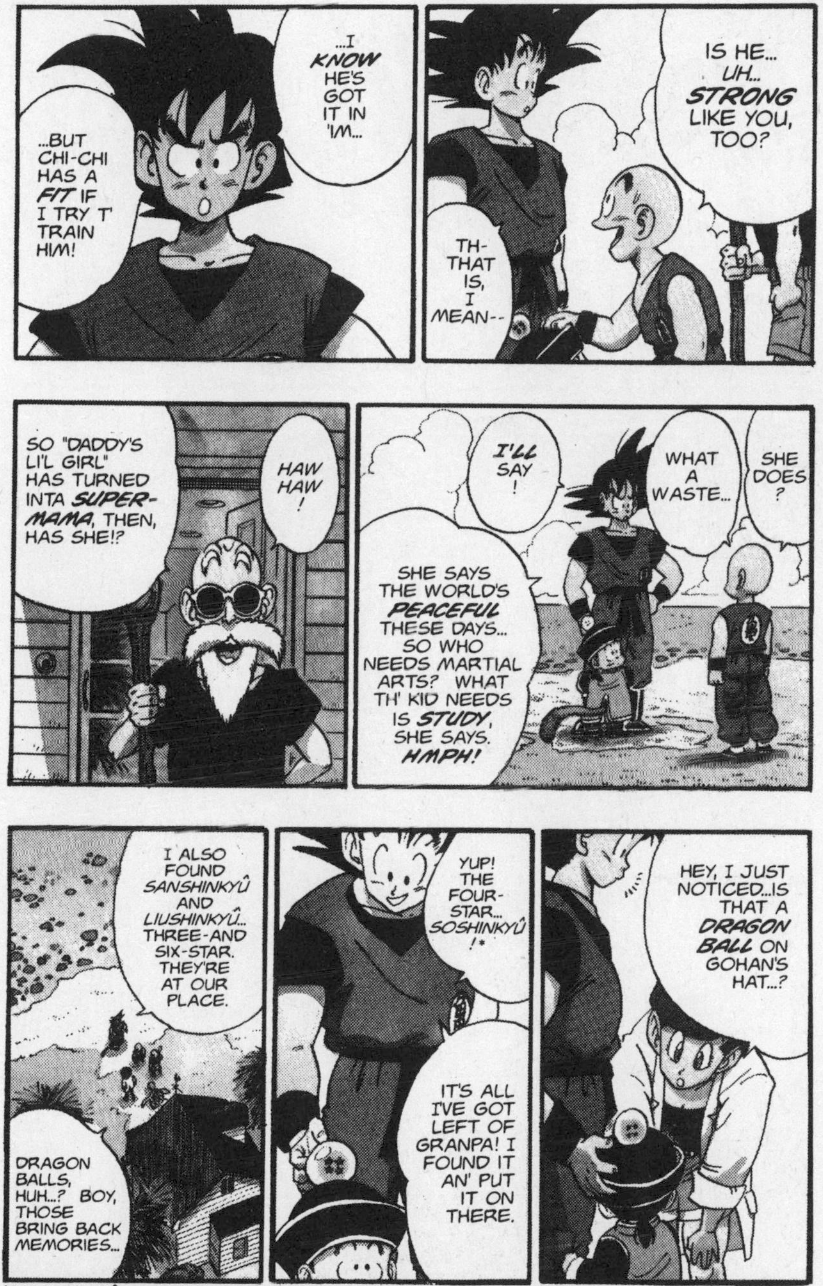
IS HE... UH... STRONG LIKE YOU, TOO?
TH-THAT IS, I MEAN--
...I KNOW HE'S GOT IT IN 'IM...
...BUT CHI-CHI HAS A FIT IF I TRY T' TRAIN HIM!
SHE DOES?
WHAT A WASTE...
I'LL SAY!
SHE SAYS THE WORLD'S PEACEFUL THESE DAYS... SO WHO NEEDS MARTIAL ARTS? WHAT TH' KID NEEDS IS STUDY, SHE SAYS. HMPH!
HAW HAW!
SO "DADDY'S LI'L GIRL" HAS TURNED INTA SUPER-MAMA, THEN, HAS SHE!?
HEY, I JUST NOTICED...IS THAT A DRAGON BALL ON GOHAN'S HAT...?
YUP! THE FOUR-STAR... SOSHINKYÛ!*
IT'S ALL I'VE GOT LEFT OF GRANPA! I FOUND IT AN' PUT IT ON THERE.
I ALSO FOUND SANSHINKYÛ AND LIUSHINKYÛ... THREE-AND SIX-STAR. THEY'RE AT OUR PLACE.
DRAGON BALLS, HUH...? BOY, THOSE BRING BACK MEMORIES...

*THE SOSHINKYÛ DRAGON BALL WAS GOKU'S ONLY KEEPSAKE OF HIS GRANDFATHER (SEE **DRAGON BALL** VOL. 1 FOR DETAILS).

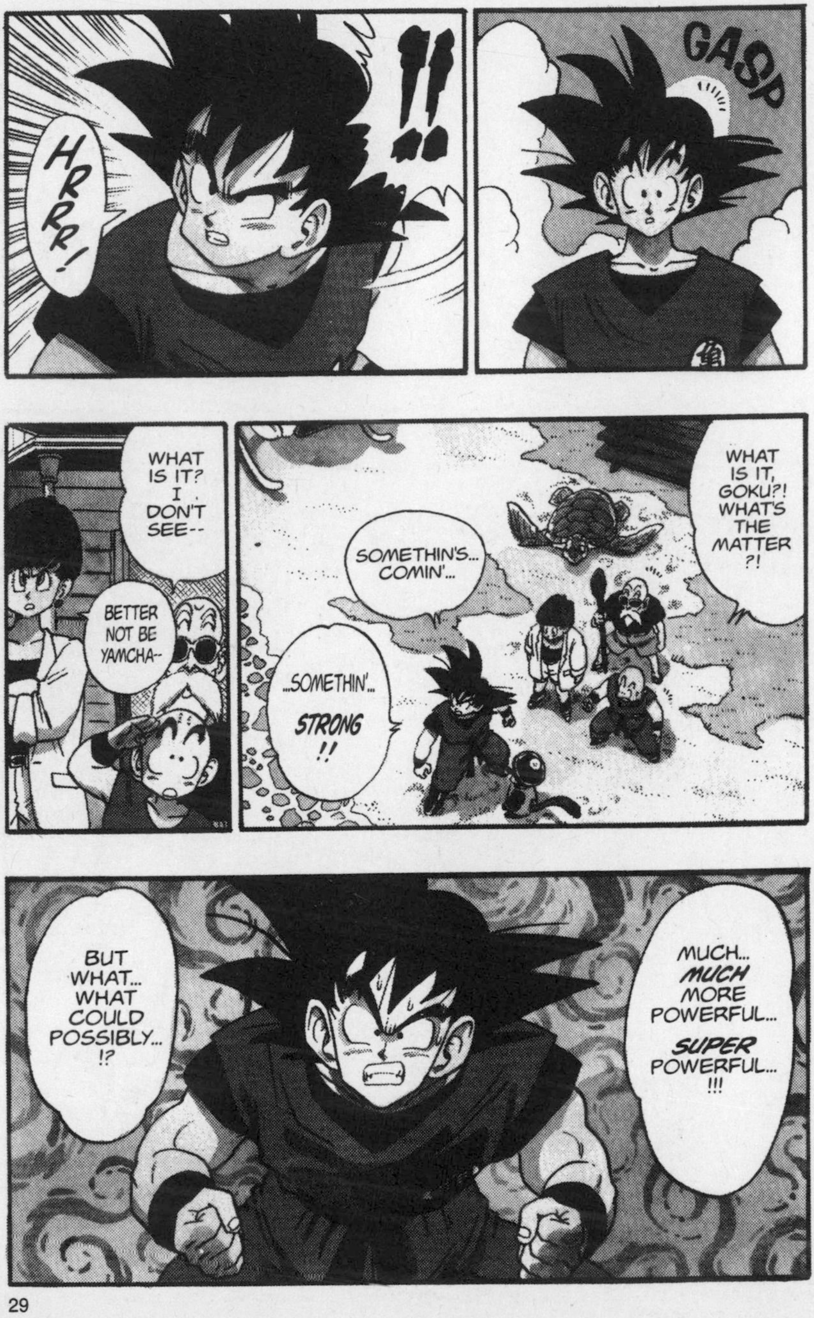
GASP
HRRR!
!!
WHAT IS IT, GOKU?! WHAT'S THE MATTER ?!
SOMETHIN'S... COMIN'...
...SOMETHIN'... STRONG !!
WHAT IS IT? I DON'T SEE--
BETTER NOT BE YAMCHA-
MUCH... MUCH MORE POWERFUL... SUPER POWERFUL... !!!
BUT WHAT... WHAT COULD POSSIBLY... !?

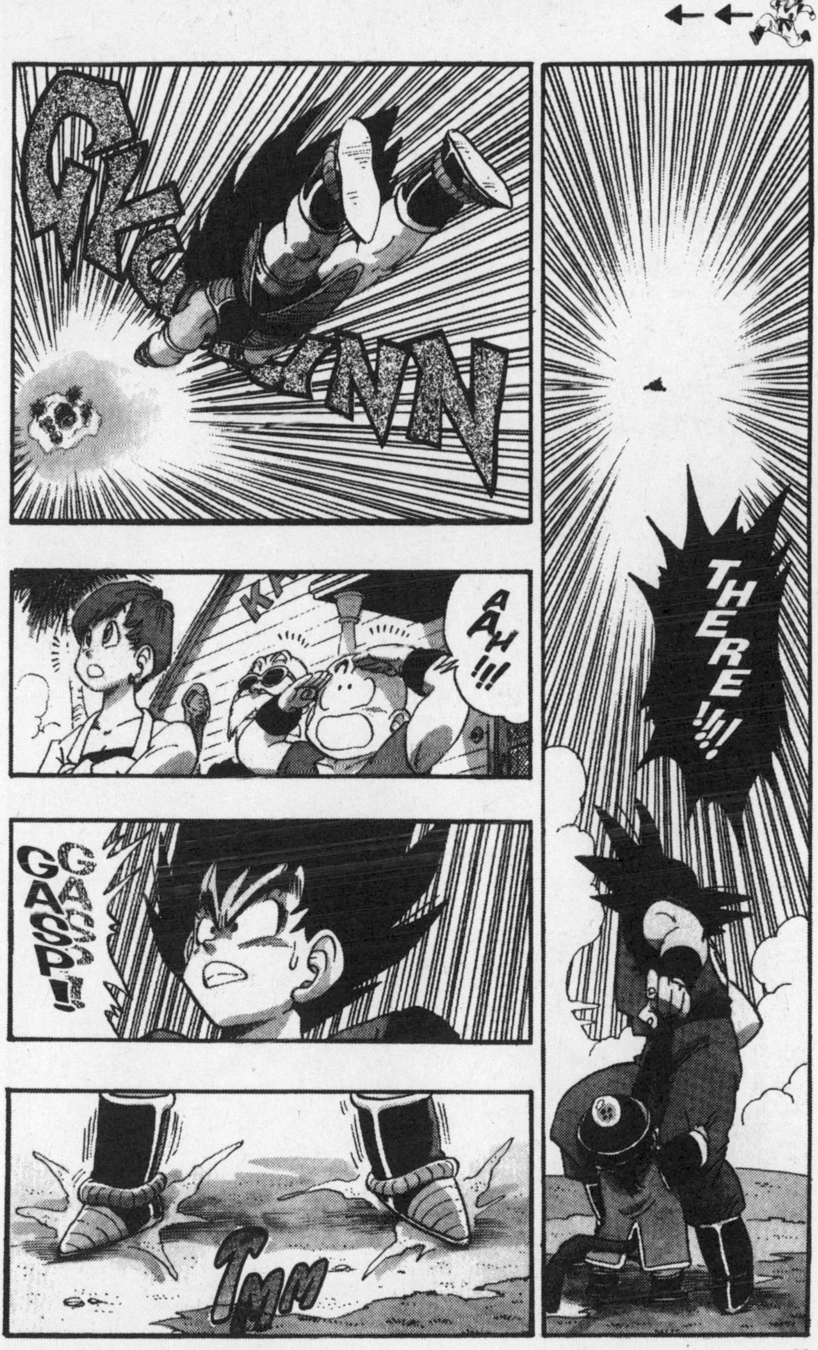
THERE!!!
AAH!!!
GASP GASP!

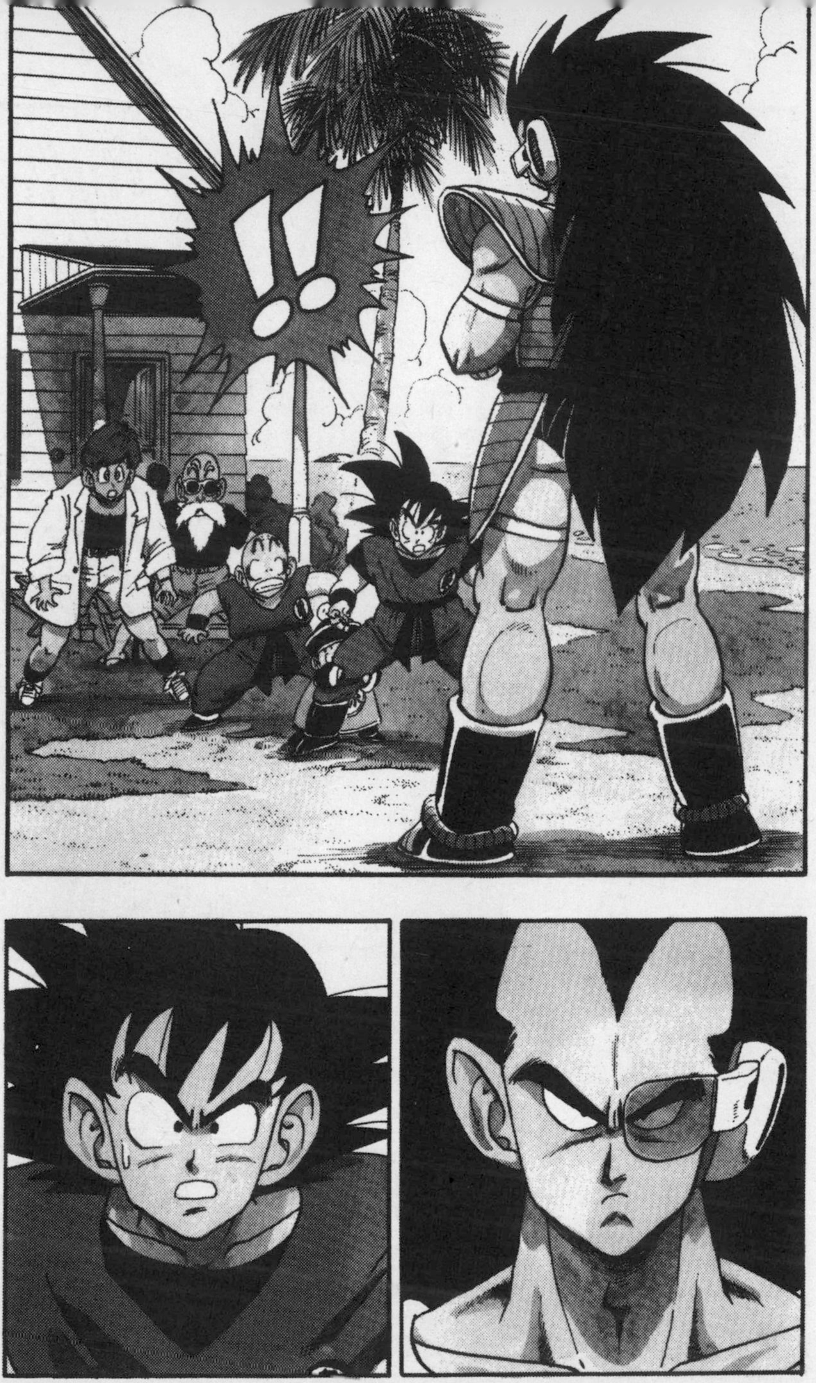
!!

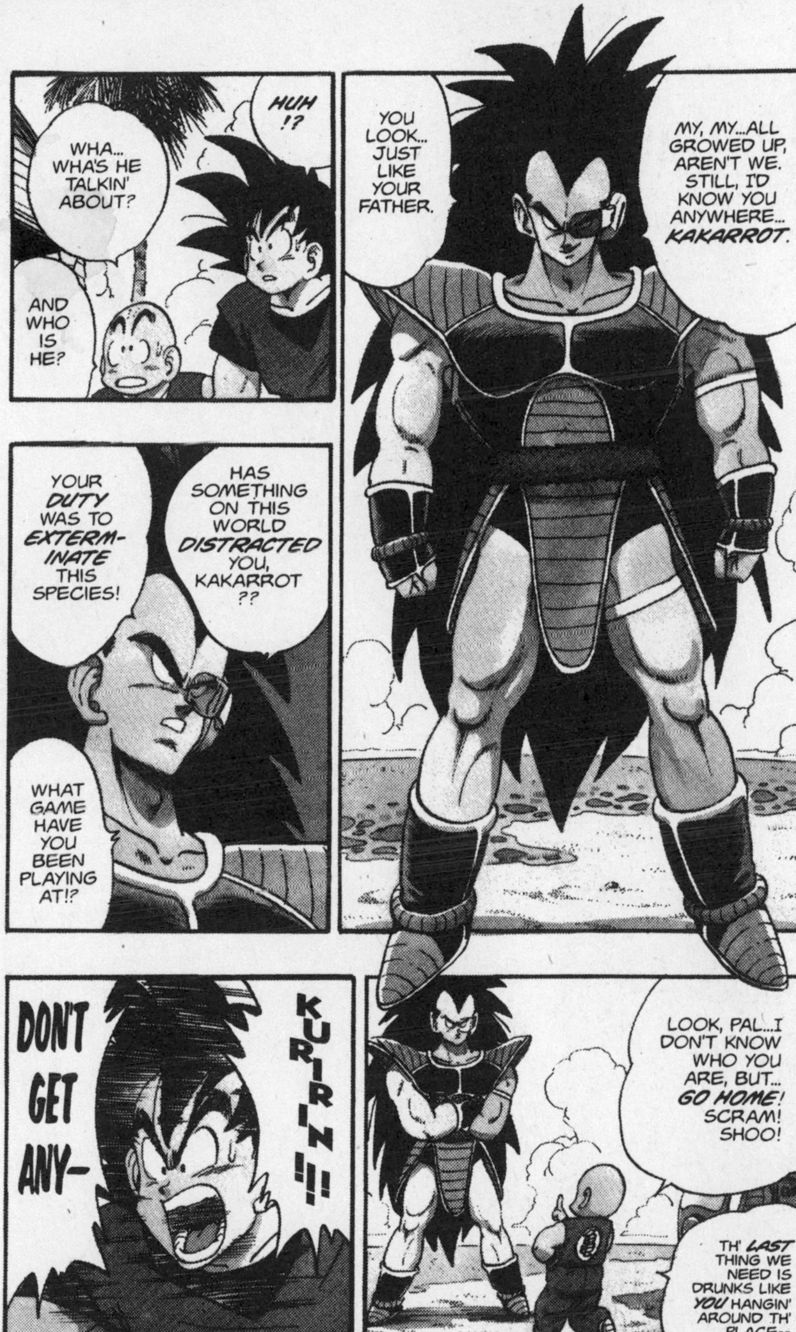
MY, MY...ALL GROWED UP, AREN'T WE. STILL, I'D KNOW YOU ANYWHERE... KAKARROT.
YOU LOOK... JUST LIKE YOUR FATHER.
HUH !?
WHA... WHA'S HE TALKIN' ABOUT?
AND WHO IS HE?
HAS SOMETHING ON THIS WORLD DISTRACTED YOU, KAKARROT ??
YOUR DUTY WAS TO EXTERMINATE THIS SPECIES!
WHAT GAME HAVE YOU BEEN PLAYING AT!?
LOOK, PAL...I DON'T KNOW WHO YOU ARE, BUT... GO HOME! SCRAM! SHOO!
TH' LAST THING WE NEED IS DRUNKS LIKE YOU HANGIN' AROUND TH' PLACE--
KURIRIN!!!
DON'T GET ANY-

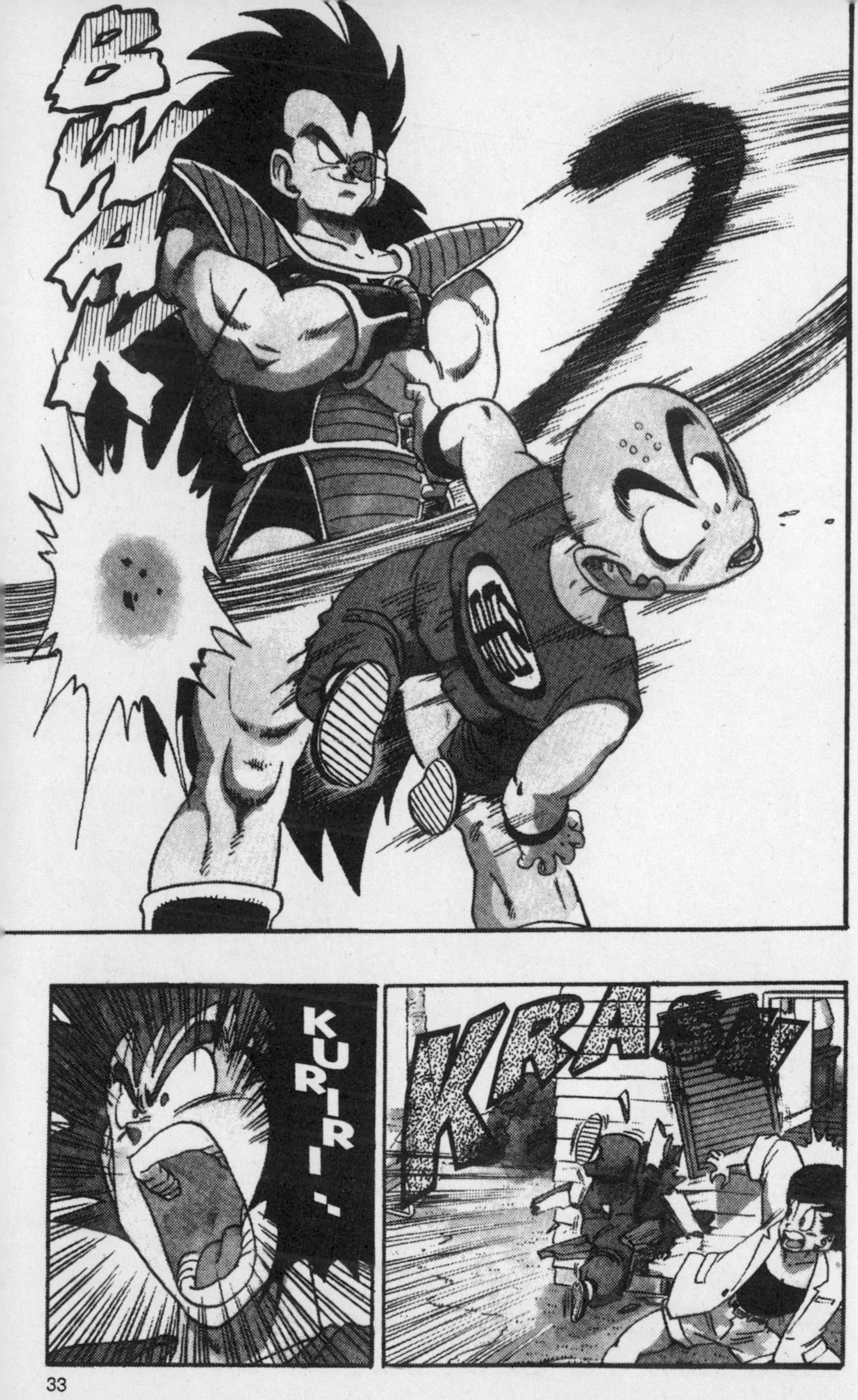
KRASH
KURIRI!!

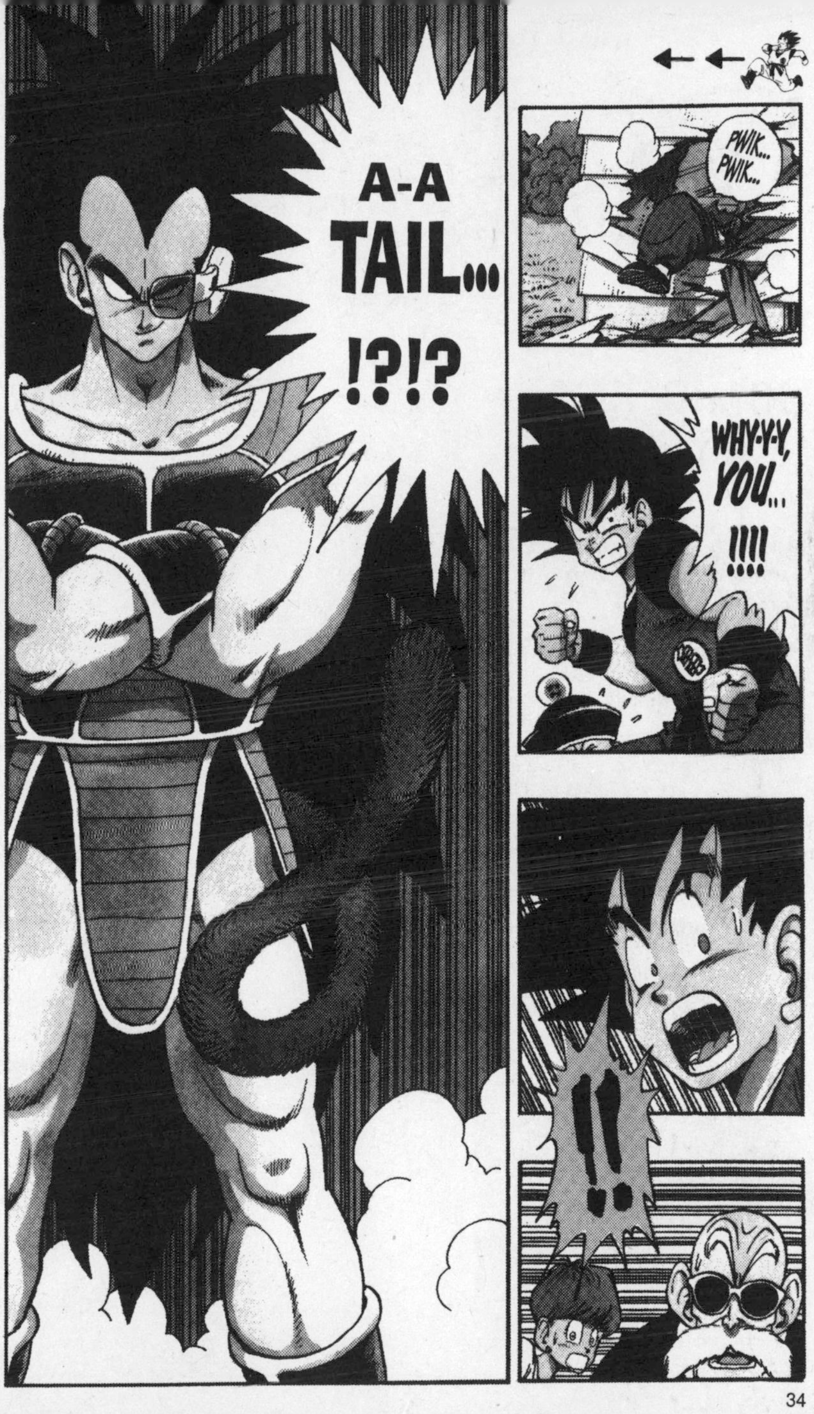
PWIK... PWIK...
WHY-Y-Y, YOU... !!!!
!!
A-A TAIL... !?!?

ドラゴンボール

DRAGON BALL

SOMETHING SAIYAN THIS WAY COMES!

DBZ:03 • Tails of Future Not-Quite Past

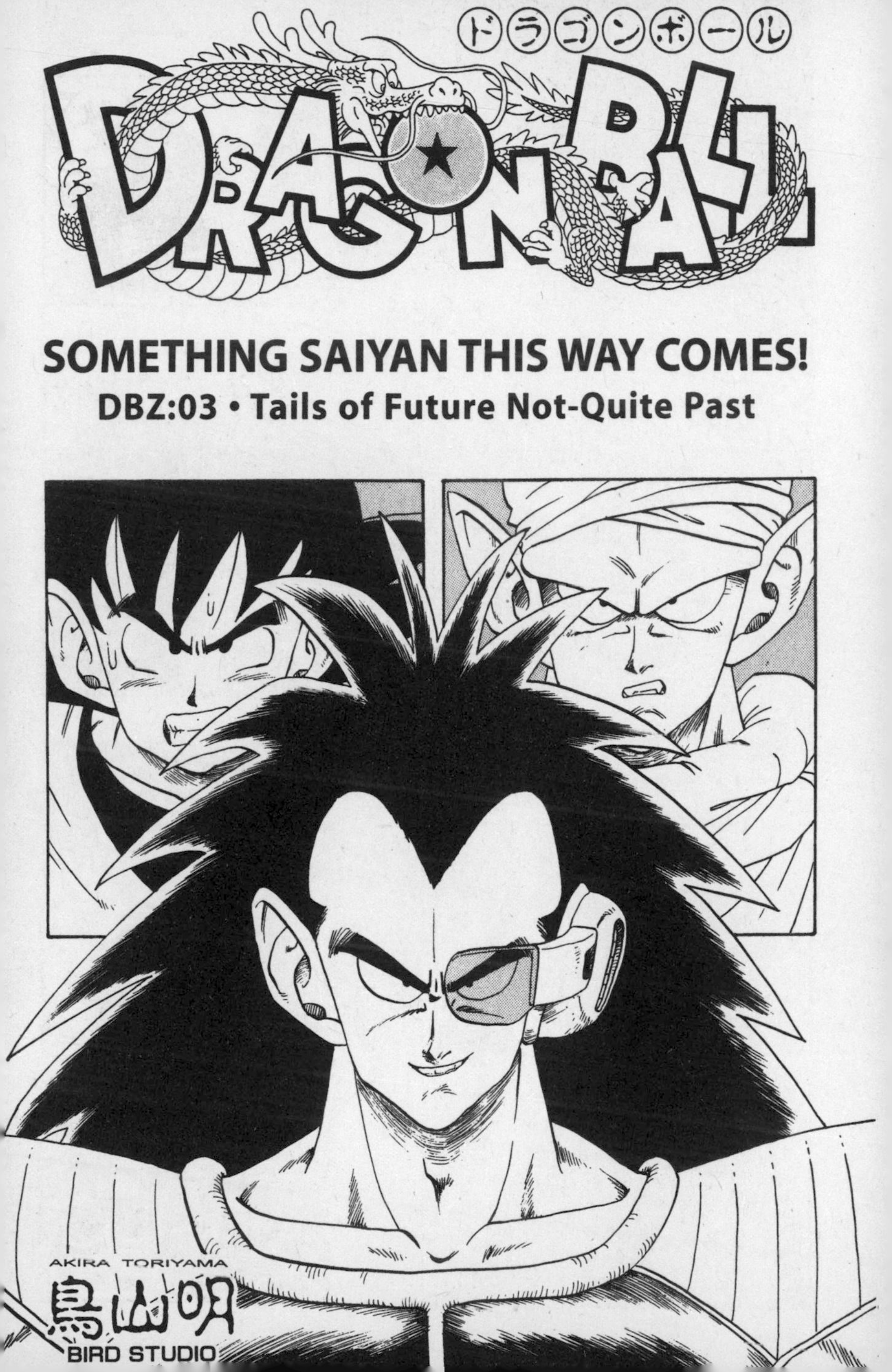
AKIRA TORIYAMA
鳥山明
BIRD STUDIO

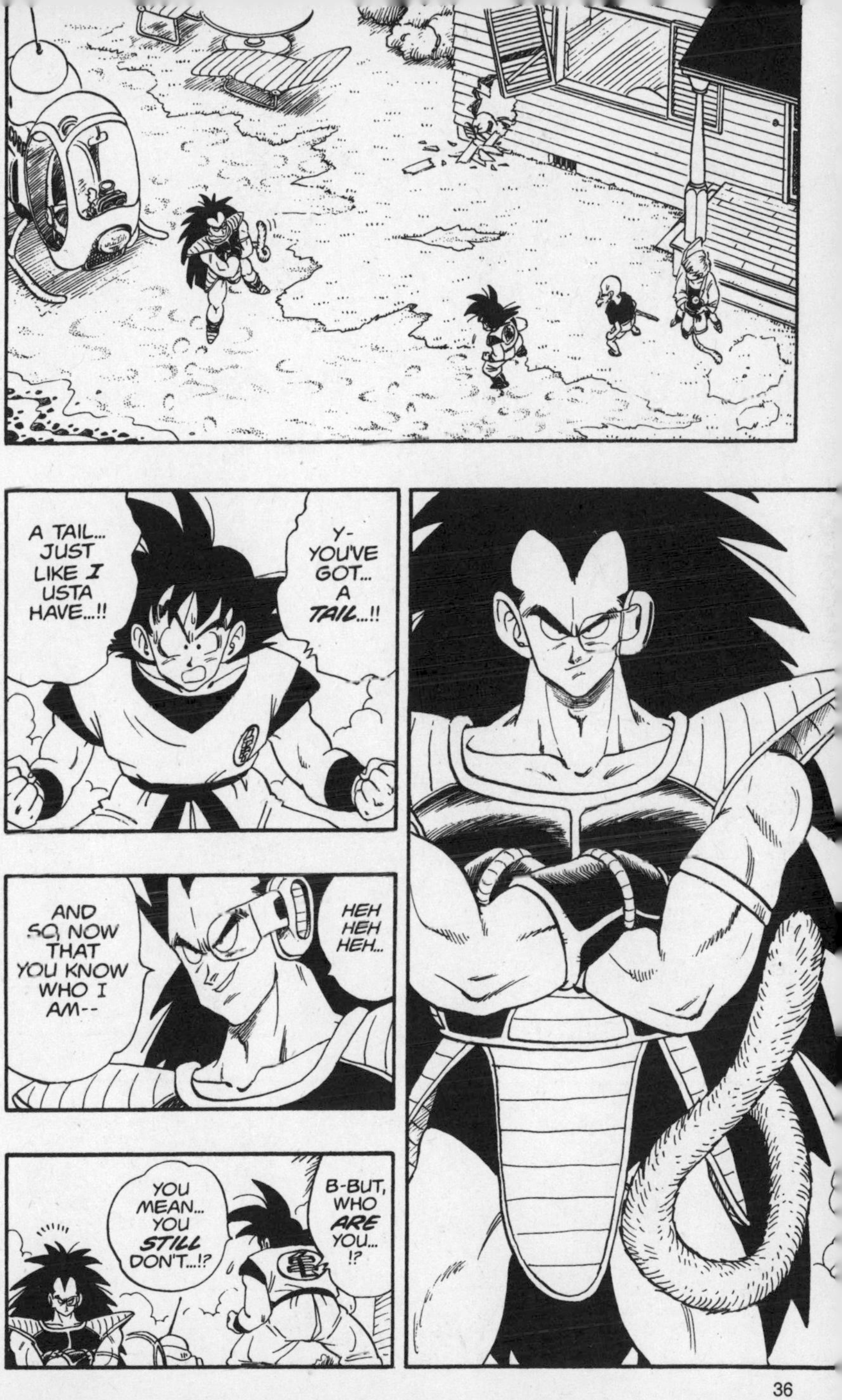
Y-
YOU'VE GOT... A TAIL...!!
A TAIL... JUST LIKE I USTA HAVE...!!
HEH HEH HEH...
AND SO, NOW THAT YOU KNOW WHO I AM--
B-BUT, WHO ARE YOU...!?
YOU MEAN... YOU STILL DON'T...!?

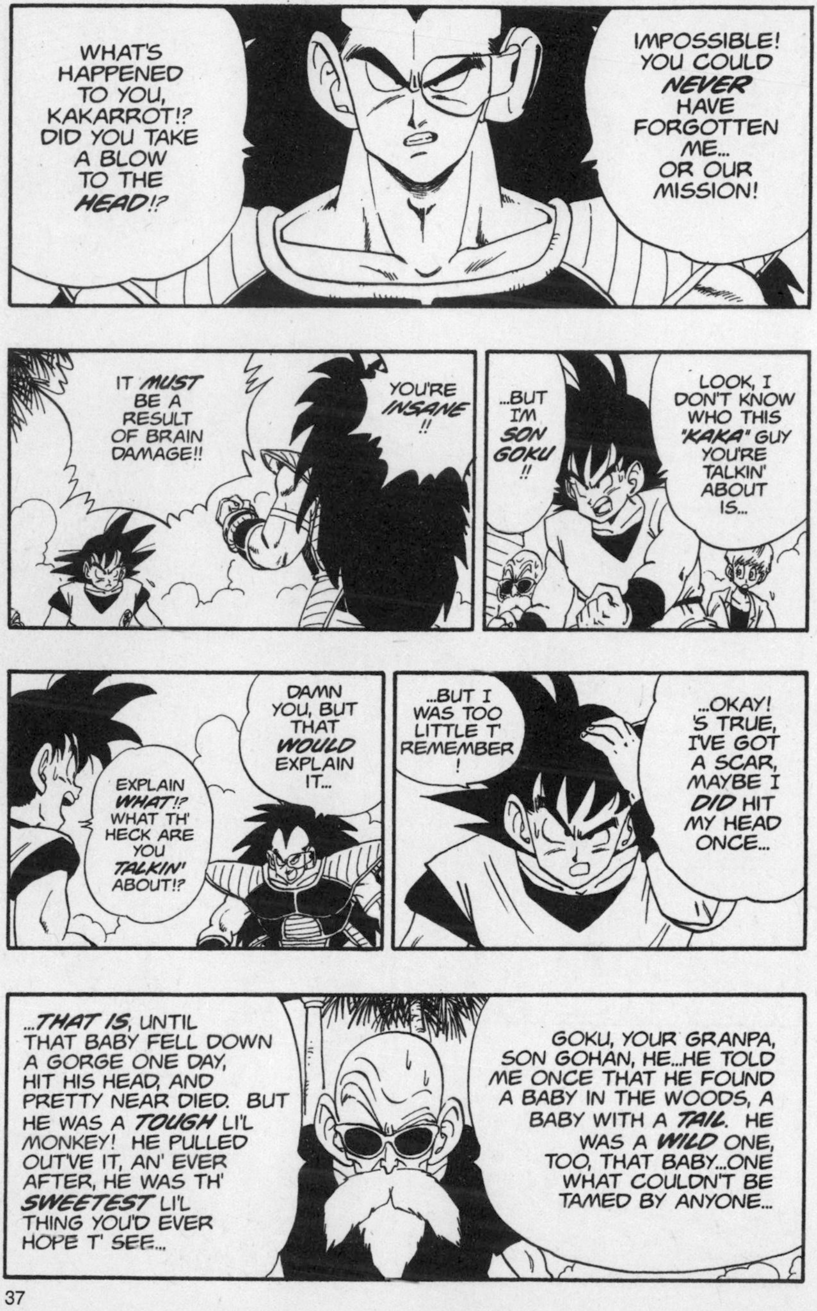
IMPOSSIBLE! YOU COULD *NEVER* HAVE FORGOTTEN ME... OR OUR MISSION!
WHAT'S HAPPENED TO YOU, KAKARROT!? DID YOU TAKE A BLOW TO THE *HEAD*!?
LOOK, I DON'T KNOW WHO THIS *"KAKA"* GUY YOU'RE TALKIN' ABOUT IS...
...BUT I'M *SON GOKU* !!
YOU'RE *INSANE* !!
IT *MUST* BE A RESULT OF BRAIN DAMAGE!!
...OKAY! 'S TRUE, I'VE GOT A SCAR, MAYBE I *DID* HIT MY HEAD ONCE...
...BUT I WAS TOO LITTLE T' REMEMBER !
DAMN YOU, BUT THAT *WOULD* EXPLAIN IT...
EXPLAIN *WHAT*!? WHAT TH' HECK ARE YOU *TALKIN'* ABOUT!?
GOKU, YOUR GRANPA, SON GOHAN, HE...HE TOLD ME ONCE THAT HE FOUND A BABY IN THE WOODS, A BABY WITH A *TAIL*. HE WAS A *WILD* ONE, TOO, THAT BABY...ONE WHAT COULDN'T BE TAMED BY ANYONE...
...*THAT IS*, UNTIL THAT BABY FELL DOWN A GORGE ONE DAY, HIT HIS HEAD, AND PRETTY NEAR DIED. BUT HE WAS A *TOUGH* LI'L MONKEY! HE PULLED OUT'VE IT, AN' EVER AFTER, HE WAS TH' *SWEETEST* LI'L THING YOU'D EVER HOPE T' SEE...

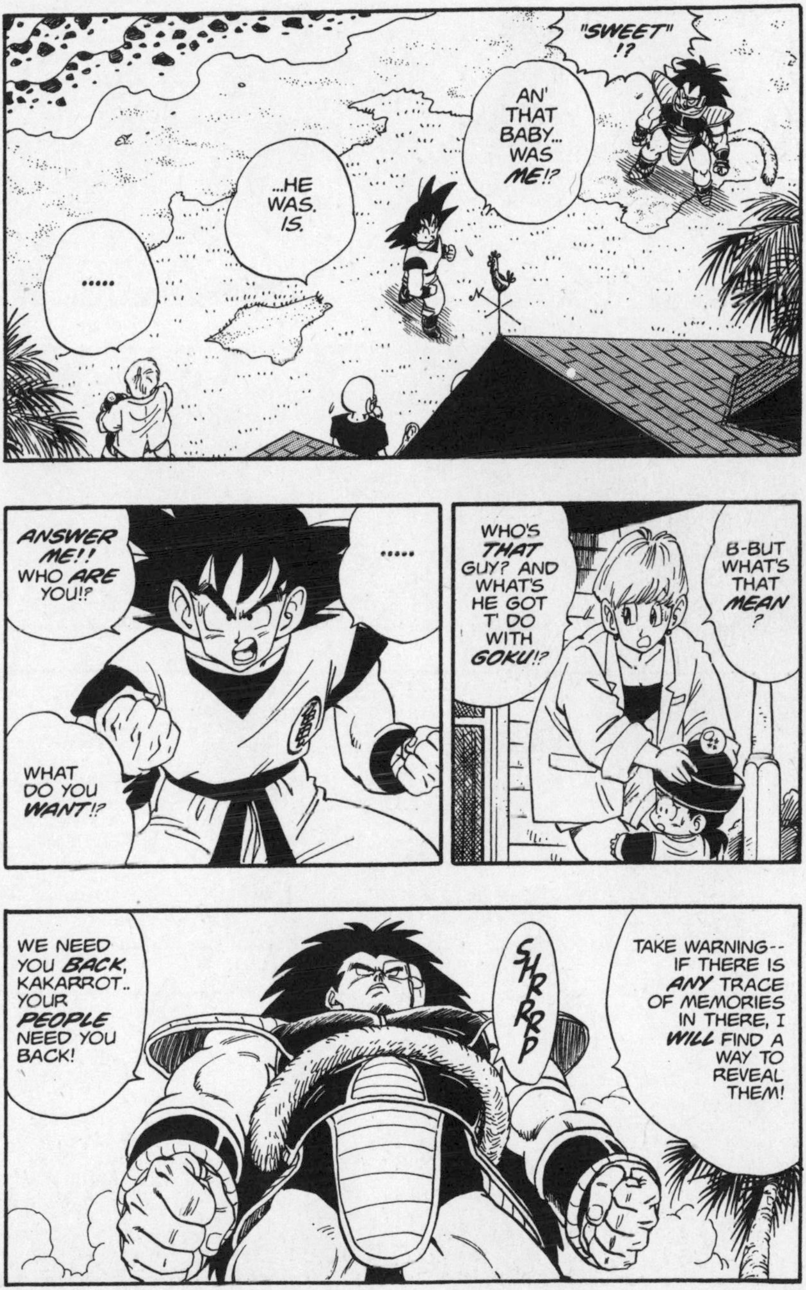
"SWEET" !?
AN' THAT BABY... WAS ME!?
...HE WAS. IS.
......
B-BUT WHAT'S THAT MEAN?
WHO'S THAT GUY? AND WHAT'S HE GOT T' DO WITH GOKU!?
......
ANSWER ME!! WHO ARE YOU!?
WHAT DO YOU WANT!?
TAKE WARNING-- IF THERE IS ANY TRACE OF MEMORIES IN THERE, I WILL FIND A WAY TO REVEAL THEM!
SHRRRP
WE NEED YOU BACK, KAKARROT.. YOUR PEOPLE NEED YOU BACK!

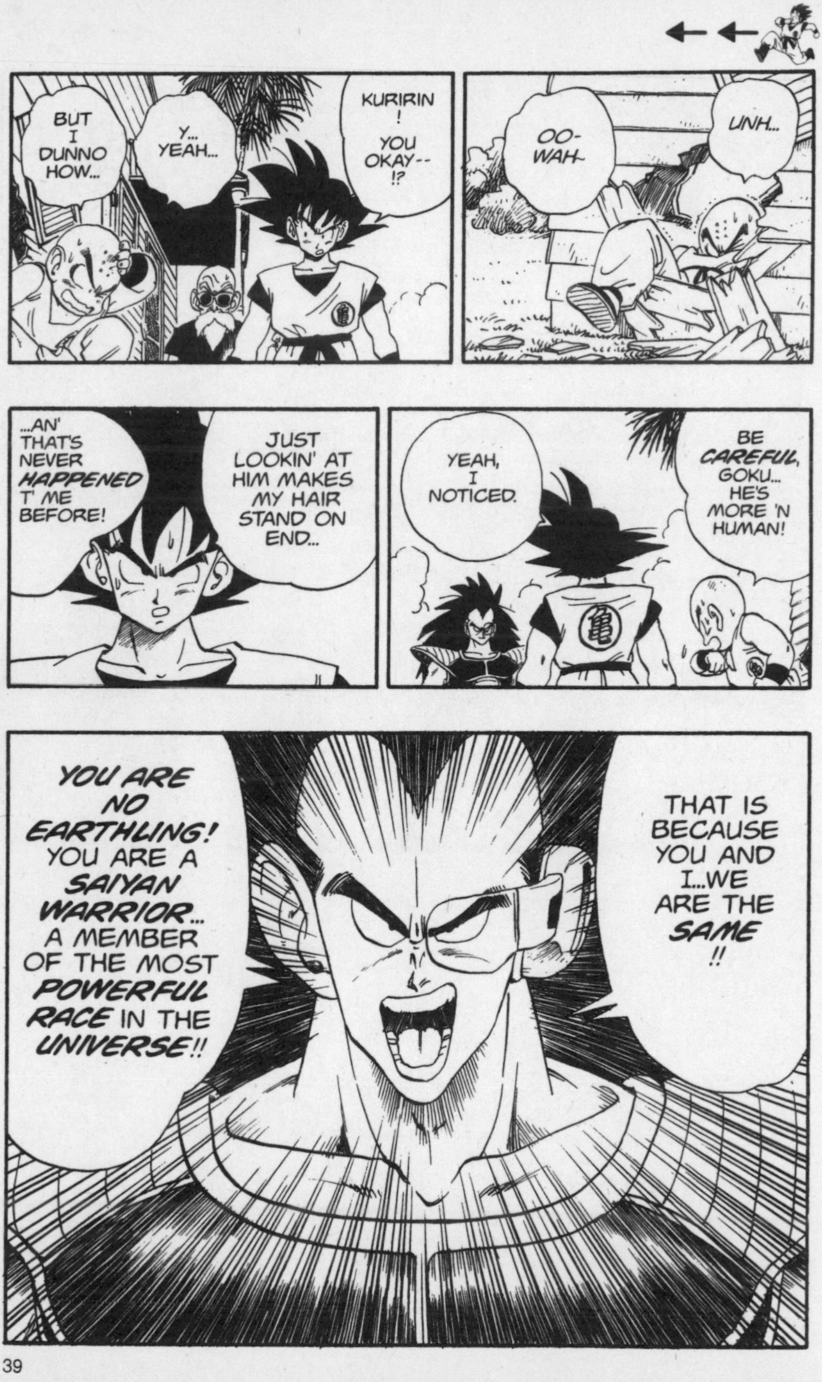
UNH...
OO-WAH
KURIRIN! YOU OKAY--!?
Y... YEAH...
BUT I DUNNO HOW...
BE CAREFUL, GOKU... HE'S MORE 'N HUMAN!
YEAH, I NOTICED.
JUST LOOKIN' AT HIM MAKES MY HAIR STAND ON END...
...AN' THAT'S NEVER HAPPENED T' ME BEFORE!
THAT IS BECAUSE YOU AND I...WE ARE THE SAME!!
YOU ARE NO EARTHLING! YOU ARE A SAIYAN WARRIOR... A MEMBER OF THE MOST POWERFUL RACE IN THE UNIVERSE!!

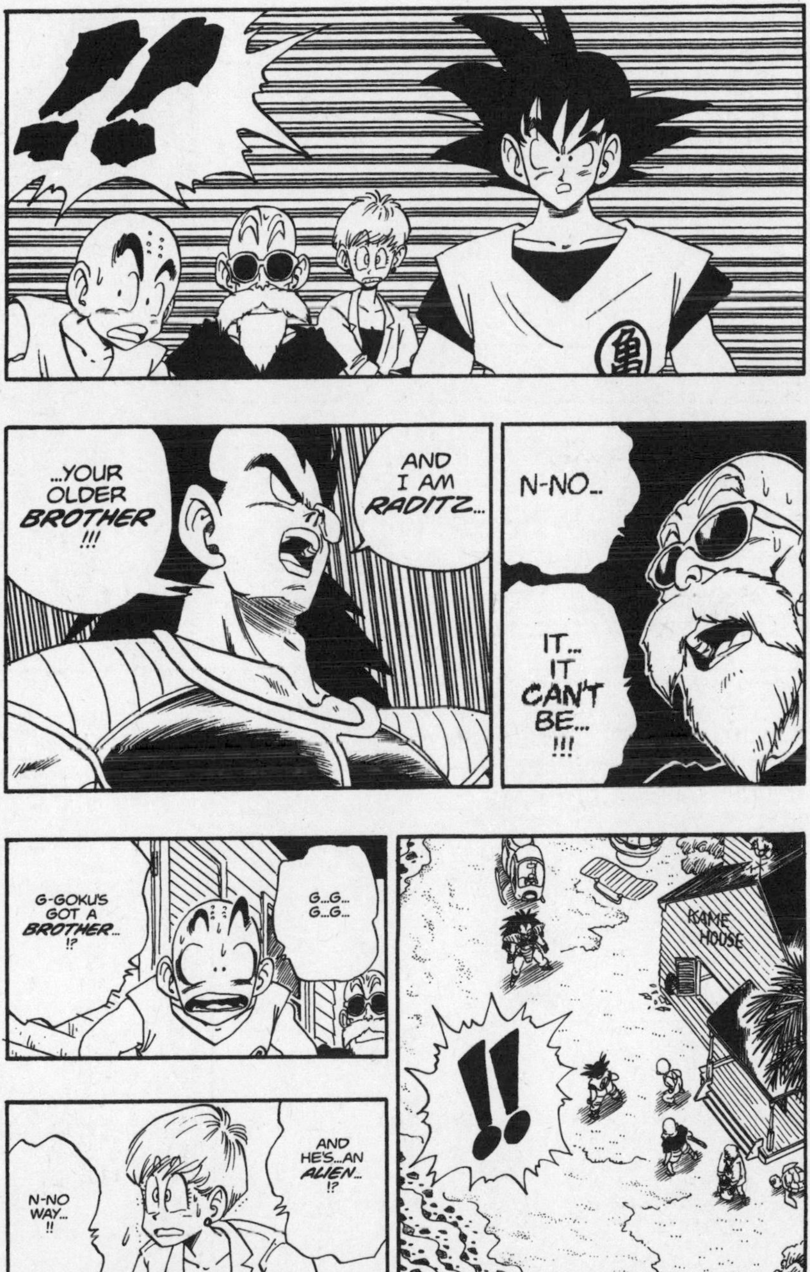
!!
N-NO..
IT... IT CAN'T BE... !!!
AND I AM RADITZ...
...YOUR OLDER BROTHER !!!
KAME HOUSE
!!
G...G... G...G...
G-GOKU'S GOT A BROTHER... !?
AND HE'S...AN ALIEN... !?
N-NO WAY... !!

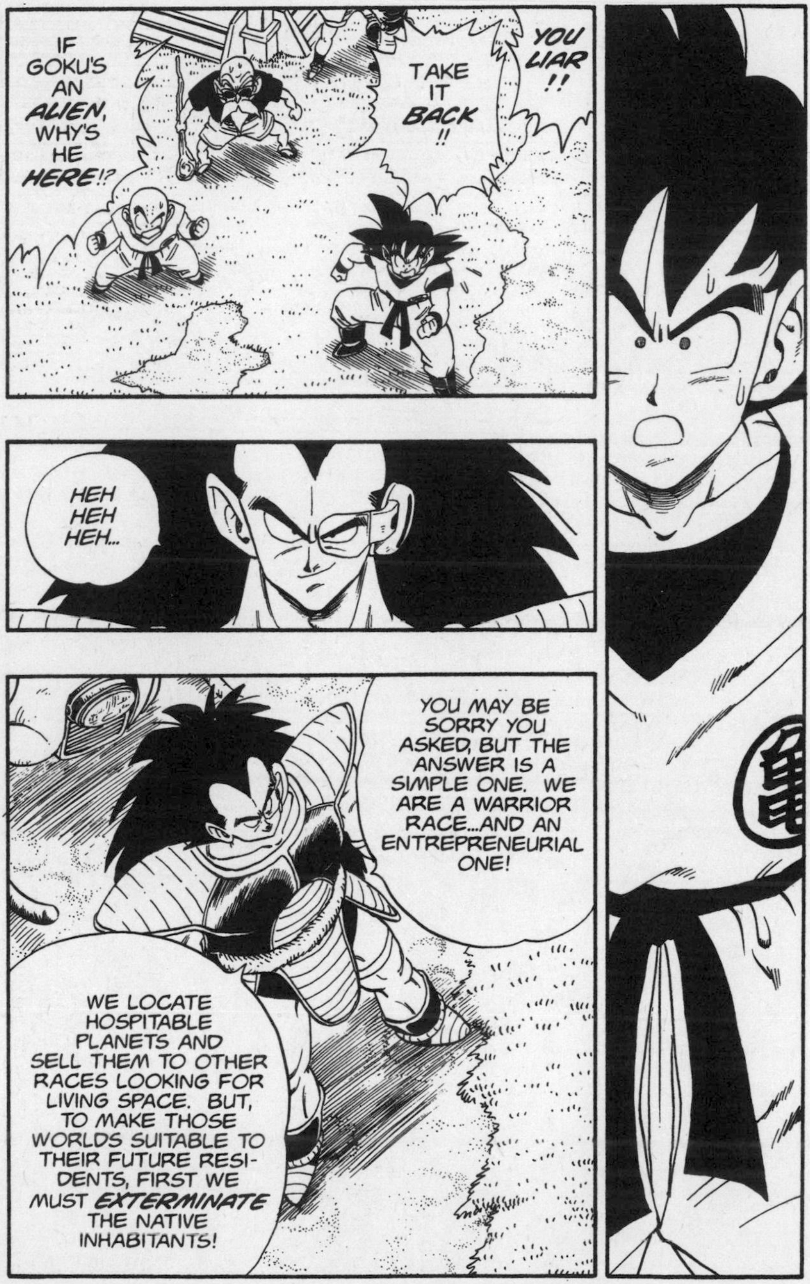
YOU LIAR!!
TAKE IT BACK!!
IF GOKU'S AN ALIEN, WHY'S HE HERE!?
HEH HEH HEH...
YOU MAY BE SORRY YOU ASKED, BUT THE ANSWER IS A SIMPLE ONE. WE ARE A WARRIOR RACE...AND AN ENTREPRENEURIAL ONE!
WE LOCATE HOSPITABLE PLANETS AND SELL THEM TO OTHER RACES LOOKING FOR LIVING SPACE. BUT, TO MAKE THOSE WORLDS SUITABLE TO THEIR FUTURE RESI-DENTS, FIRST WE MUST EXTERMINATE THE NATIVE INHABITANTS!

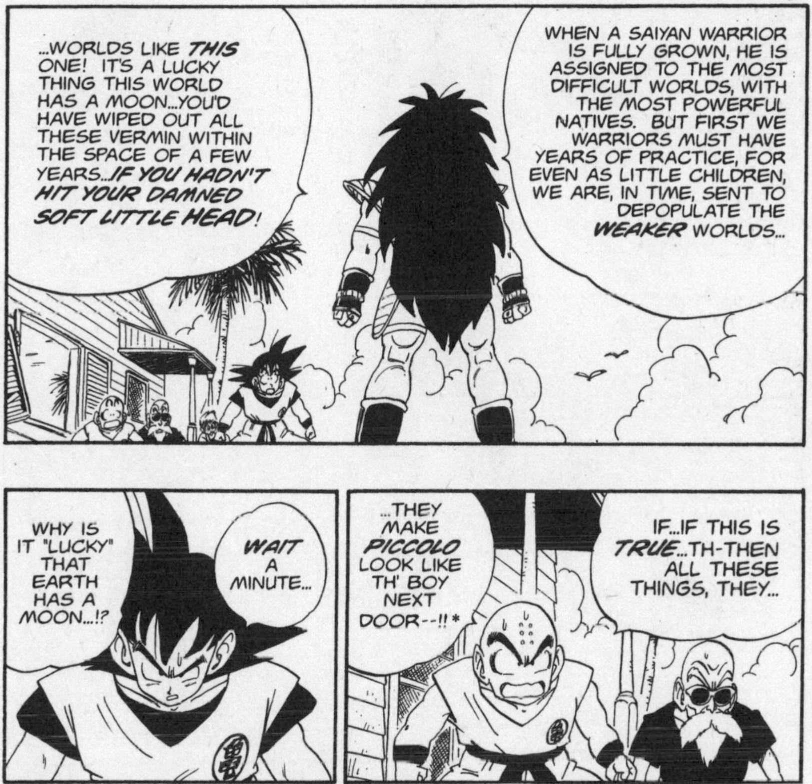
WHEN A SAIYAN WARRIOR IS FULLY GROWN, HE IS ASSIGNED TO THE MOST DIFFICULT WORLDS, WITH THE MOST POWERFUL NATIVES. BUT FIRST WE WARRIORS MUST HAVE YEARS OF PRACTICE, FOR EVEN AS LITTLE CHILDREN, WE ARE, IN TIME, SENT TO DEPOPULATE THE WEAKER WORLDS...
...WORLDS LIKE THIS ONE! IT'S A LUCKY THING THIS WORLD HAS A MOON...YOU'D HAVE WIPED OUT ALL THESE VERMIN WITHIN THE SPACE OF A FEW YEARS...IF YOU HADN'T HIT YOUR DAMNED SOFT LITTLE HEAD!
IF...IF THIS IS TRUE...TH-THEN ALL THESE THINGS, THEY...
...THEY MAKE PICCOLO LOOK LIKE TH' BOY NEXT DOOR--!!*
WAIT A MINUTE...
WHY IS IT "LUCKY" THAT EARTH HAS A MOON...!?

*PICCOLO'S MANY EVIL DEEDS ARE SHOWN IN THE LATER VOLUMES OF **DRAGON BALL**, WHICH TAKE PLACE BEFORE **DRAGON BALL Z**.

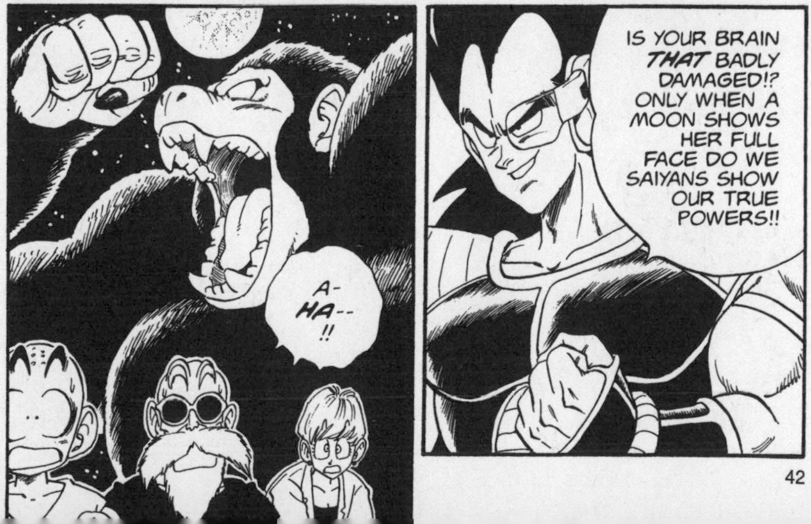
IS YOUR BRAIN THAT BADLY DAMAGED!? ONLY WHEN A MOON SHOWS HER FULL FACE DO WE SAIYANS SHOW OUR TRUE POWERS!!
A-HA--!!

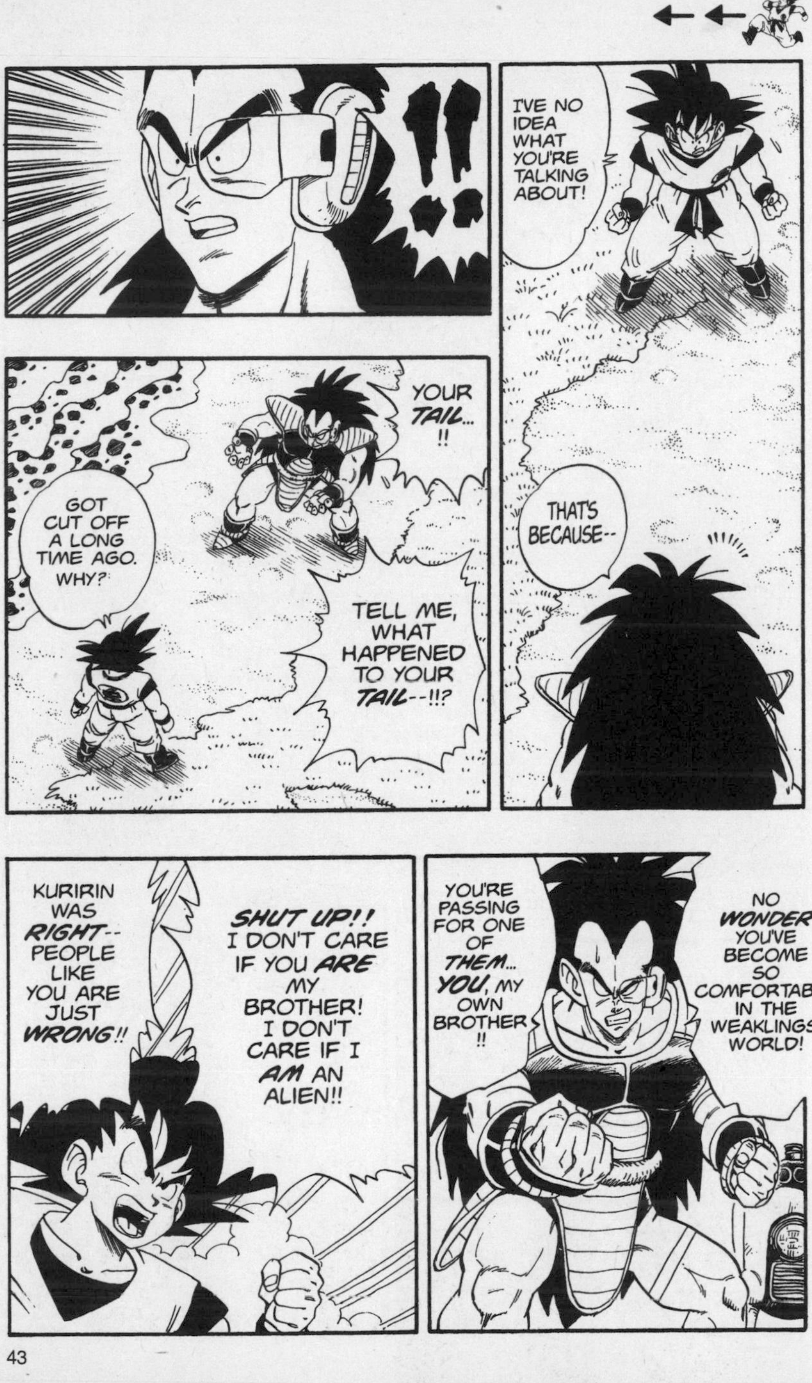

YOUR TAIL... !!
GOT CUT OFF A LONG TIME AGO. WHY?
TELL ME, WHAT HAPPENED TO YOUR TAIL--!!?
I'VE NO IDEA WHAT YOU'RE TALKING ABOUT!
THAT'S BECAUSE--
NO WONDER YOU'VE BECOME SO COMFORTABLE IN THE WEAKLINGS' WORLD!
YOU'RE PASSING FOR ONE OF THEM... YOU, MY OWN BROTHER !!
SHUT UP!! I DON'T CARE IF YOU ARE MY BROTHER! I DON'T CARE IF I AM AN ALIEN!!
KURIRIN WAS RIGHT--PEOPLE LIKE YOU ARE JUST WRONG!!

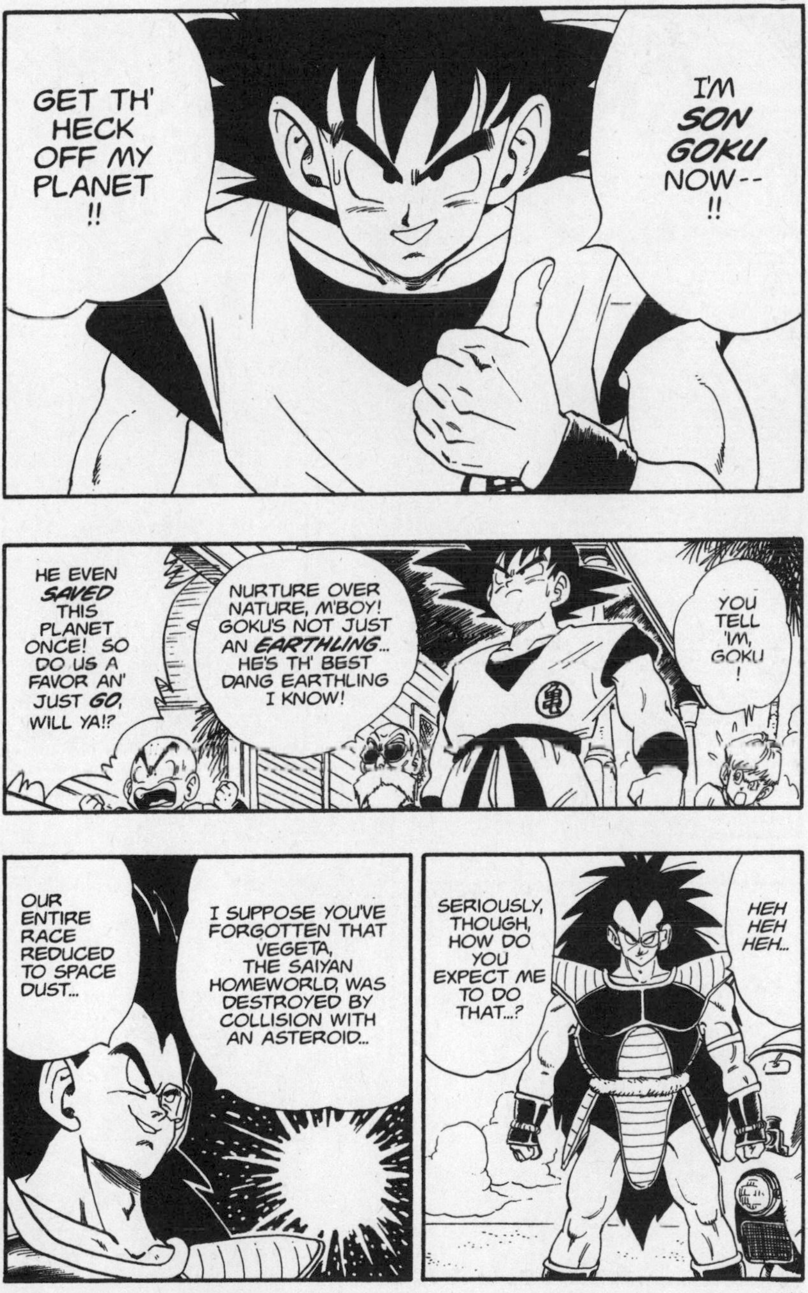
I'M SON GOKU NOW--!!
GET TH' HECK OFF MY PLANET!!
YOU TELL 'IM, GOKU!
NURTURE OVER NATURE, M'BOY! GOKU'S NOT JUST AN EARTHLING... HE'S TH' BEST DANG EARTHLING I KNOW!
HE EVEN SAVED THIS PLANET ONCE! SO DO US A FAVOR AN' JUST GO, WILL YA!?
HEH HEH HEH...
SERIOUSLY, THOUGH, HOW DO YOU EXPECT ME TO DO THAT...?
I SUPPOSE YOU'VE FORGOTTEN THAT VEGETA, THE SAIYAN HOMEWORLD, WAS DESTROYED BY COLLISION WITH AN ASTEROID...
OUR ENTIRE RACE REDUCED TO SPACE DUST...

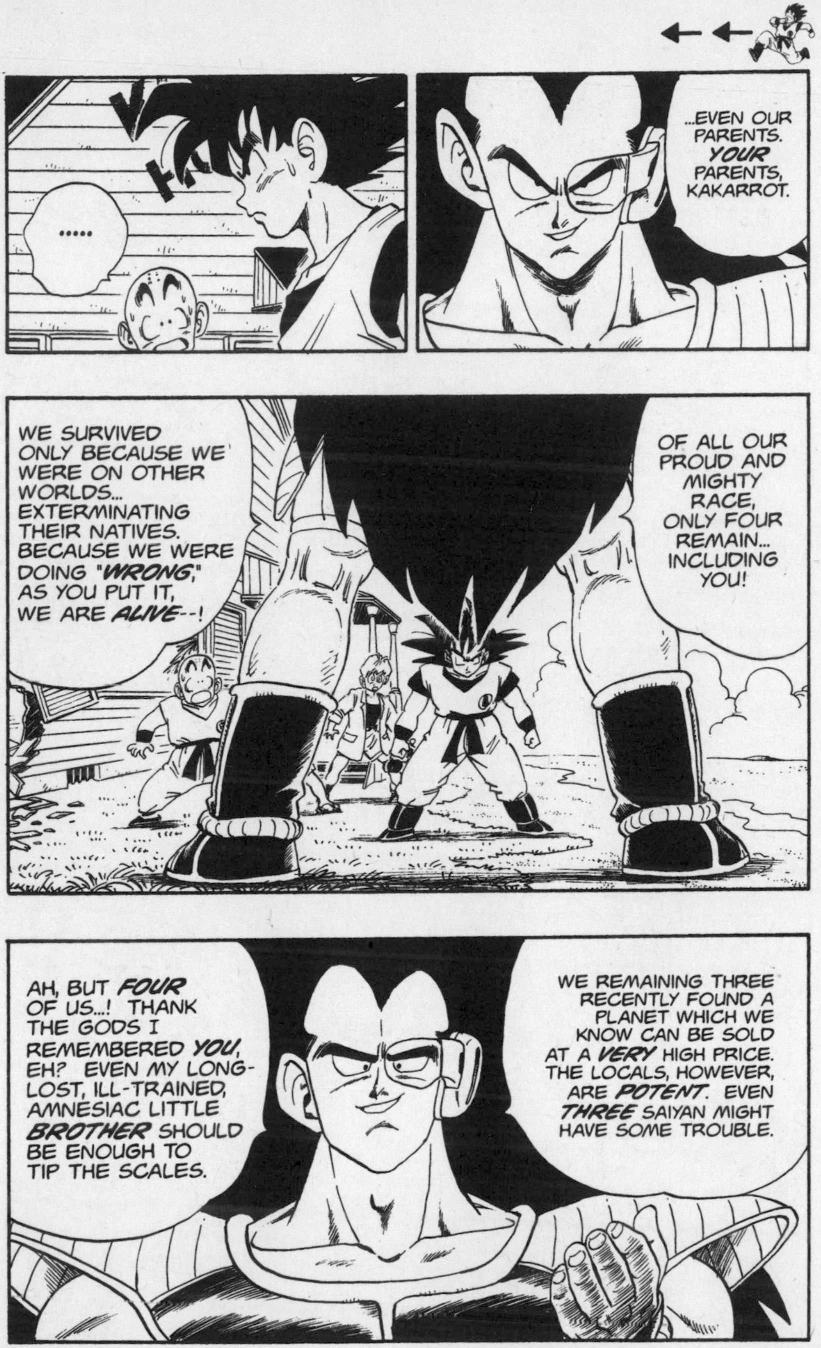
...EVEN OUR PARENTS. YOUR PARENTS, KAKARROT.
.....
OF ALL OUR PROUD AND MIGHTY RACE, ONLY FOUR REMAIN... INCLUDING YOU!
WE SURVIVED ONLY BECAUSE WE WERE ON OTHER WORLDS... EXTERMINATING THEIR NATIVES. BECAUSE WE WERE DOING "WRONG," AS YOU PUT IT, WE ARE ALIVE--!
WE REMAINING THREE RECENTLY FOUND A PLANET WHICH WE KNOW CAN BE SOLD AT A VERY HIGH PRICE. THE LOCALS, HOWEVER, ARE POTENT. EVEN THREE SAIYAN MIGHT HAVE SOME TROUBLE.
AH, BUT FOUR OF US...! THANK THE GODS I REMEMBERED YOU, EH? EVEN MY LONG-LOST, ILL-TRAINED, AMNESIAC LITTLE BROTHER SHOULD BE ENOUGH TO TIP THE SCALES.

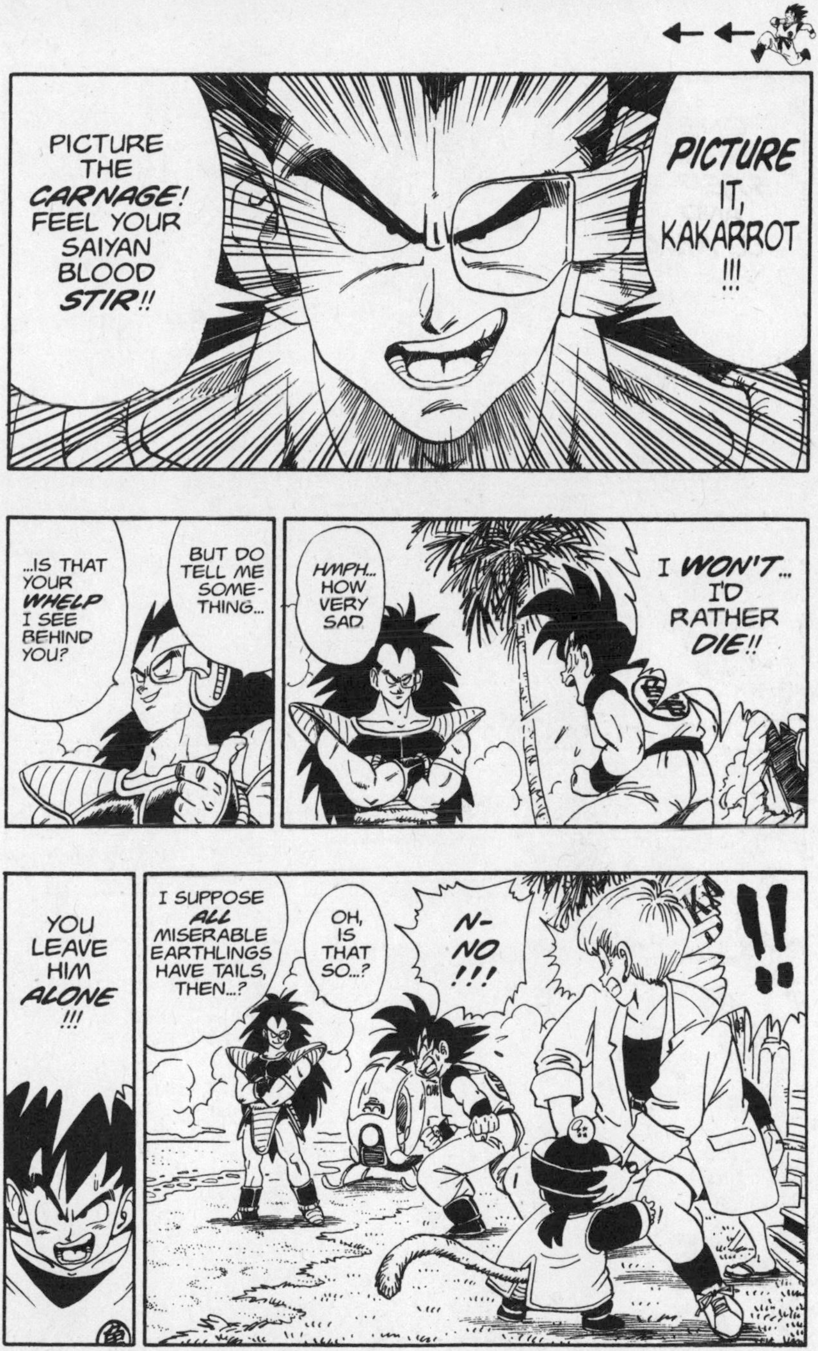
PICTURE IT, KAKARROT!!!
PICTURE THE CARNAGE! FEEL YOUR SAIYAN BLOOD STIR!!
I WON'T... I'D RATHER DIE!!
HMPH... HOW VERY SAD.
BUT DO TELL ME SOMETHING...
...IS THAT YOUR WHELP I SEE BEHIND YOU?
!!
KA
N-NO!!!
OH, IS THAT SO...?
I SUPPOSE ALL MISERABLE EARTHLINGS HAVE TAILS, THEN...?
YOU LEAVE HIM ALONE!!!

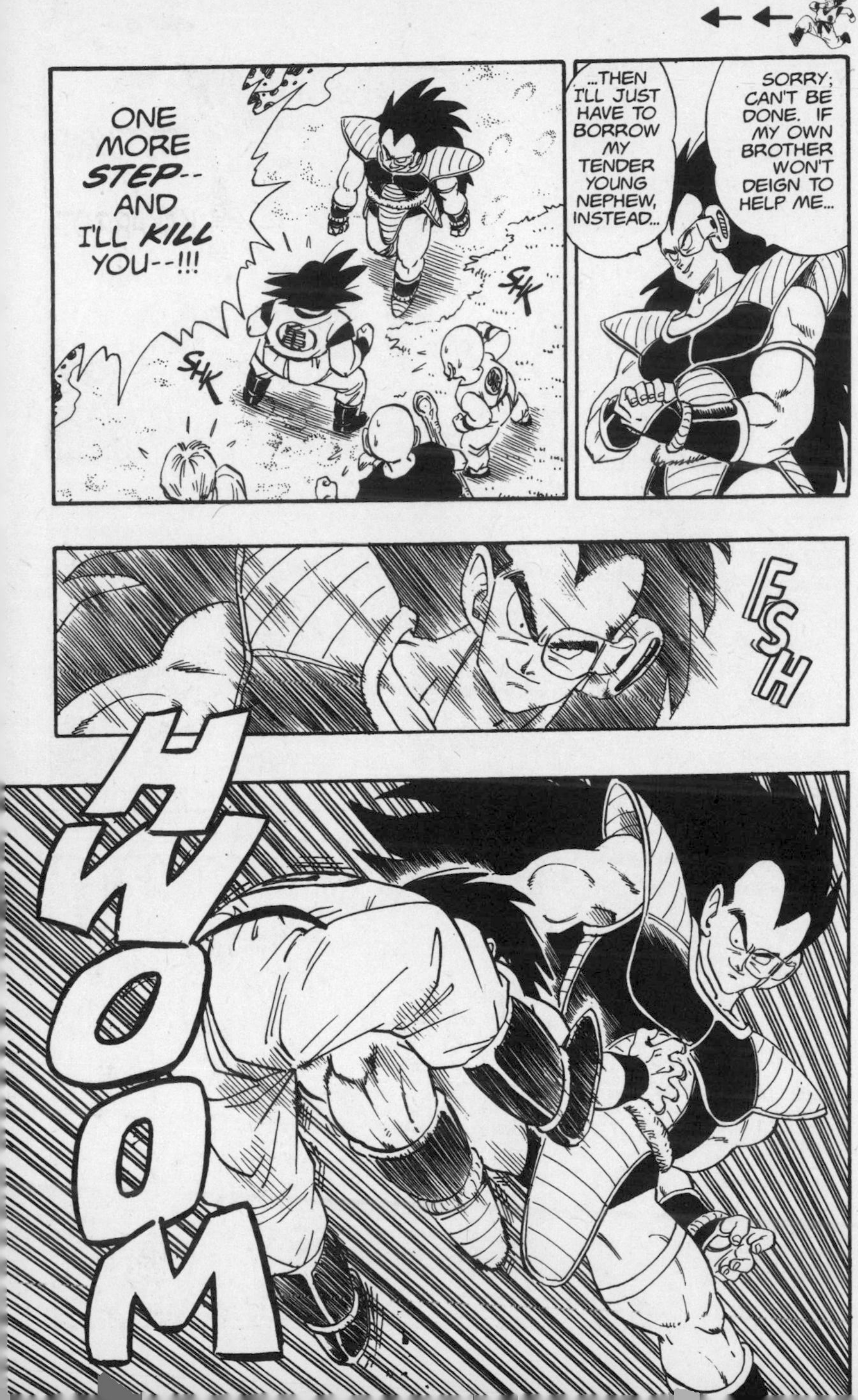
SORRY; CAN'T BE DONE. IF MY OWN BROTHER WON'T DEIGN TO HELP ME...
...THEN I'LL JUST HAVE TO BORROW MY TENDER YOUNG NEPHEW, INSTEAD...
SHK
ONE MORE STEP-- AND I'LL KILL YOU--!!!
SHK
FSH
WHOOM

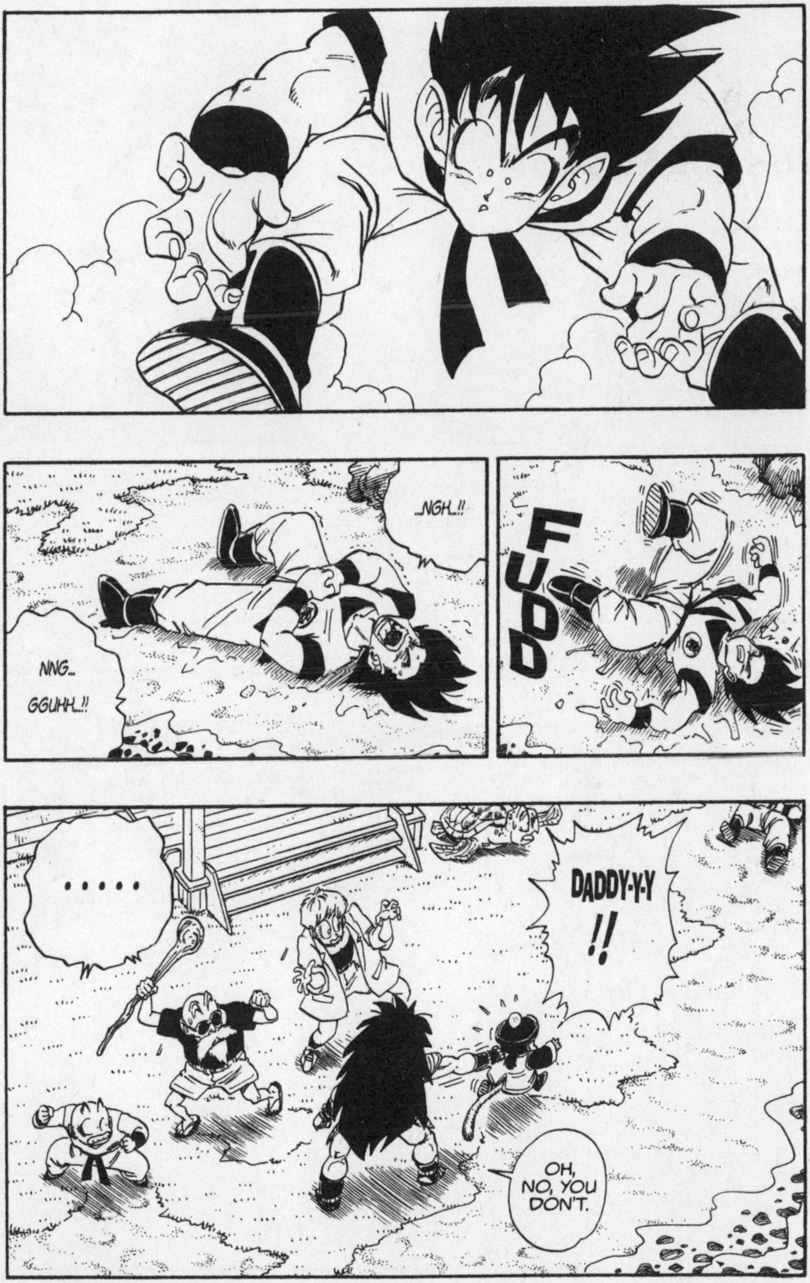
FUDD
...NGH...!!
NNG...
GGUHH...!!
DADDY-Y-Y
!!
.....
OH, NO, YOU DON'T.

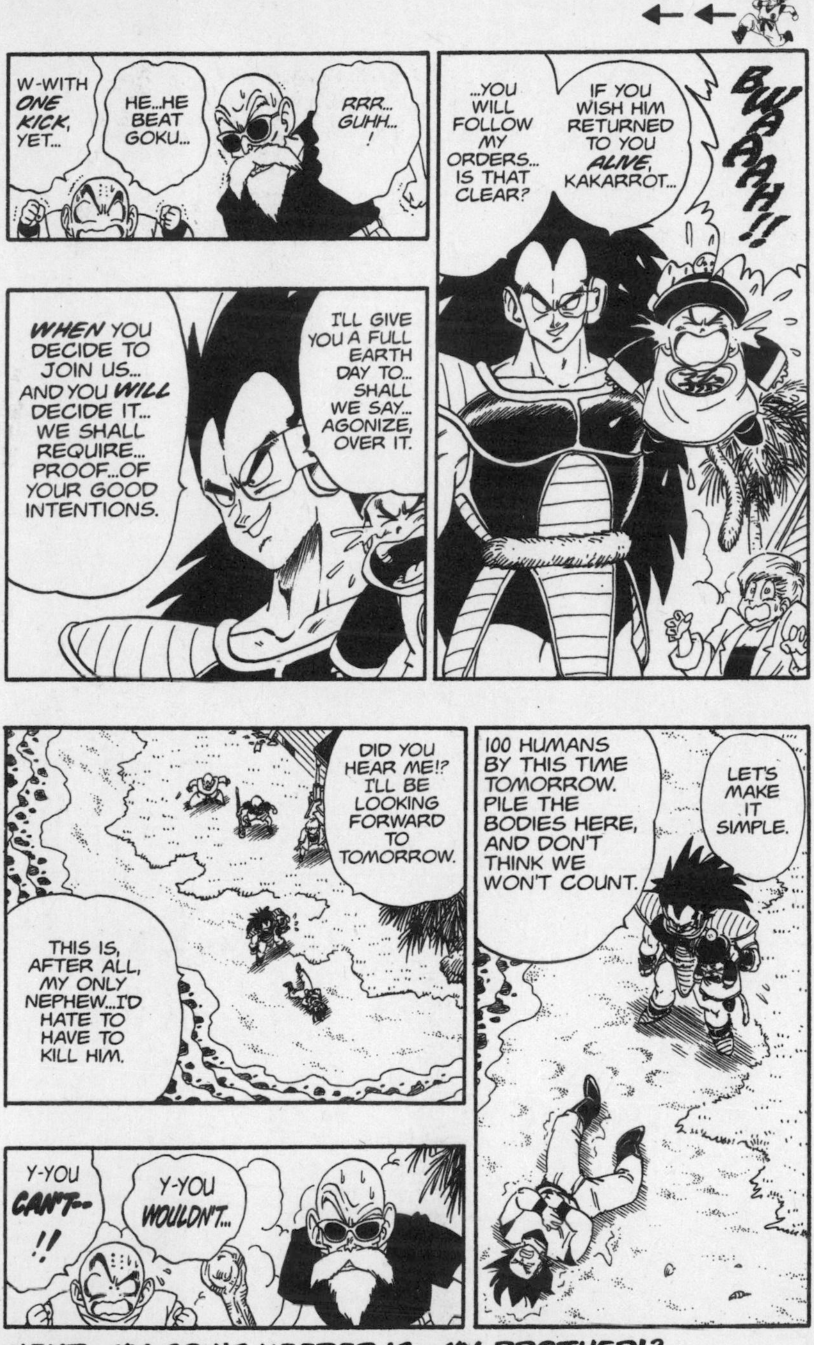
BWAAAH!!
IF YOU WISH HIM RETURNED TO YOU ALIVE, KAKARROT...
...YOU WILL FOLLOW MY ORDERS... IS THAT CLEAR?
RRR... GUHH...!
HE...HE BEAT GOKU...
W-WITH ONE KICK, YET...
I'LL GIVE YOU A FULL EARTH DAY TO... SHALL WE SAY... AGONIZE, OVER IT.
WHEN YOU DECIDE TO JOIN US... AND YOU WILL DECIDE IT... WE SHALL REQUIRE... PROOF...OF YOUR GOOD INTENTIONS.
LET'S MAKE IT SIMPLE.
100 HUMANS BY THIS TIME TOMORROW. PILE THE BODIES HERE, AND DON'T THINK WE WON'T COUNT.
DID YOU HEAR ME!? I'LL BE LOOKING FORWARD TO TOMORROW.
THIS IS, AFTER ALL, MY ONLY NEPHEW...I'D HATE TO HAVE TO KILL HIM.
Y-YOU WOULDN'T...
Y-YOU CAN'T--!!

NEXT: MY SON'S KEEPER IS...MY BROTHER!?

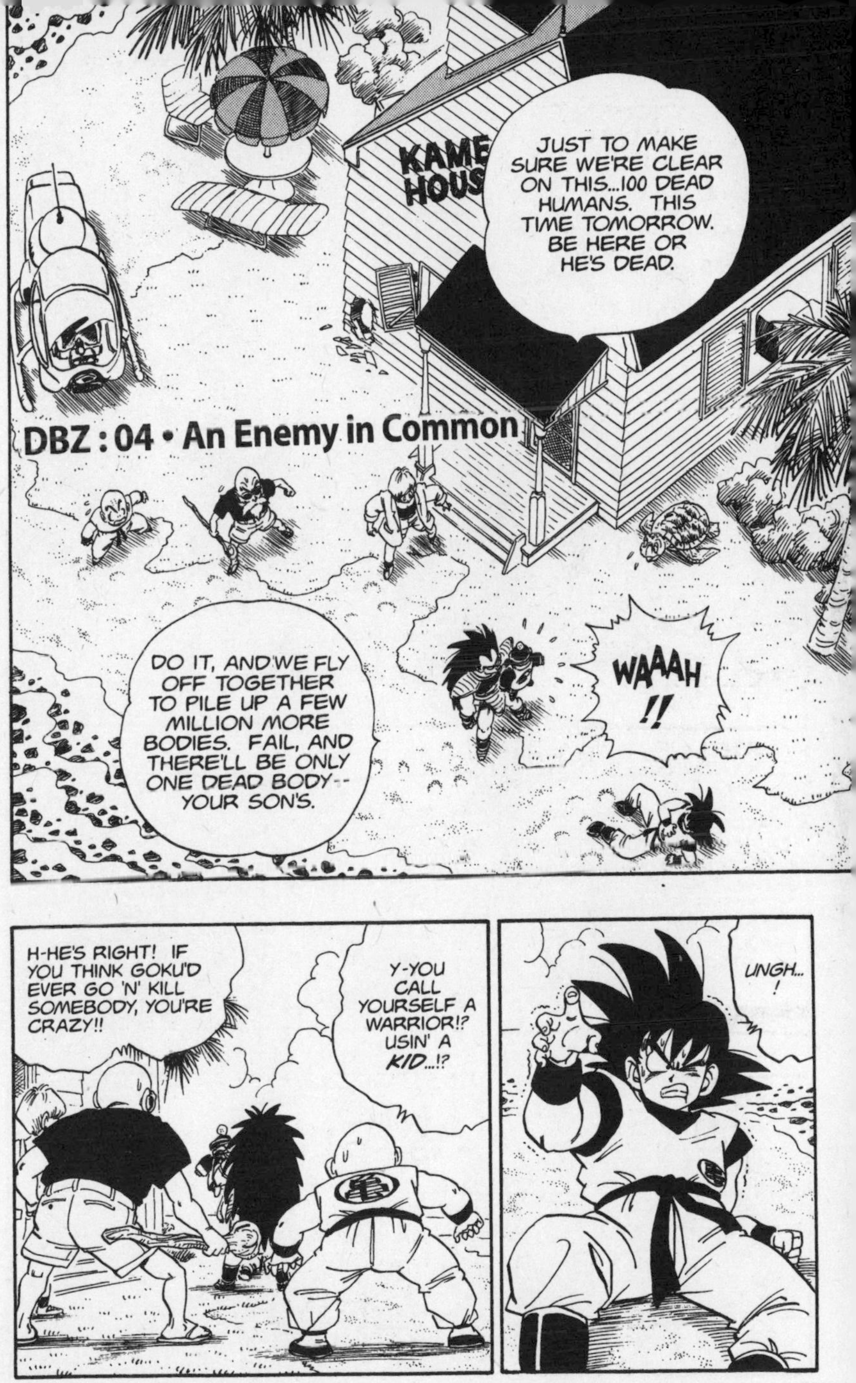
KAME HOUS
JUST TO MAKE SURE WE'RE CLEAR ON THIS...100 DEAD HUMANS. THIS TIME TOMORROW. BE HERE OR HE'S DEAD.
DBZ : 04 • An Enemy in Common
WAAAH !!
DO IT, AND WE FLY OFF TOGETHER TO PILE UP A FEW MILLION MORE BODIES. FAIL, AND THERE'LL BE ONLY ONE DEAD BODY-- YOUR SON'S.
UNGH... !
Y-YOU CALL YOURSELF A WARRIOR!? USIN' A *KID*...!?
H-HE'S RIGHT! IF YOU THINK GOKU'D EVER GO 'N' KILL SOMEBODY, YOU'RE CRAZY!!

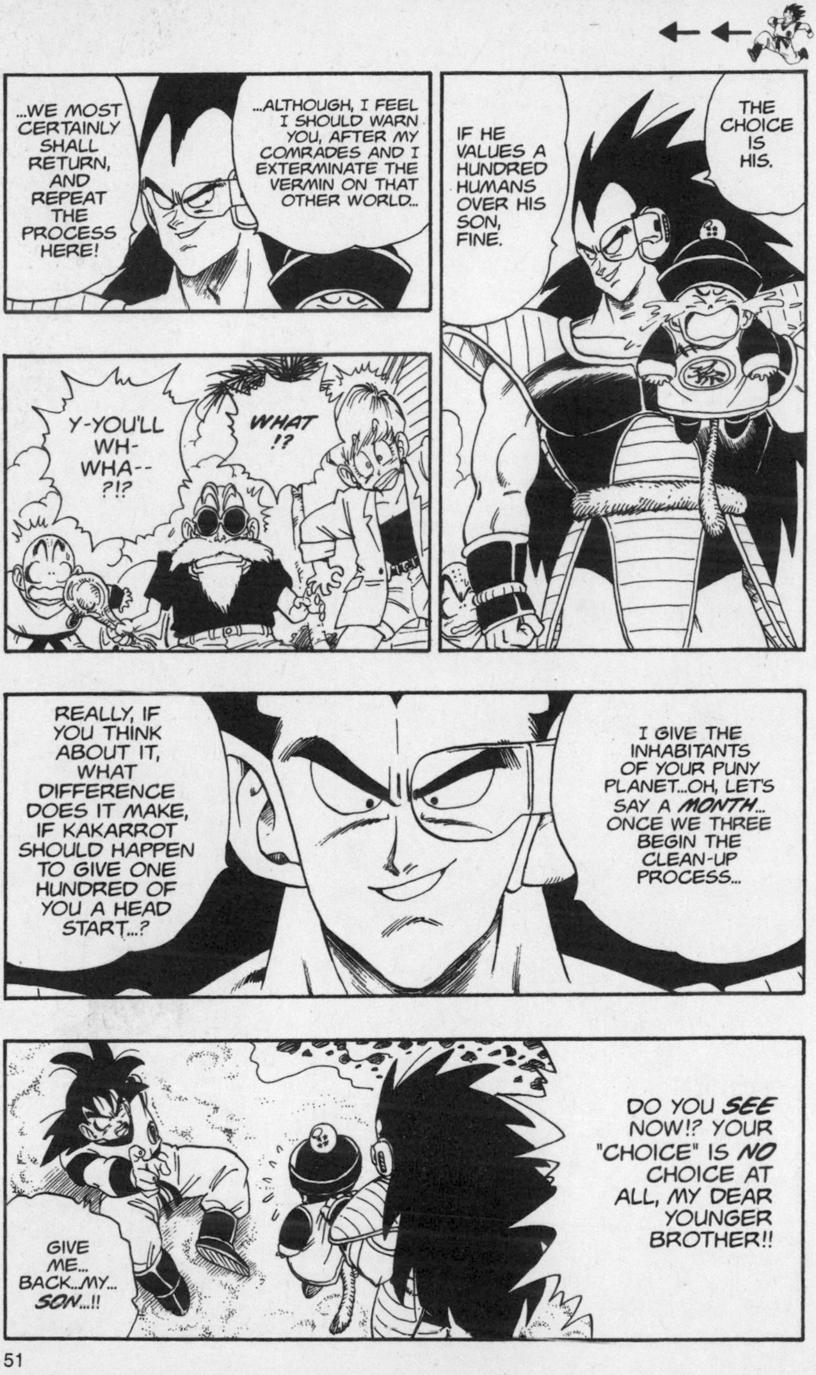
THE CHOICE IS HIS.
IF HE VALUES A HUNDRED HUMANS OVER HIS SON, FINE.
...ALTHOUGH, I FEEL I SHOULD WARN YOU, AFTER MY COMRADES AND I EXTERMINATE THE VERMIN ON THAT OTHER WORLD...
...WE MOST CERTAINLY SHALL RETURN, AND REPEAT THE PROCESS HERE!
WHAT!?
Y-YOU'LL WH- WHA--?!?
I GIVE THE INHABITANTS OF YOUR PUNY PLANET...OH, LET'S SAY A *MONTH*... ONCE WE THREE BEGIN THE CLEAN-UP PROCESS...
REALLY, IF YOU THINK ABOUT IT, WHAT DIFFERENCE DOES IT MAKE, IF KAKARROT SHOULD HAPPEN TO GIVE ONE HUNDRED OF YOU A HEAD START...?
DO YOU *SEE* NOW!? YOUR "CHOICE" IS *NO* CHOICE AT ALL, MY DEAR YOUNGER BROTHER!!
GIVE ME... BACK...MY... *SON*...!!

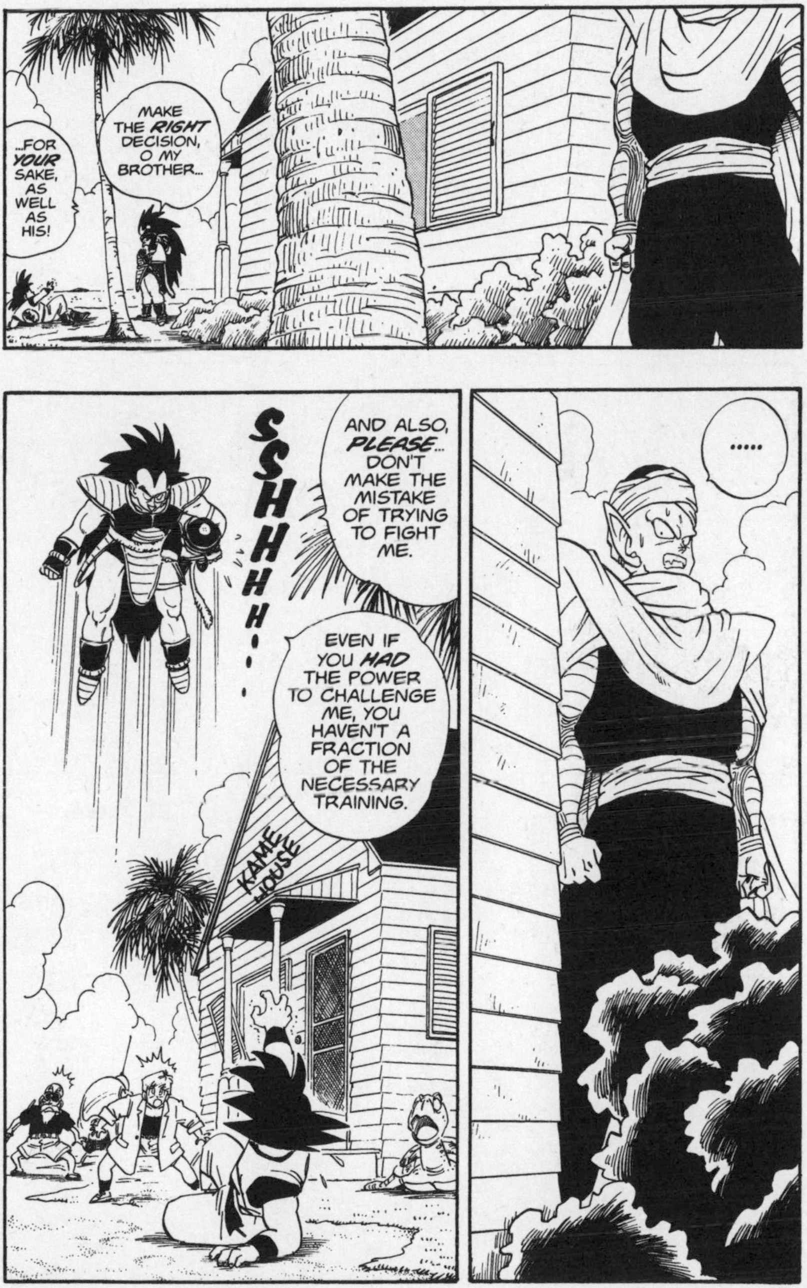
MAKE THE *RIGHT* DECISION, O MY BROTHER...
...FOR *YOUR* SAKE, AS WELL AS HIS!
......
AND ALSO, *PLEASE*... DON'T MAKE THE MISTAKE OF TRYING TO FIGHT ME.
SSHHHH...
EVEN IF YOU *HAD* THE POWER TO CHALLENGE ME, YOU HAVEN'T A FRACTION OF THE NECESSARY TRAINING.
KAME HOUSE

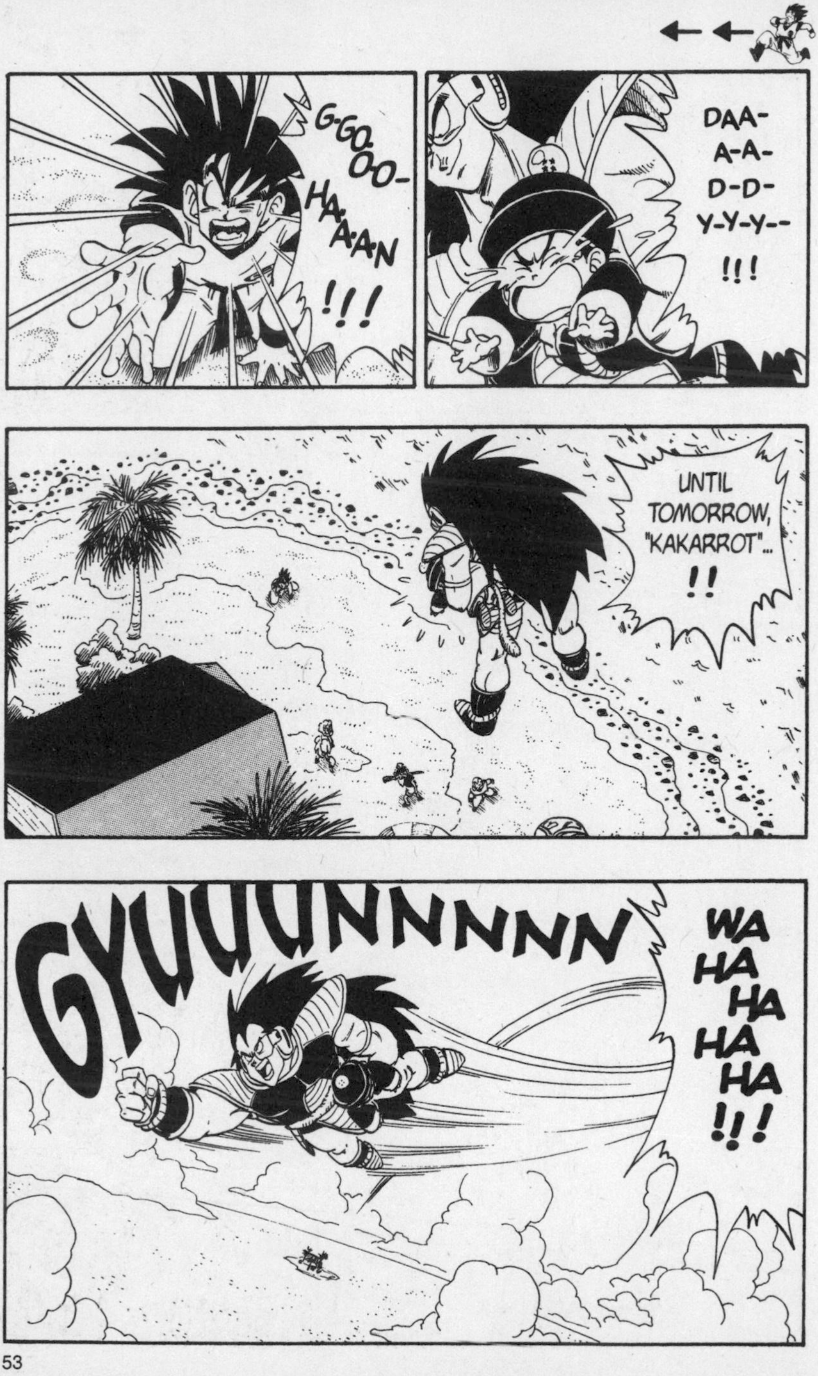
DAA-
A-A-
D-D-
Y-Y-Y--
!!!
G-GO-
O-O-
HA-A-AN
!!!
UNTIL TOMORROW, "KAKARROT"...
!!
WA HA HA HA HA HA
!!!
GYUUUNNNNN

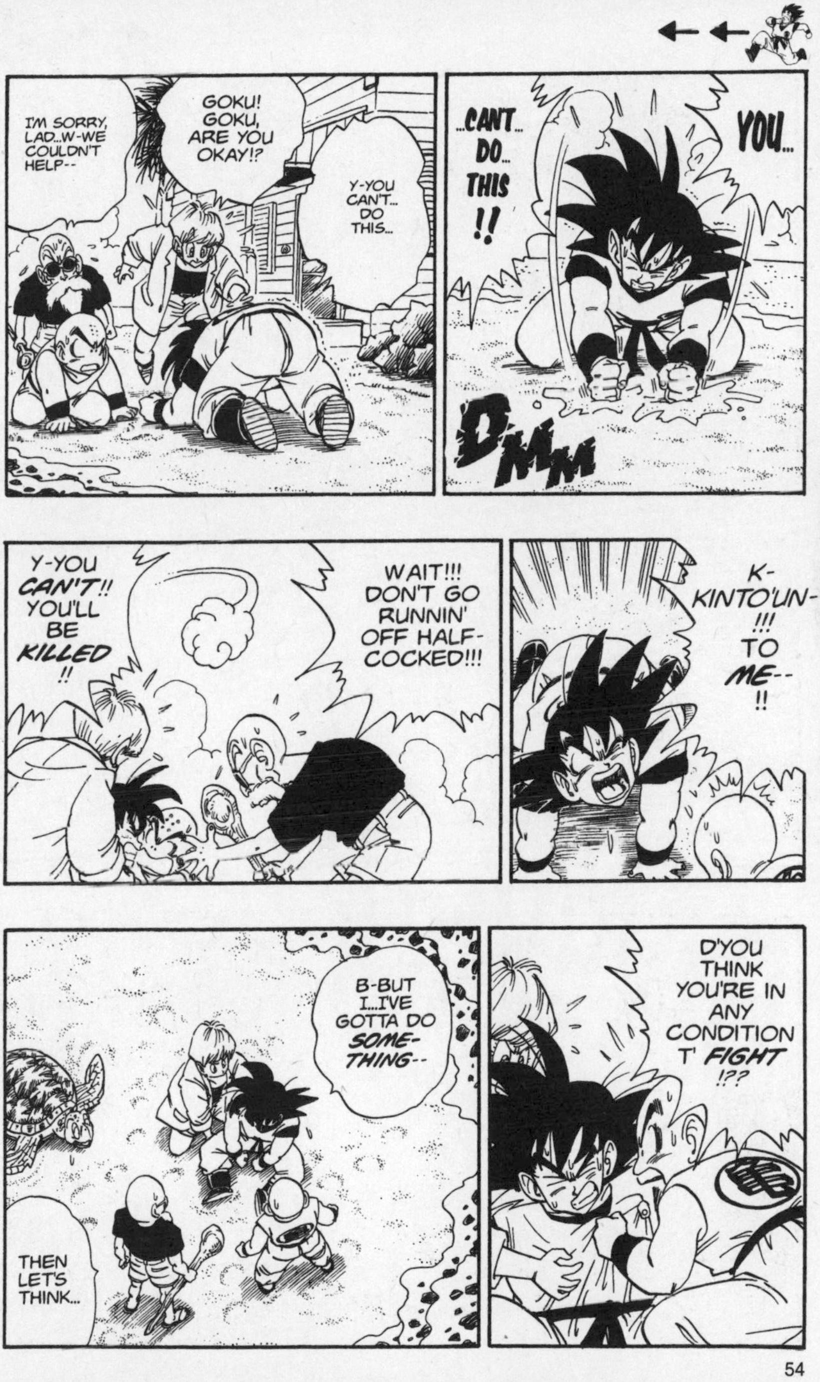
YOU...
...CAN'T... DO... THIS !!
DMM
GOKU! GOKU, ARE YOU OKAY!?
Y-YOU CAN'T... DO THIS...
I'M SORRY, LAD...W-WE COULDN'T HELP--
K-KINTO'UN-- !!! TO ME-- !!
WAIT!!! DON'T GO RUNNIN' OFF HALF-COCKED!!!
Y-YOU CAN'T!! YOU'LL BE KILLED !!
D'YOU THINK YOU'RE IN ANY CONDITION T' FIGHT !??
B-BUT I...I'VE GOTTA DO SOME-THING--
THEN LET'S THINK...

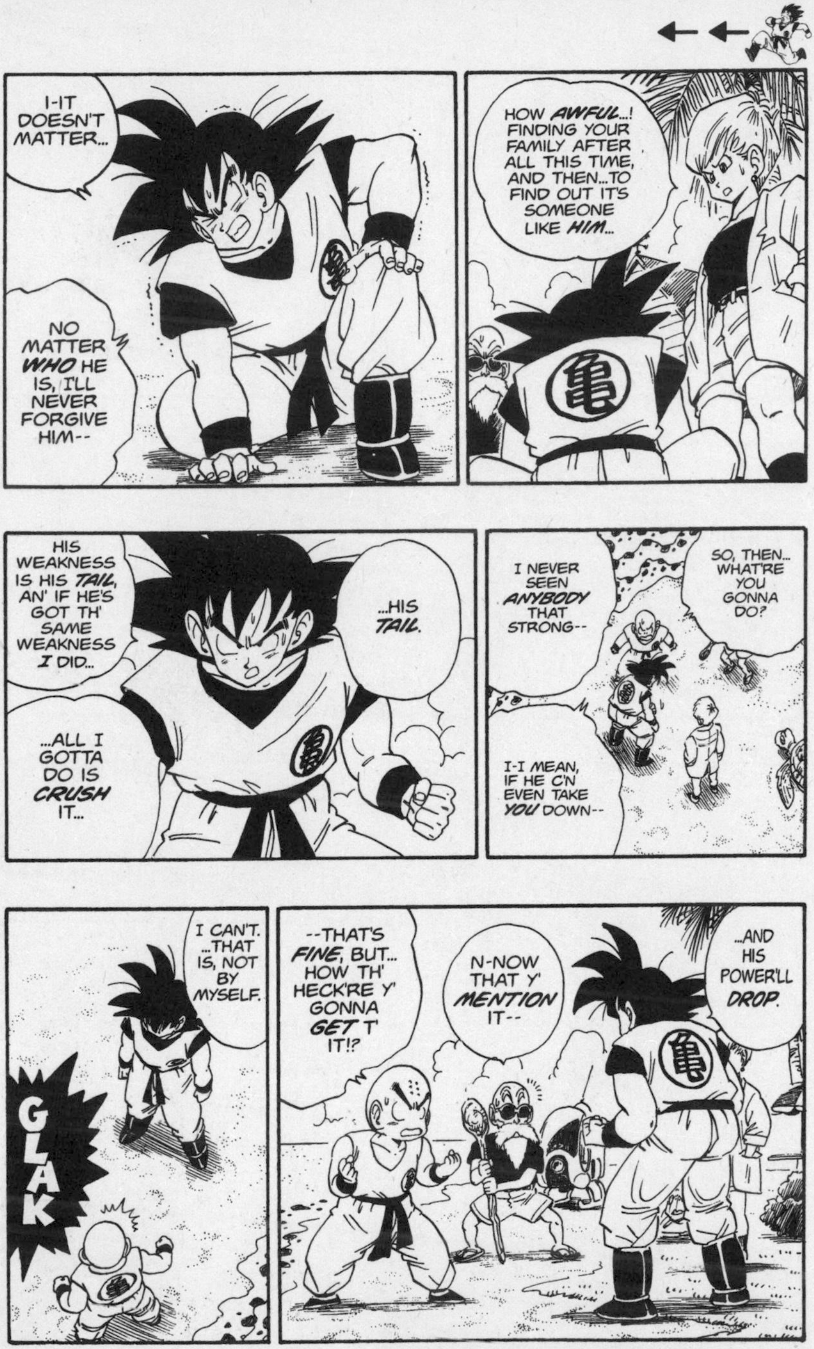
HOW AWFUL...! FINDING YOUR FAMILY AFTER ALL THIS TIME, AND THEN...TO FIND OUT IT'S SOMEONE LIKE HIM...
I-IT DOESN'T MATTER...
NO MATTER WHO HE IS, I'LL NEVER FORGIVE HIM--
SO, THEN... WHAT'RE YOU GONNA DO?
I NEVER SEEN ANYBODY THAT STRONG--
I-I MEAN, IF HE C'N EVEN TAKE YOU DOWN--
...HIS TAIL.
HIS WEAKNESS IS HIS TAIL, AN' IF HE'S GOT TH' SAME WEAKNESS I DID...
...ALL I GOTTA DO IS CRUSH IT...
...AND HIS POWER'LL DROP.
N-NOW THAT Y' MENTION IT--
--THAT'S FINE, BUT... HOW TH' HECK'RE Y' GONNA GET T' IT!?
I CAN'T. ...THAT IS, NOT BY MYSELF.
GLAK

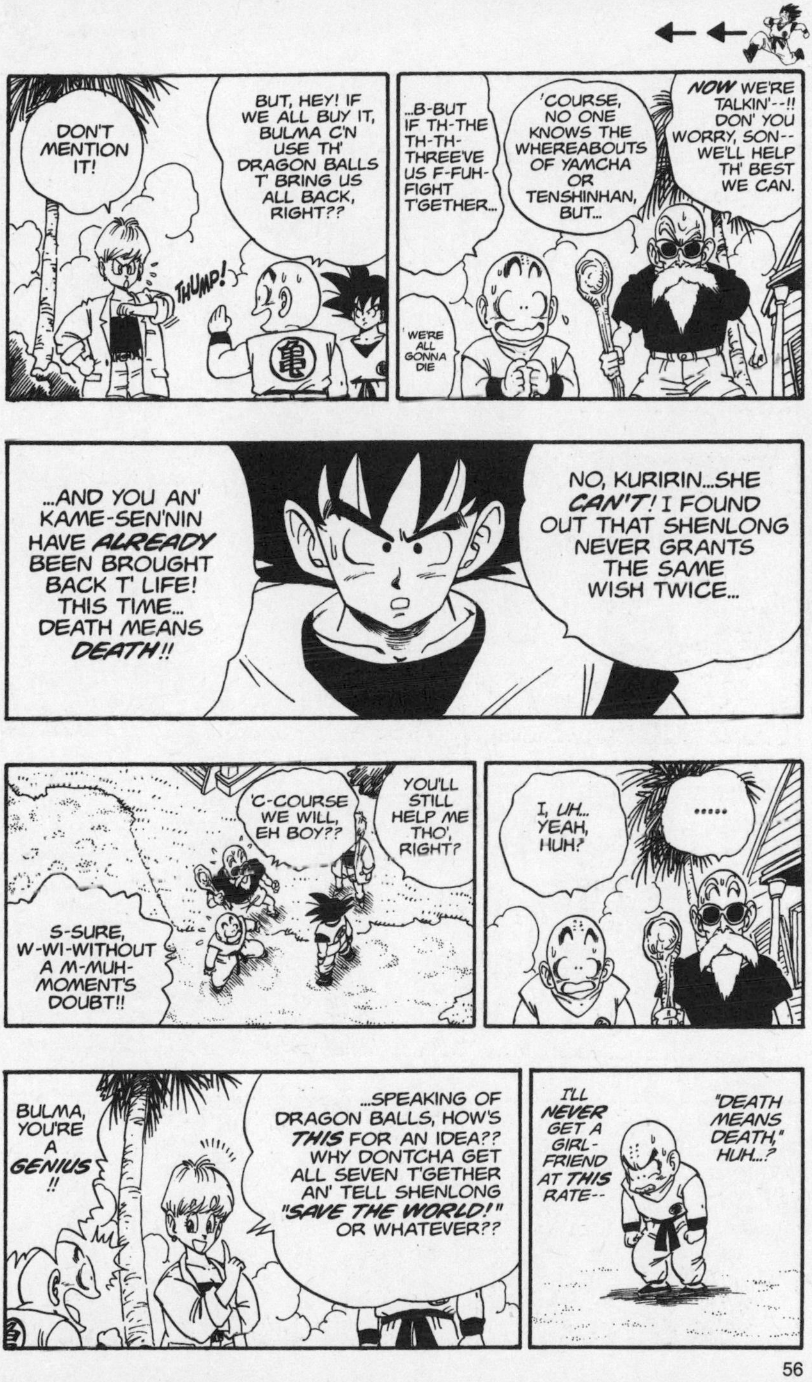
NOW WE'RE TALKIN'--!! DON' YOU WORRY, SON-- WE'LL HELP TH' BEST WE CAN.
'COURSE, NO ONE KNOWS THE WHEREABOUTS OF YAMCHA OR TENSHINHAN, BUT...
...B-BUT IF TH-THE TH-TH-THREE'VE US F-FUH-FIGHT T'GETHER...
WE'RE ALL GONNA DIE
BUT, HEY! IF WE ALL BUY IT, BULMA C'N USE TH' DRAGON BALLS T' BRING US ALL BACK, RIGHT??
THUMP!
DON'T MENTION IT!
NO, KURIRIN...SHE CAN'T! I FOUND OUT THAT SHENLONG NEVER GRANTS THE SAME WISH TWICE...
...AND YOU AN' KAME-SEN'NIN HAVE ALREADY BEEN BROUGHT BACK T' LIFE! THIS TIME... DEATH MEANS DEATH!!
......
I, UH... YEAH, HUH?
YOU'LL STILL HELP ME THO', RIGHT?
'C-COURSE WE WILL, EH BOY??
S-SURE, W-WI-WITHOUT A M-MUH-MOMENT'S DOUBT!!
"DEATH MEANS DEATH," HUH...?
I'LL NEVER GET A GIRL-FRIEND AT THIS RATE--
...SPEAKING OF DRAGON BALLS, HOW'S THIS FOR AN IDEA?? WHY DONTCHA GET ALL SEVEN T'GETHER AN' TELL SHENLONG "SAVE THE WORLD!" OR WHATEVER??
BULMA, YOU'RE A GENIUS!!

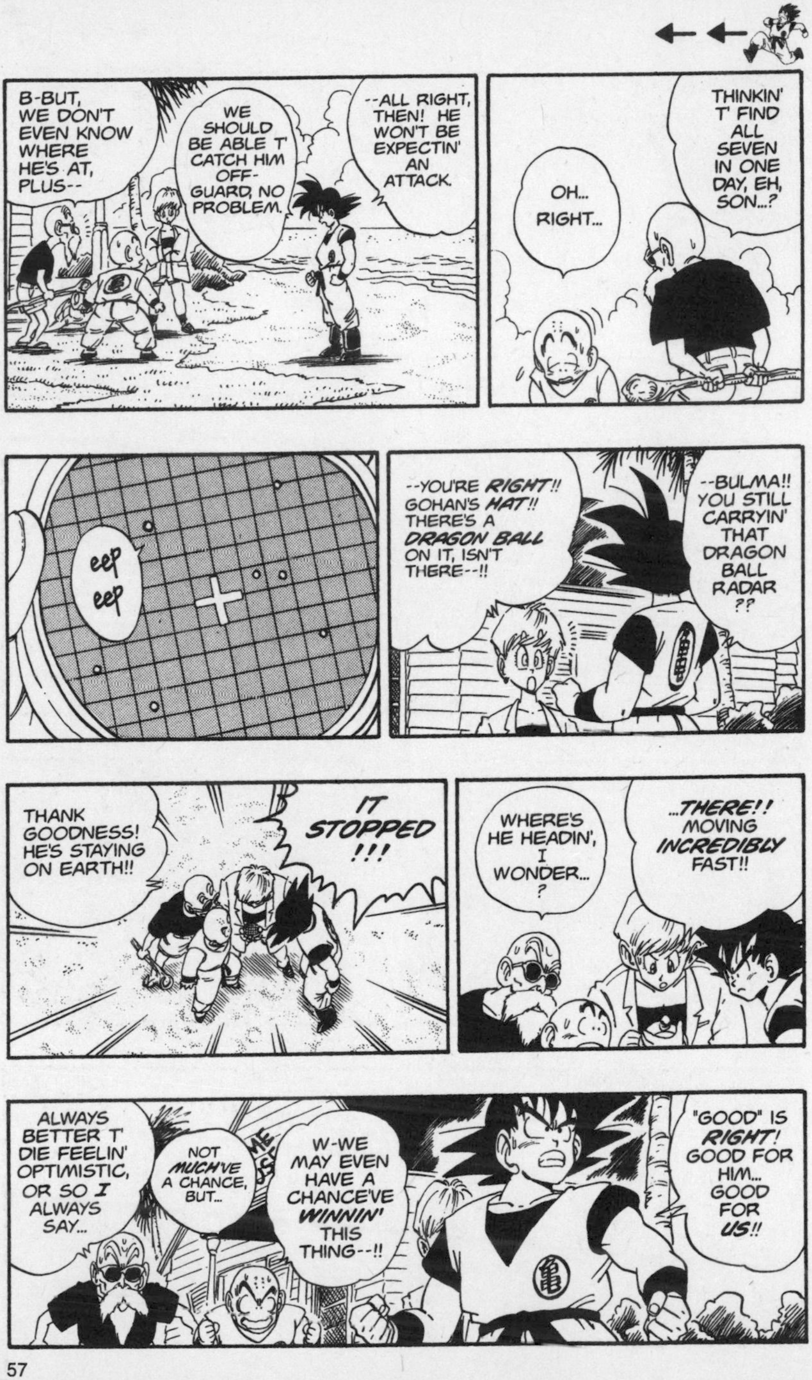
THINKIN' T' FIND ALL SEVEN IN ONE DAY, EH, SON...?
OH... RIGHT...
--ALL RIGHT, THEN! HE WON'T BE EXPECTIN' AN ATTACK.
WE SHOULD BE ABLE T' CATCH HIM OFF-GUARD, NO PROBLEM.
B-BUT, WE DON'T EVEN KNOW WHERE HE'S AT, PLUS--
--BULMA!! YOU STILL CARRYIN' THAT DRAGON BALL RADAR??
--YOU'RE RIGHT!! GOHAN'S HAT!! THERE'S A DRAGON BALL ON IT, ISN'T THERE--!!
eep eep
...THERE!! MOVING INCREDIBLY FAST!!
WHERE'S HE HEADIN', I WONDER...?
IT STOPPED!!!
THANK GOODNESS! HE'S STAYING ON EARTH!!
"GOOD" IS RIGHT! GOOD FOR HIM... GOOD FOR US!!
W-WE MAY EVEN HAVE A CHANCE'VE WINNIN' THIS THING--!!
NOT MUCH'VE A CHANCE, BUT...
ALWAYS BETTER T' DIE FEELIN' OPTIMISTIC, OR SO I ALWAYS SAY...

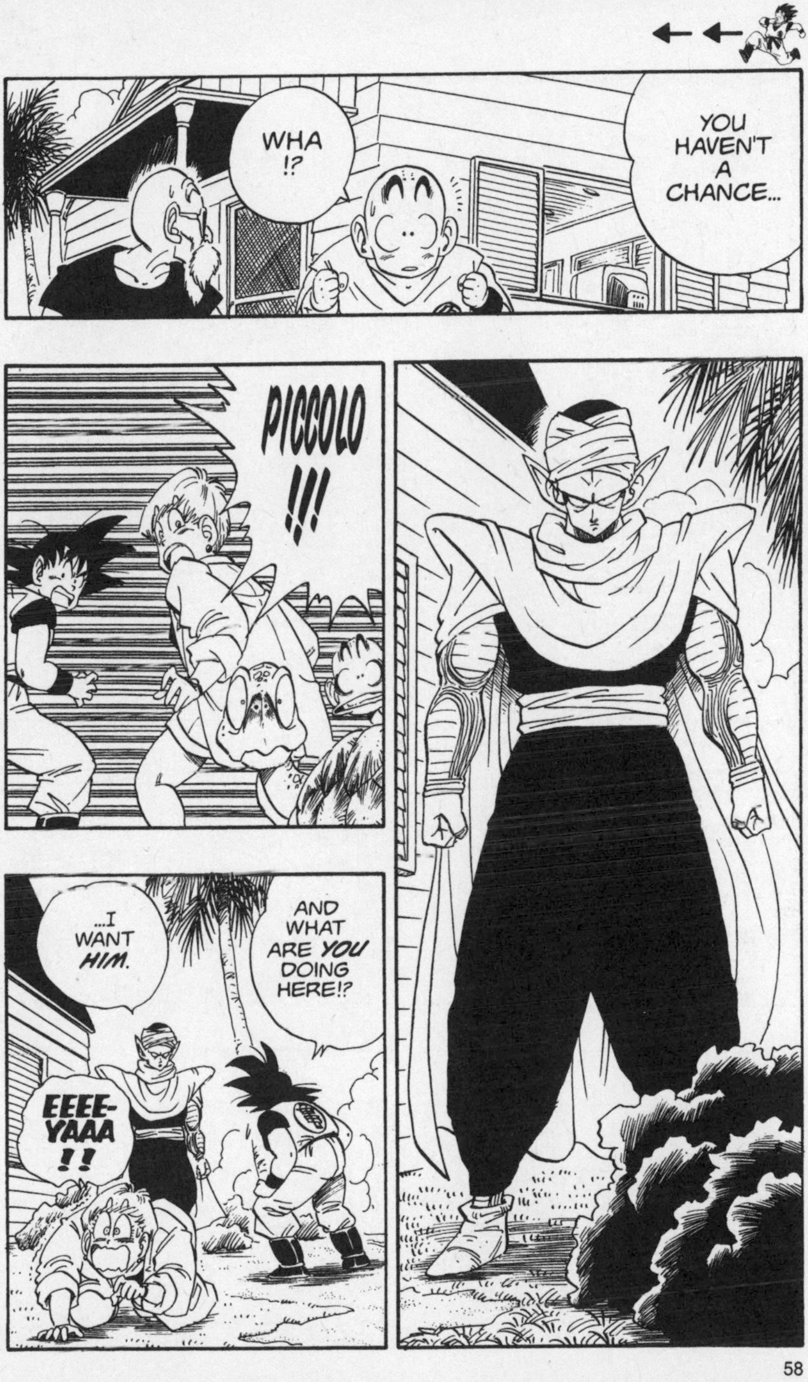
YOU HAVEN'T A CHANCE...
WHA !?
PICCOLO !!!
AND WHAT ARE *YOU* DOING HERE!?
...I WANT *HIM*.
EEEE-YAAA !!

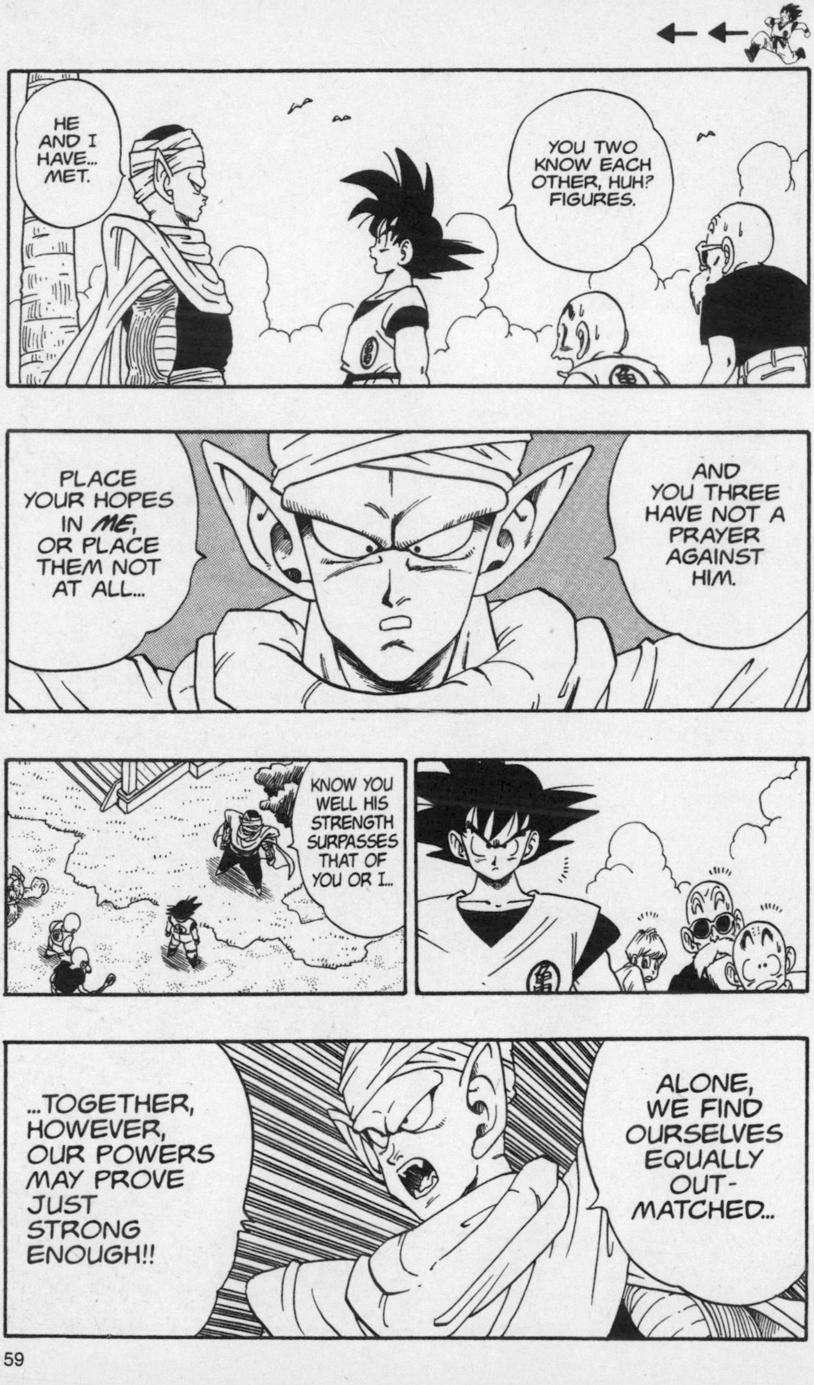
YOU TWO KNOW EACH OTHER, HUH? FIGURES.
HE AND I HAVE... MET.
AND YOU THREE HAVE NOT A PRAYER AGAINST HIM.
PLACE YOUR HOPES IN *ME*, OR PLACE THEM NOT AT ALL...
KNOW YOU WELL HIS STRENGTH SURPASSES THAT OF YOU OR I...
ALONE, WE FIND OURSELVES EQUALLY OUT-MATCHED...
...TOGETHER, HOWEVER, OUR POWERS MAY PROVE JUST STRONG ENOUGH!!

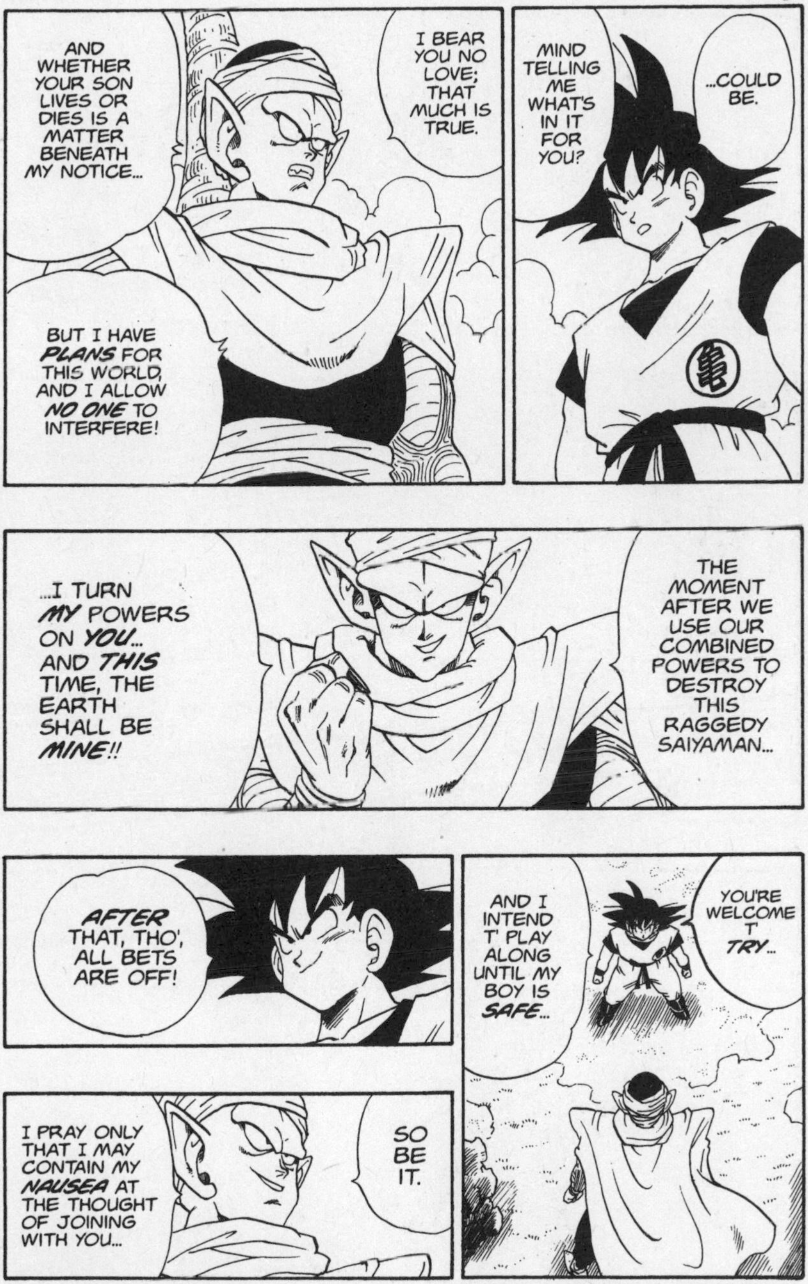
...COULD BE.
MIND TELLING ME WHAT'S IN IT FOR YOU?
I BEAR YOU NO LOVE; THAT MUCH IS TRUE.
AND WHETHER YOUR SON LIVES OR DIES IS A MATTER BENEATH MY NOTICE...
BUT I HAVE PLANS FOR THIS WORLD, AND I ALLOW NO ONE TO INTERFERE!
THE MOMENT AFTER WE USE OUR COMBINED POWERS TO DESTROY THIS RAGGEDY SAIYAMAN...
...I TURN MY POWERS ON YOU... AND THIS TIME, THE EARTH SHALL BE MINE!!
YOU'RE WELCOME T' TRY...
AND I INTEND T' PLAY ALONG UNTIL MY BOY IS SAFE...
AFTER THAT, THO', ALL BETS ARE OFF!
SO BE IT.
I PRAY ONLY THAT I MAY CONTAIN MY NAUSEA AT THE THOUGHT OF JOINING WITH YOU...

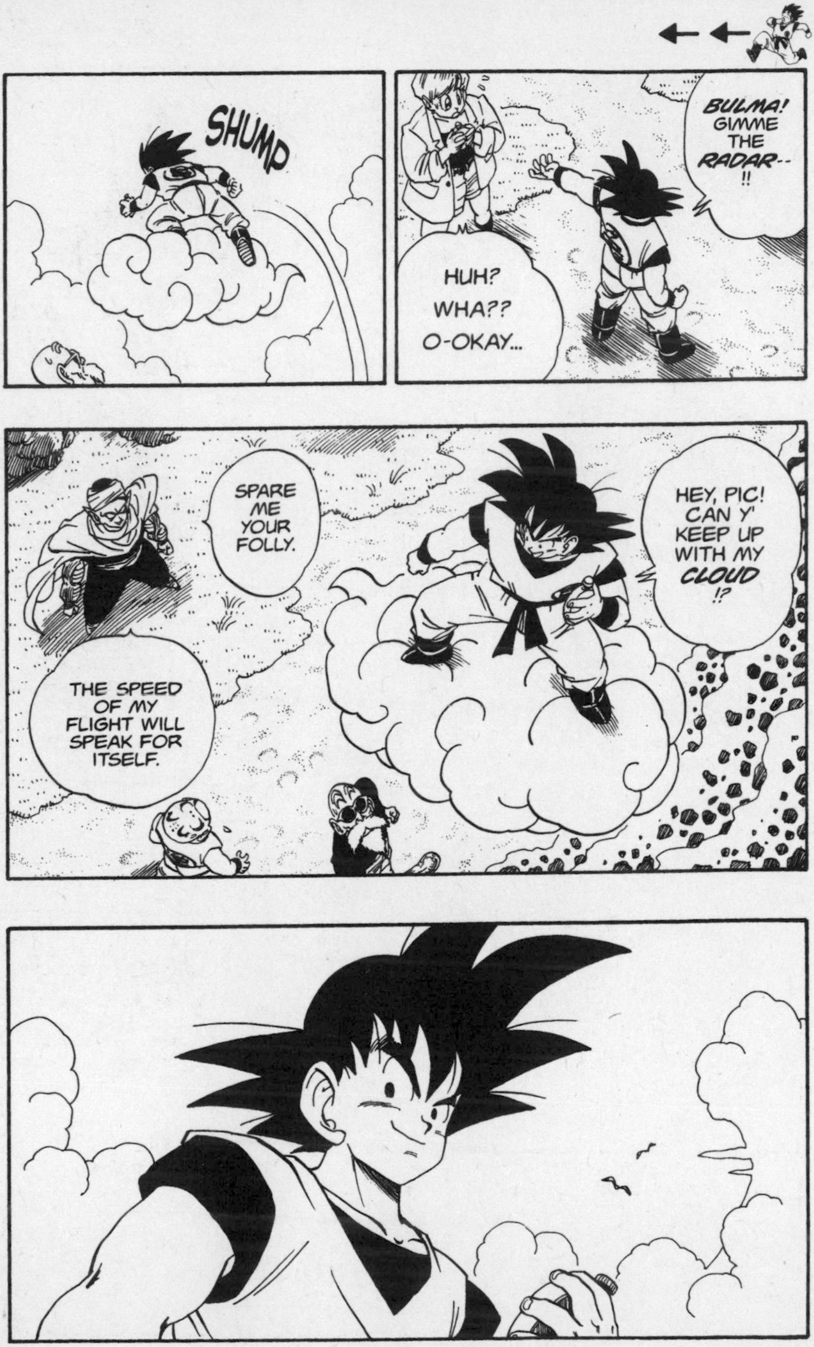
BULMA! GIMME THE RADAR-- !!
HUH? WHA?? O-OKAY...
SHUMP
HEY, PIC! CAN Y' KEEP UP WITH MY CLOUD !?
SPARE ME YOUR FOLLY.
THE SPEED OF MY FLIGHT WILL SPEAK FOR ITSELF.

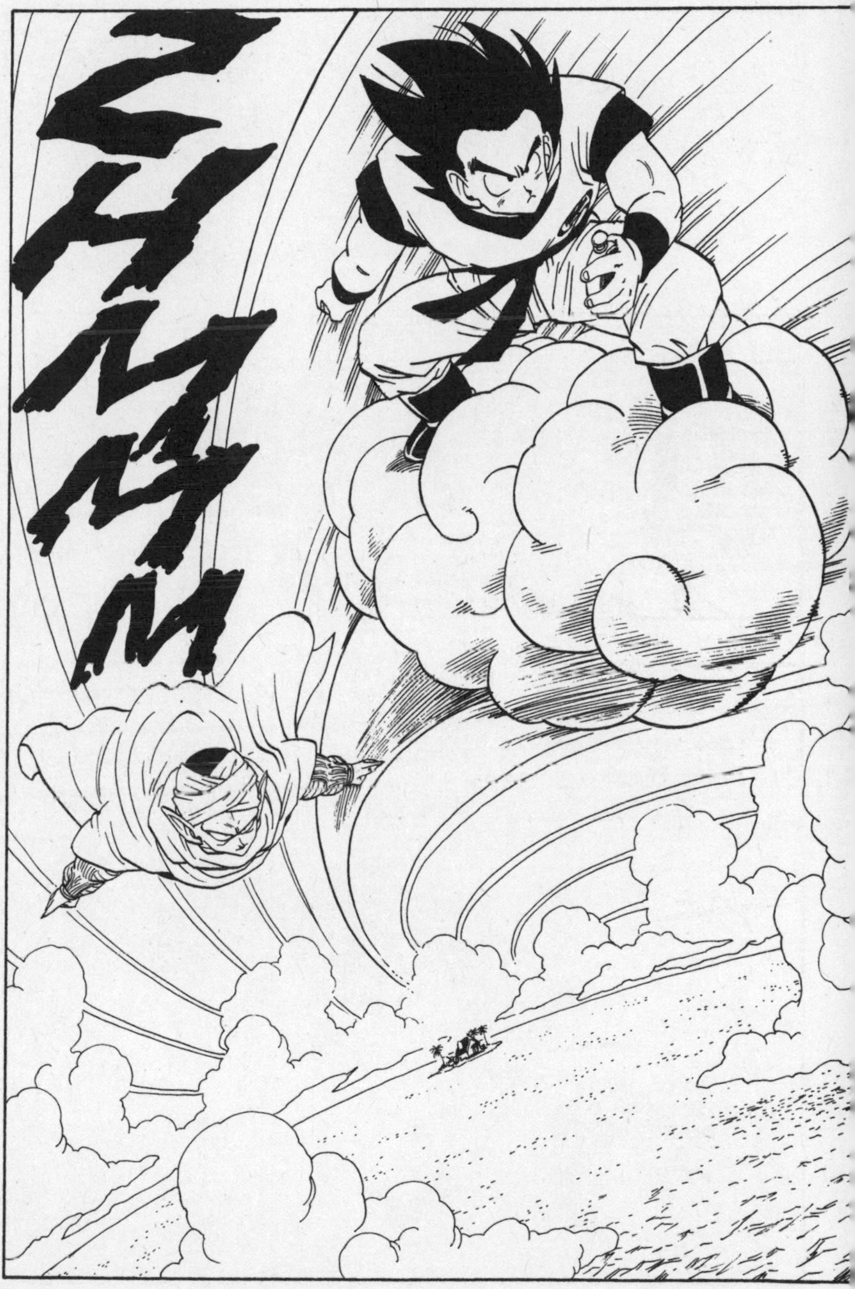
ZMMMM

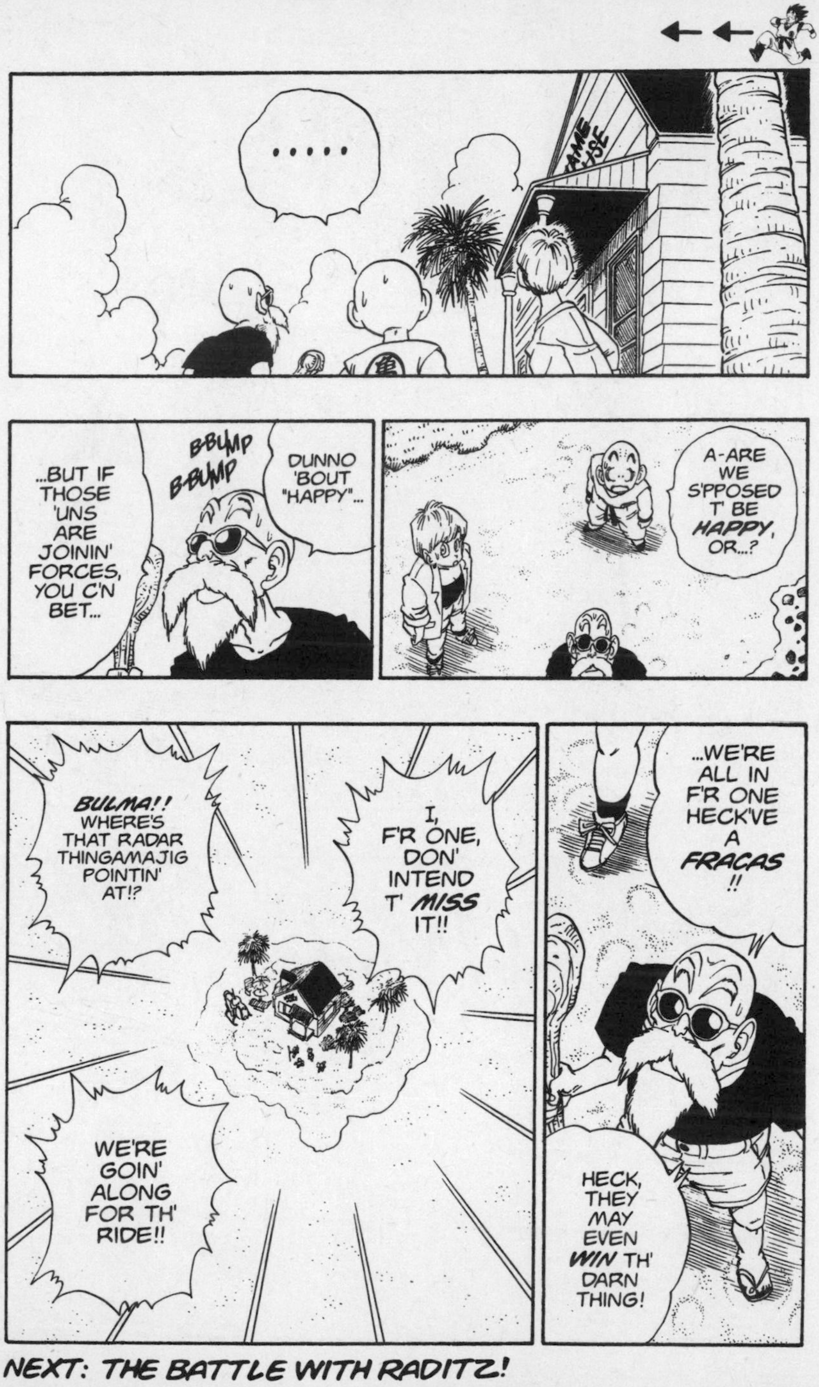
......
A-ARE WE S'PPOSED T' BE *HAPPY*, OR...?
DUNNO 'BOUT "HAPPY"...
B-BUMP B-BUMP
...BUT IF THOSE 'UNS ARE JOININ' FORCES, YOU C'N BET...
...WE'RE ALL IN F'R ONE HECK'VE A *FRACAS*!!
HECK, THEY MAY EVEN *WIN* TH' DARN THING!
I, F'R ONE, DON' INTEND T' *MISS* IT!!
BULMA!! WHERE'S THAT RADAR THINGAMAJIG POINTIN' AT!?
WE'RE GOIN' ALONG FOR TH' RIDE!!

NEXT: THE BATTLE WITH RADITZ!

DBZ : 05 • An Unexpected Strength

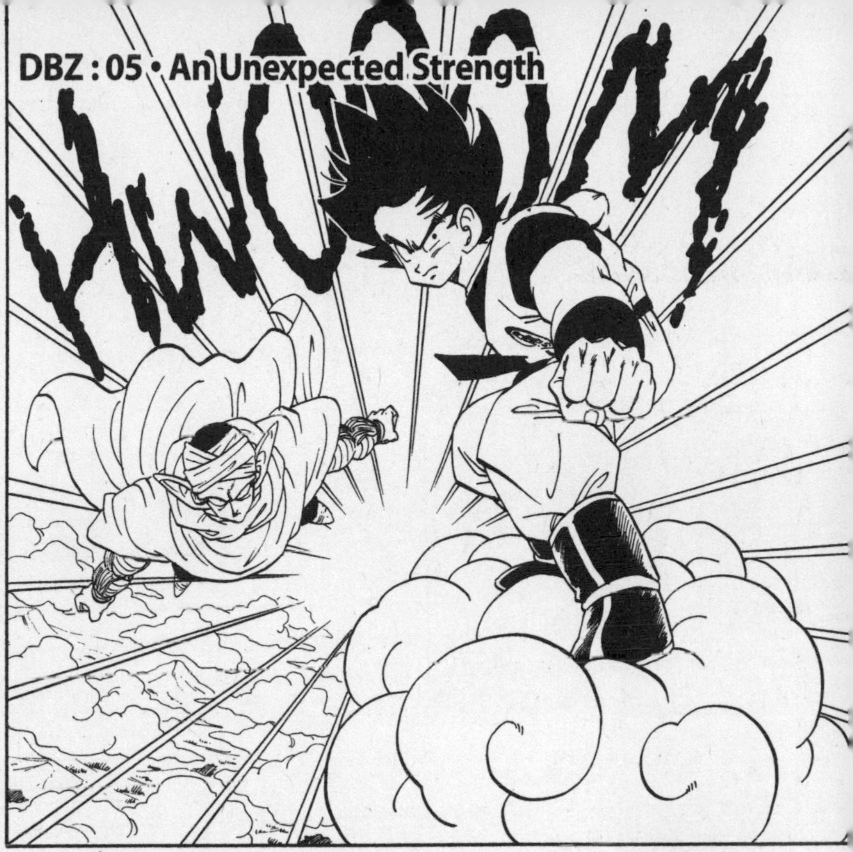

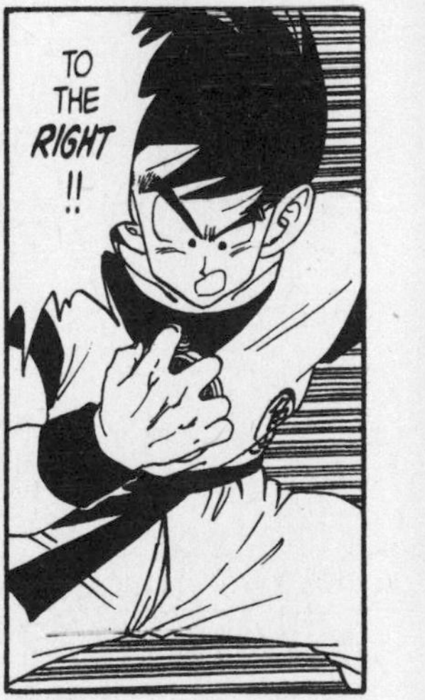
TO THE RIGHT !!

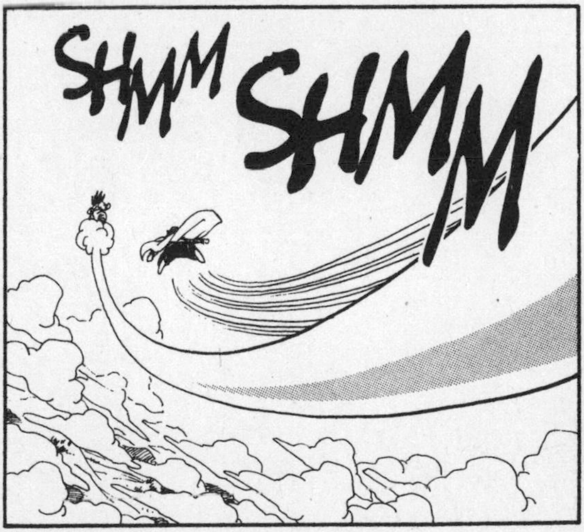
SHMM SHMM

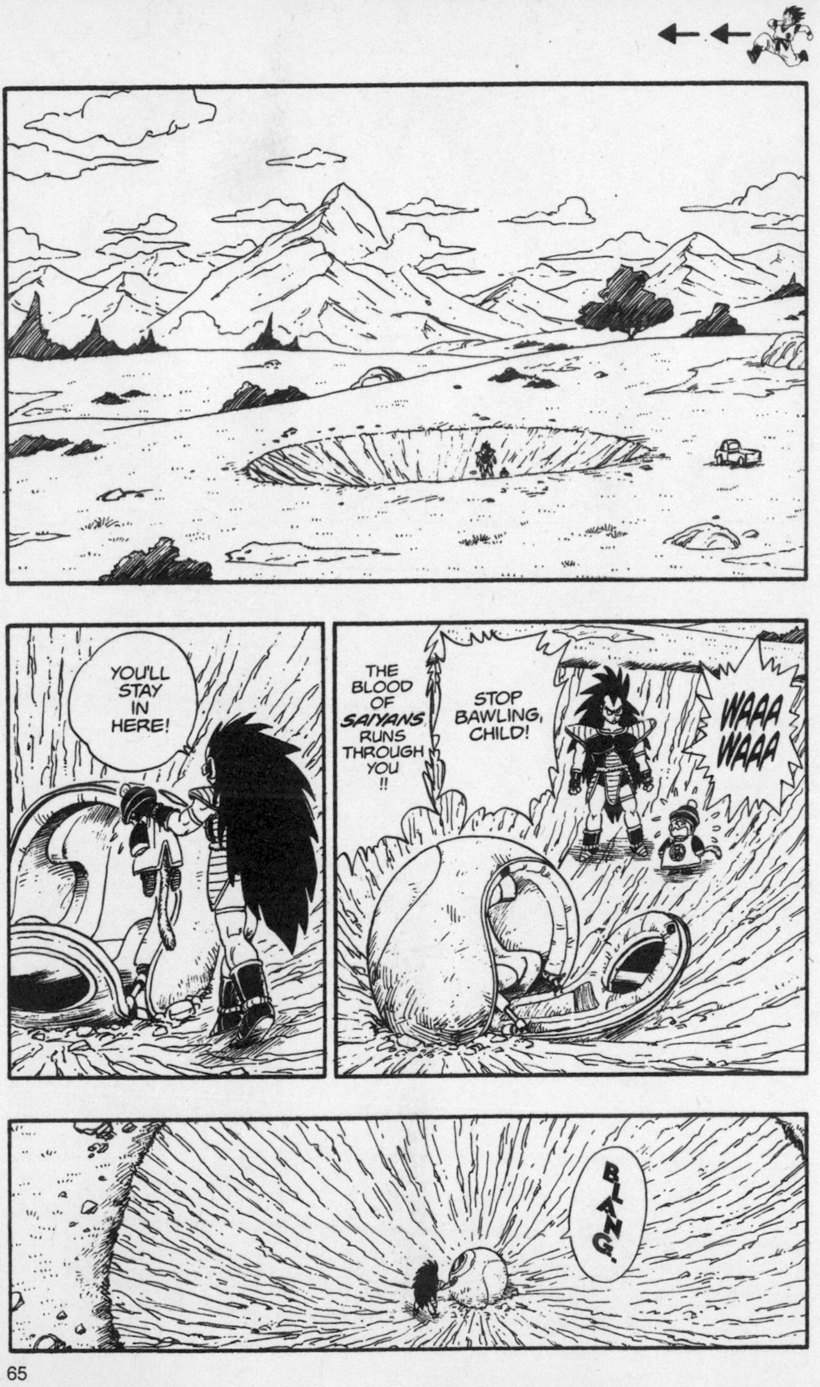
WAAA WAAA
STOP BAWLING, CHILD!
THE BLOOD OF SAIYANS RUNS THROUGH YOU !!
YOU'LL STAY IN HERE!
BLANG.

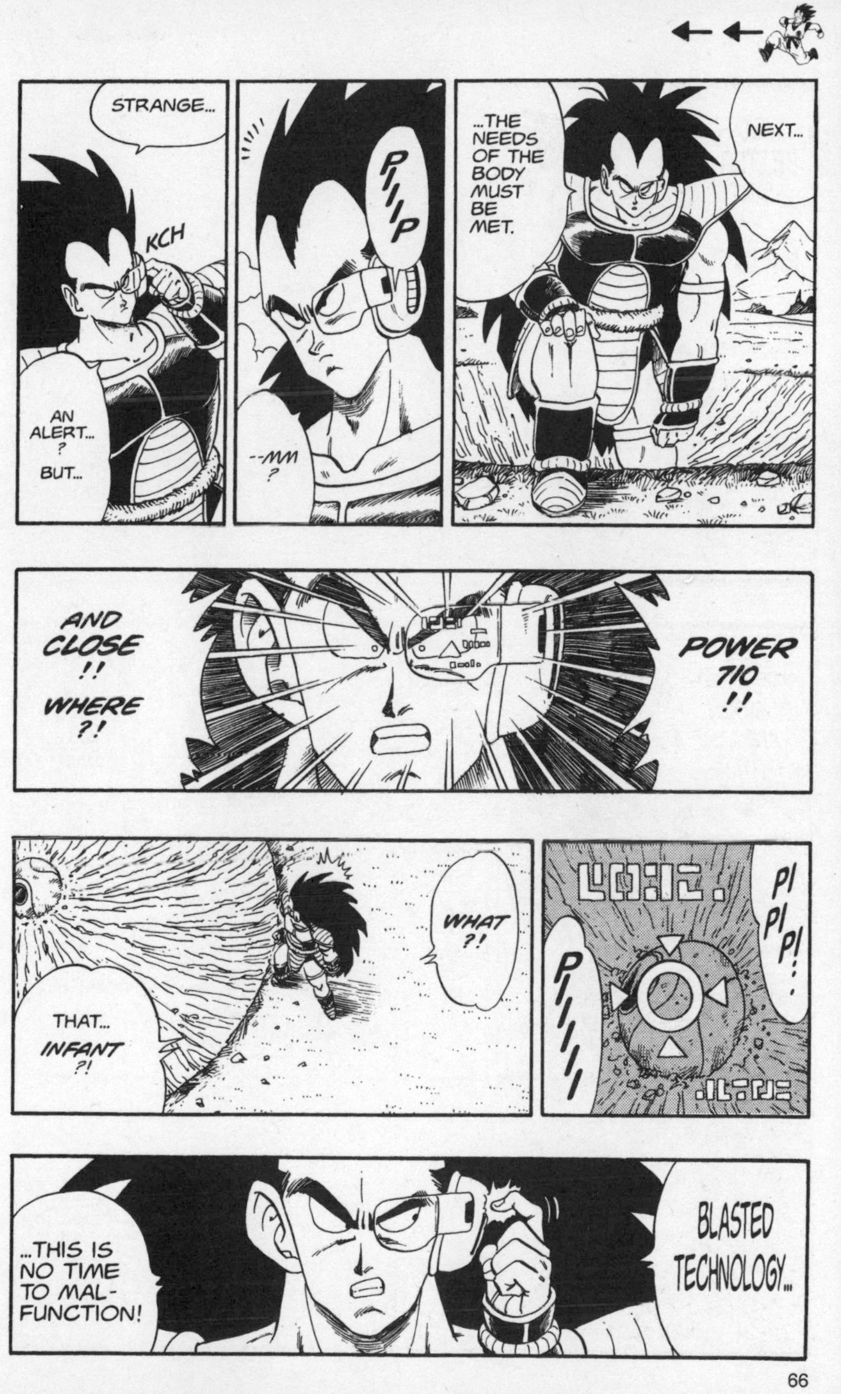

NEXT...
...THE NEEDS OF THE BODY MUST BE MET.
PIIIP
--MM ?
STRANGE...
KCH
AN ALERT... ? BUT...
POWER 710 !!
AND CLOSE !! WHERE ?!
PI PI PI!
PIIIII
WHAT ?!
THAT... INFANT ?!
BLASTED TECHNOLOGY...
...THIS IS NO TIME TO MAL-FUNCTION!

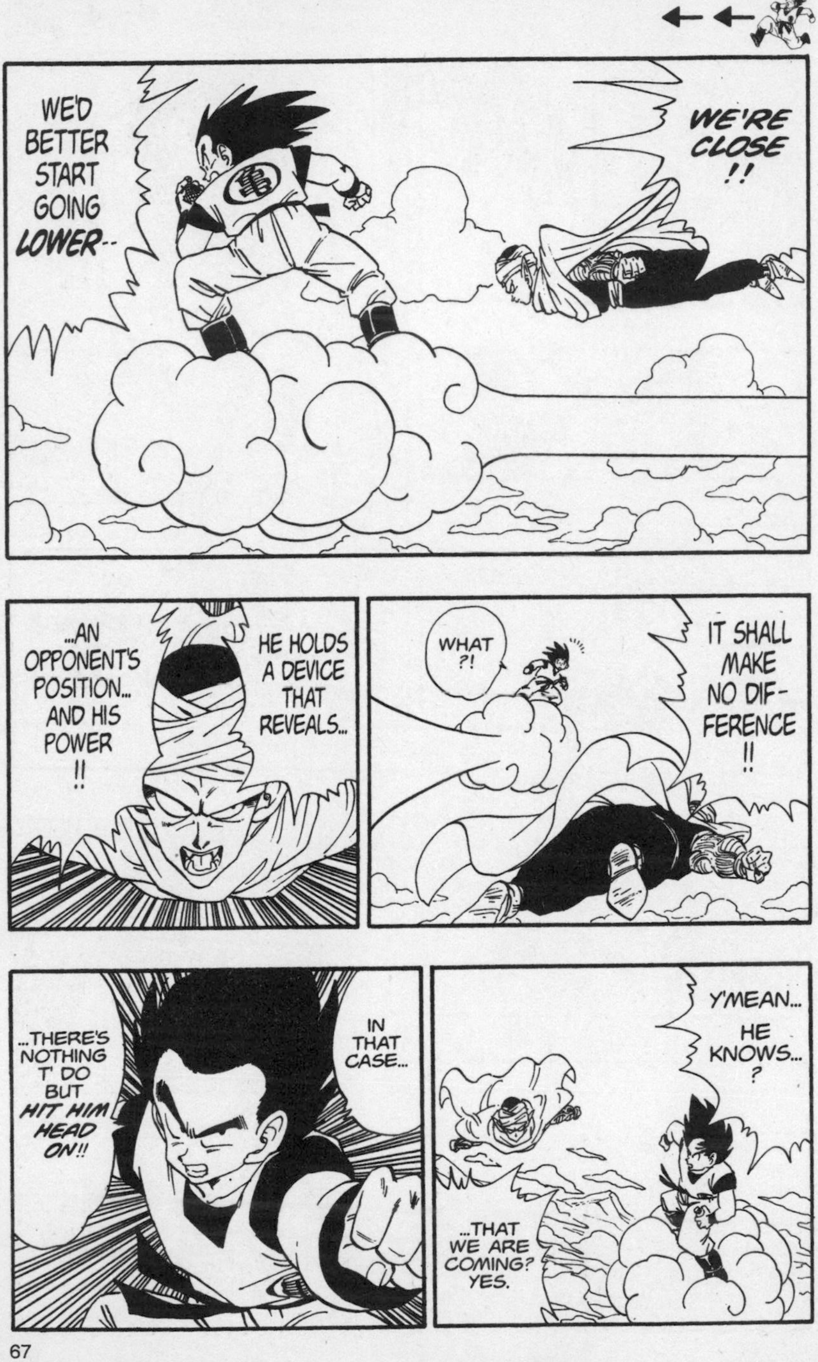
WE'RE CLOSE !!
WE'D BETTER START GOING LOWER--
IT SHALL MAKE NO DIF-FERENCE !!
WHAT ?!
HE HOLDS A DEVICE THAT REVEALS...
...AN OPPONENT'S POSITION... AND HIS POWER !!
Y'MEAN... HE KNOWS... ?
...THAT WE ARE COMING? YES.
IN THAT CASE...
...THERE'S NOTHING T' DO BUT HIT HIM HEAD ON!!

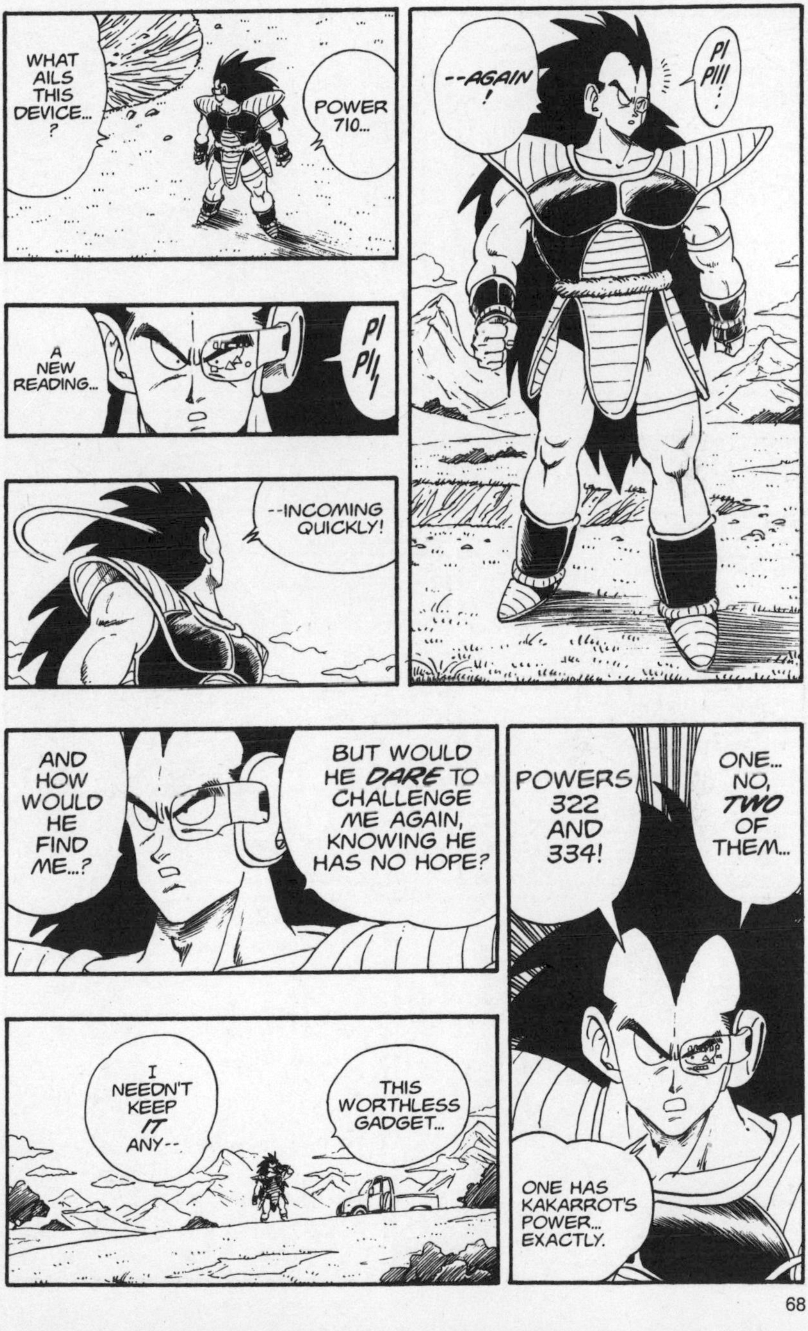
PI PI!!
--AGAIN!
POWER 710...
WHAT AILS THIS DEVICE...?
PI PI!
A NEW READING...
--INCOMING QUICKLY!
BUT WOULD HE *DARE* TO CHALLENGE ME AGAIN, KNOWING HE HAS NO HOPE?
AND HOW WOULD HE FIND ME...?
THIS WORTHLESS GADGET...
I NEEDN'T KEEP *IT* ANY--
ONE... NO, *TWO* OF THEM...
POWERS 322 AND 334!
ONE HAS KAKARROT'S POWER... EXACTLY.

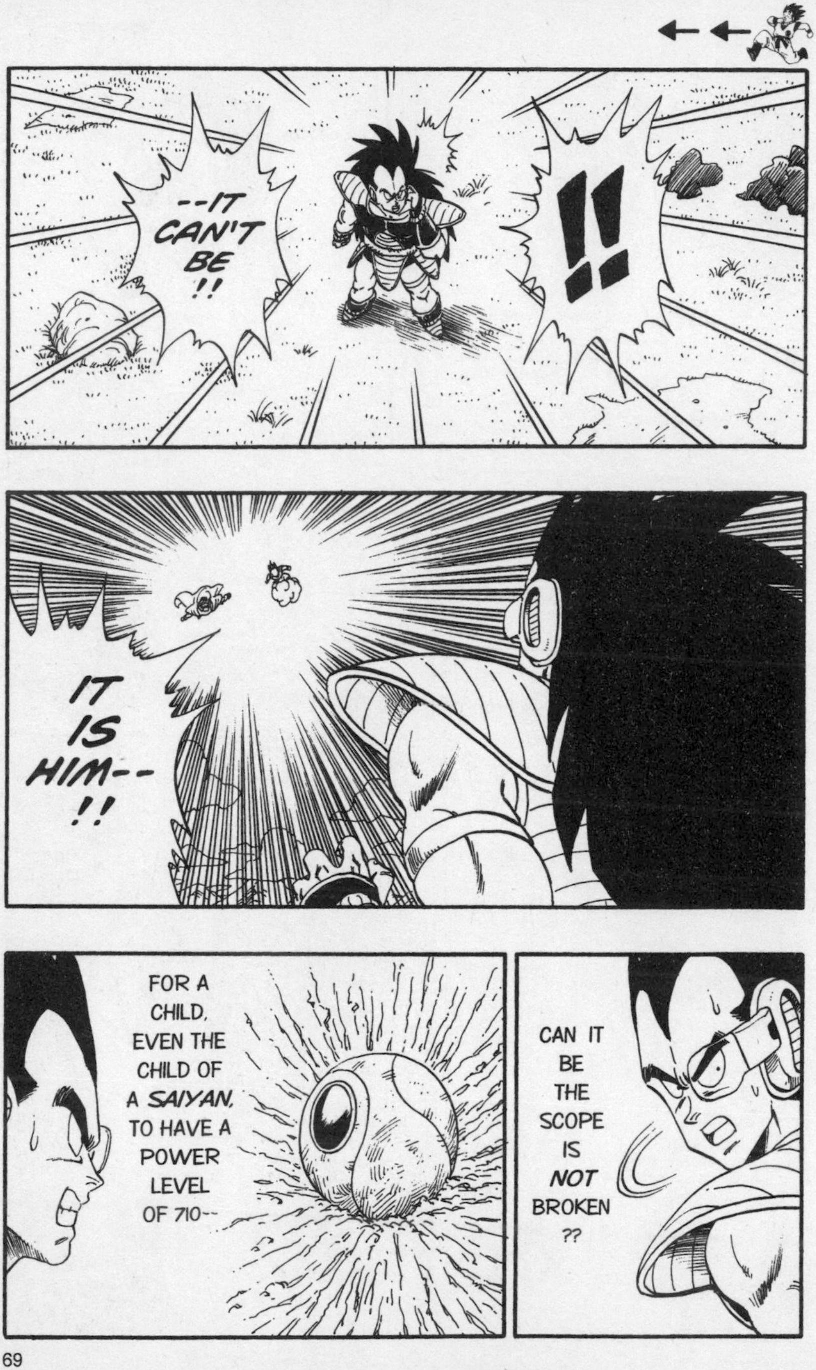
!!
--IT CAN'T BE!!
IT IS HIM--!!
CAN IT BE THE SCOPE IS *NOT* BROKEN??
FOR A CHILD, EVEN THE CHILD OF A *SAIYAN,* TO HAVE A POWER LEVEL OF 710--

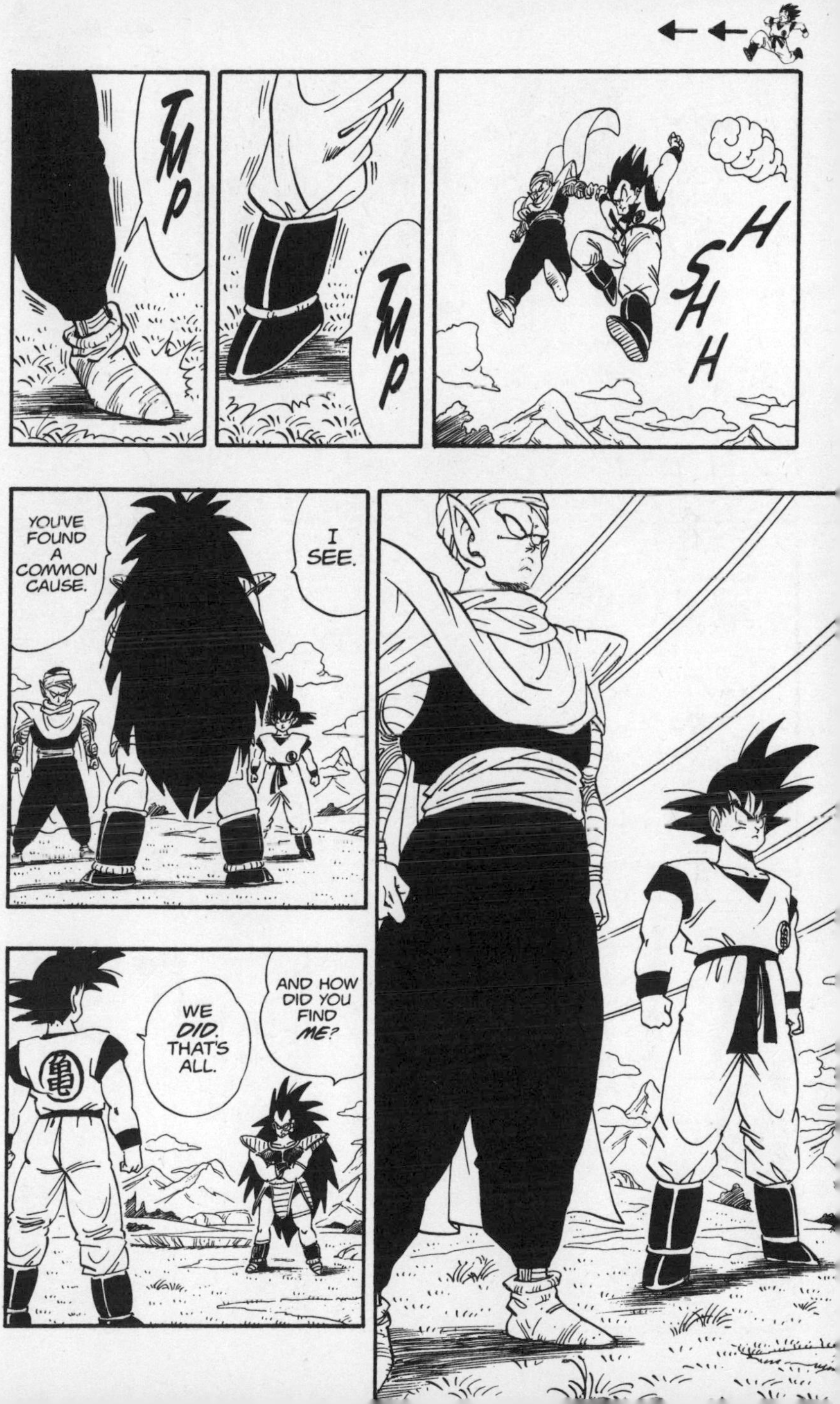
SHHH
TMP
TMP
I SEE.
YOU'VE FOUND A COMMON CAUSE.
AND HOW DID YOU FIND *ME?*
WE *DID*. THAT'S ALL.

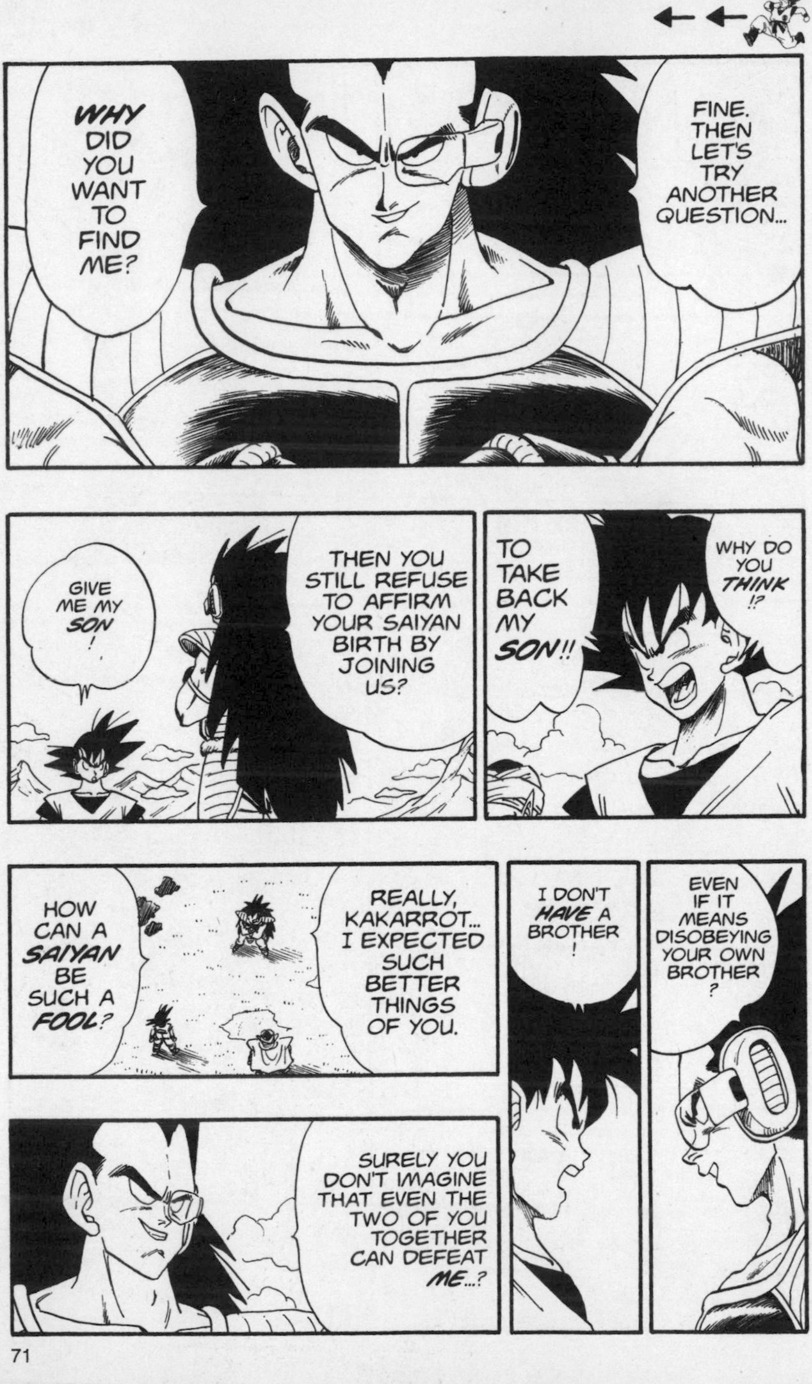
FINE. THEN LET'S TRY ANOTHER QUESTION...
WHY DID YOU WANT TO FIND ME?
WHY DO YOU THINK!?
TO TAKE BACK MY SON!!
THEN YOU STILL REFUSE TO AFFIRM YOUR SAIYAN BIRTH BY JOINING US?
GIVE ME MY SON!
EVEN IF IT MEANS DISOBEYING YOUR OWN BROTHER?
I DON'T HAVE A BROTHER!
REALLY, KAKARROT... I EXPECTED SUCH BETTER THINGS OF YOU.
HOW CAN A SAIYAN BE SUCH A FOOL?
SURELY YOU DON'T IMAGINE THAT EVEN THE TWO OF YOU TOGETHER CAN DEFEAT ME...?

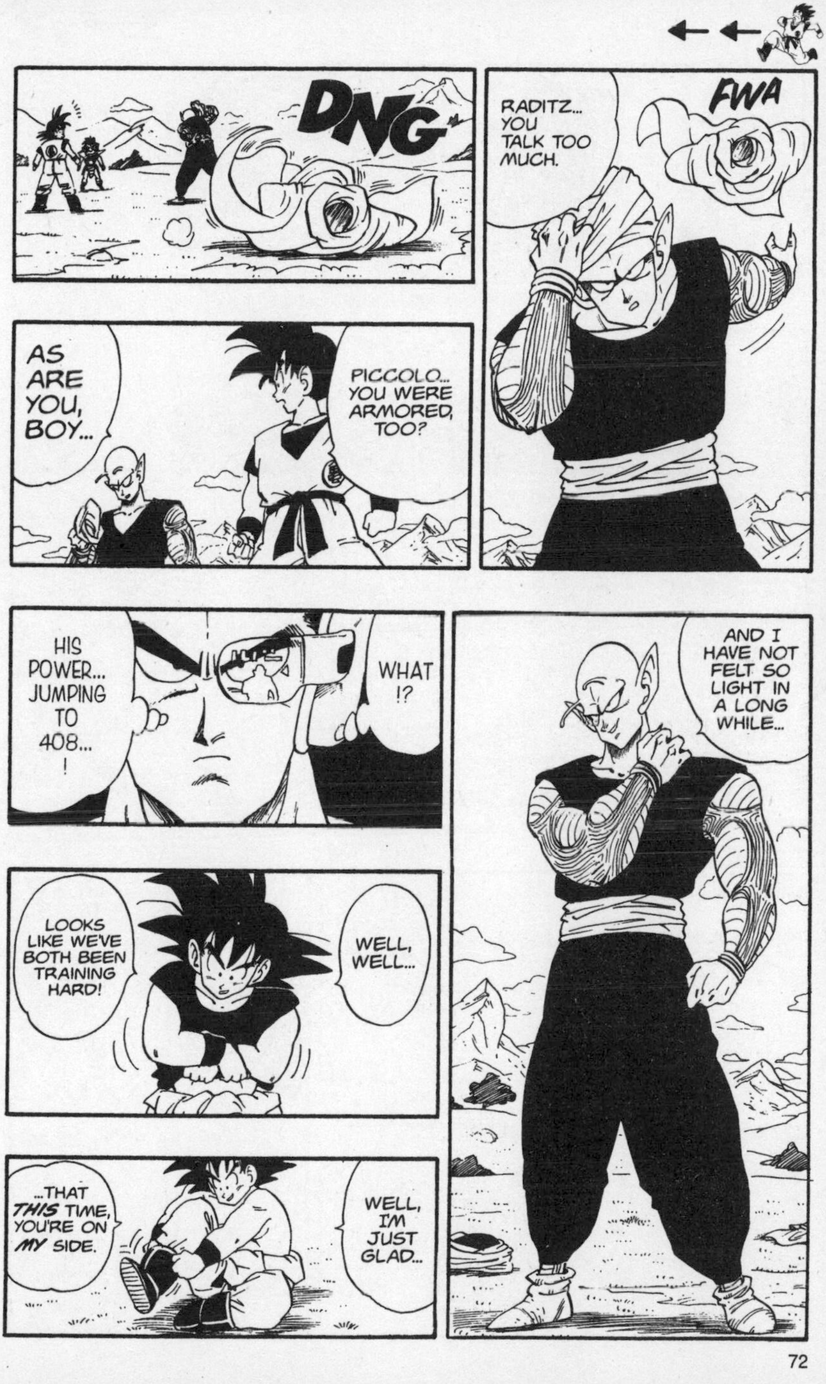
FWA
RADITZ... YOU TALK TOO MUCH.
DNG
PICCOLO... YOU WERE ARMORED, TOO?
AS ARE YOU, BOY...
AND I HAVE NOT FELT SO LIGHT IN A LONG WHILE...
WHAT!?
HIS POWER... JUMPING TO 408...!
WELL, WELL...
LOOKS LIKE WE'VE BOTH BEEN TRAINING HARD!
WELL, I'M JUST GLAD...
...THAT ***THIS*** TIME, YOU'RE ON ***MY*** SIDE.

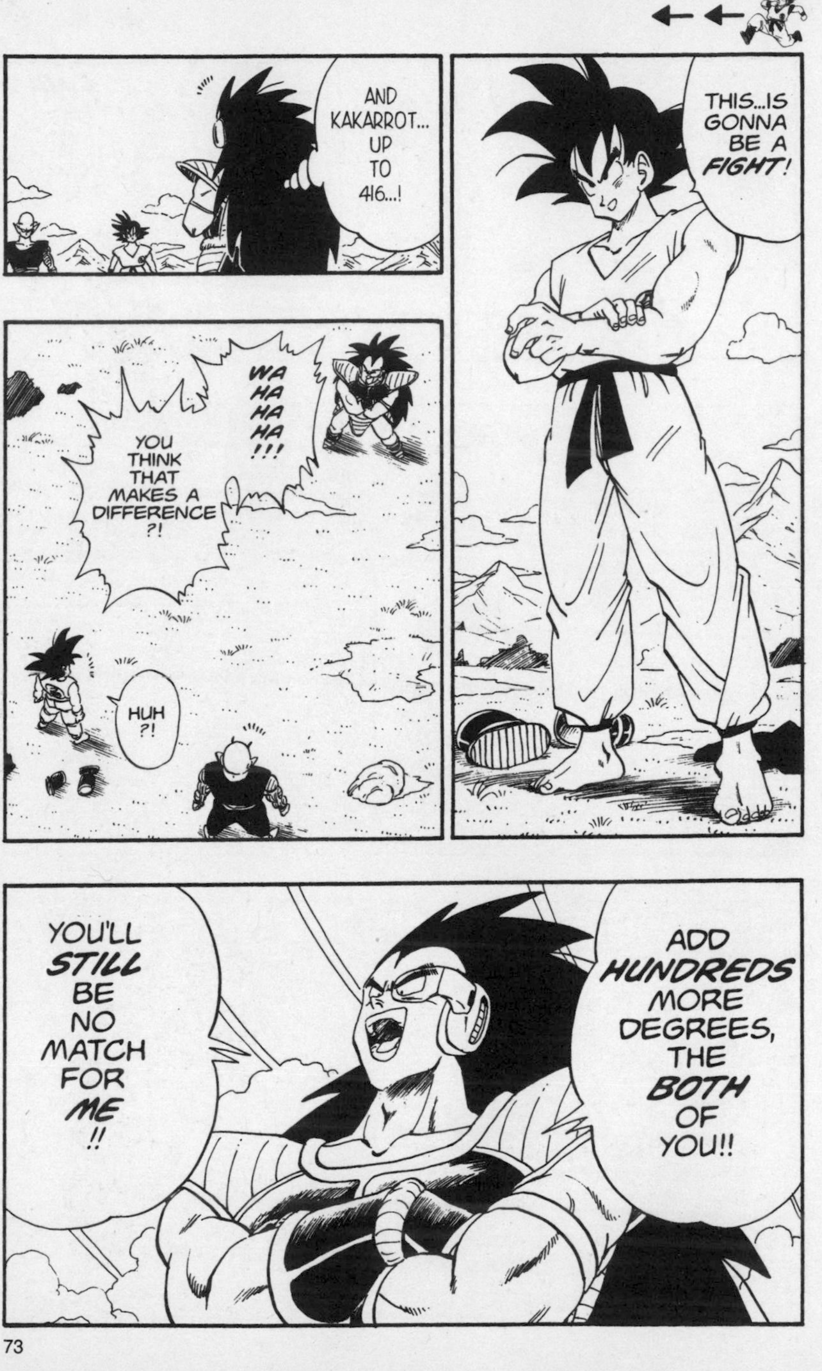
THIS...IS GONNA BE A FIGHT!
AND KAKAROT... UP TO 416...!
WA HA HA HA!!!
YOU THINK THAT MAKES A DIFFERENCE?!
HUH?!
ADD HUNDREDS MORE DEGREES, THE BOTH OF YOU!!
YOU'LL STILL BE NO MATCH FOR ME!!

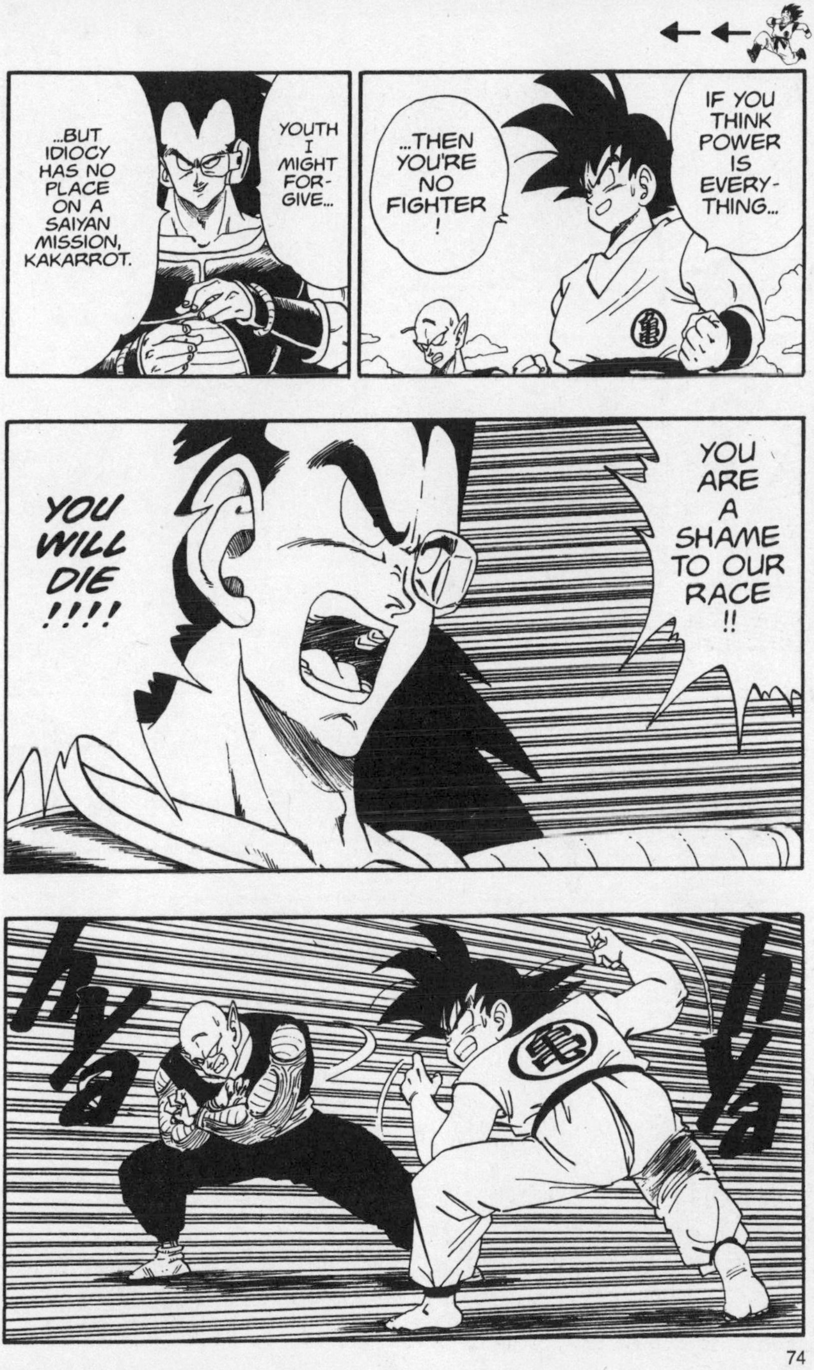
IF YOU THINK POWER IS EVERYTHING...
...THEN YOU'RE NO FIGHTER!
YOUTH I MIGHT FORGIVE...
...BUT IDIOCY HAS NO PLACE ON A SAIYAN MISSION, KAKARROT.
YOU ARE A SHAME TO OUR RACE!!
YOU WILL DIE!!!!
hya
hya

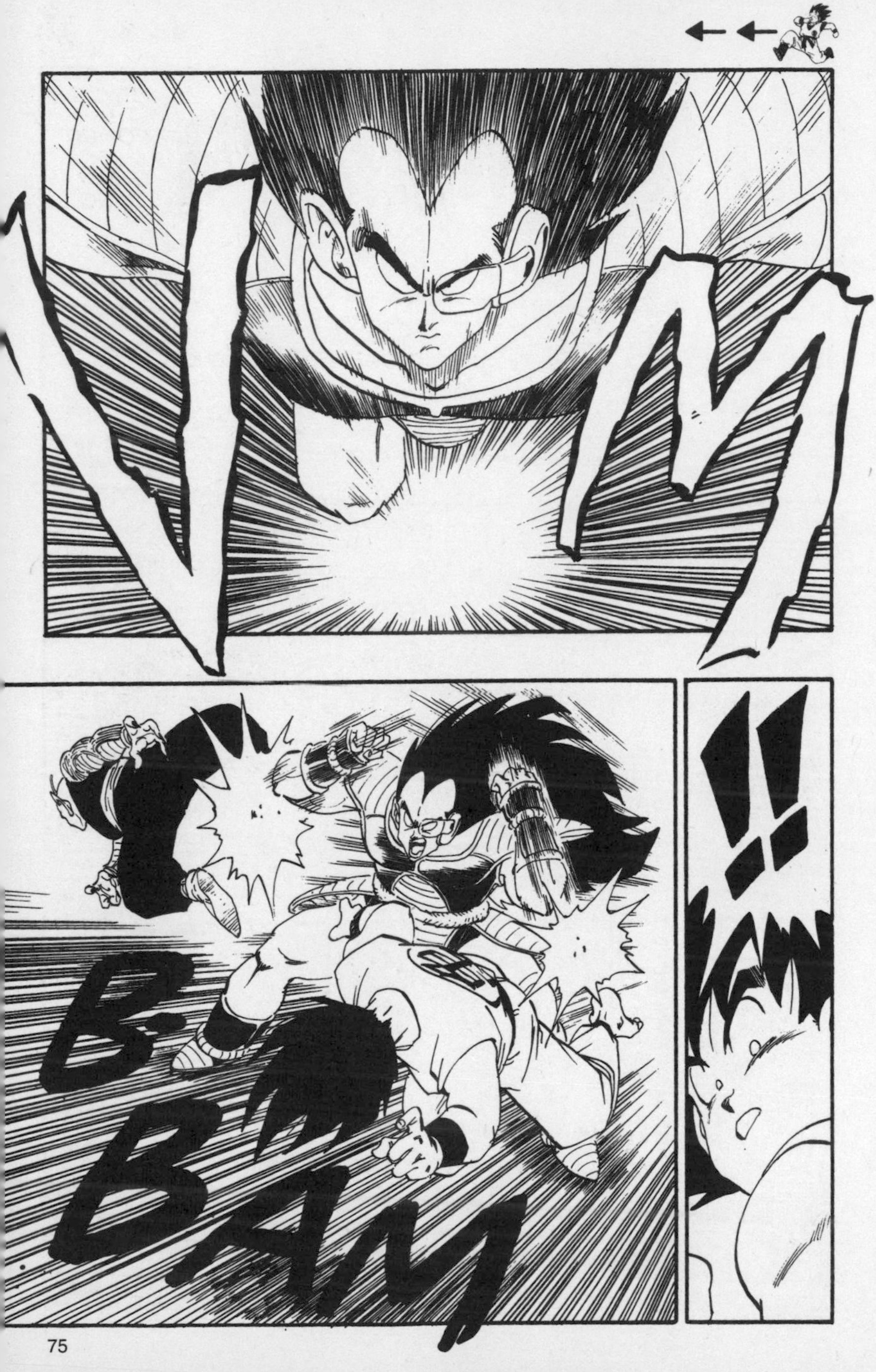
VM
!!
B-BAM

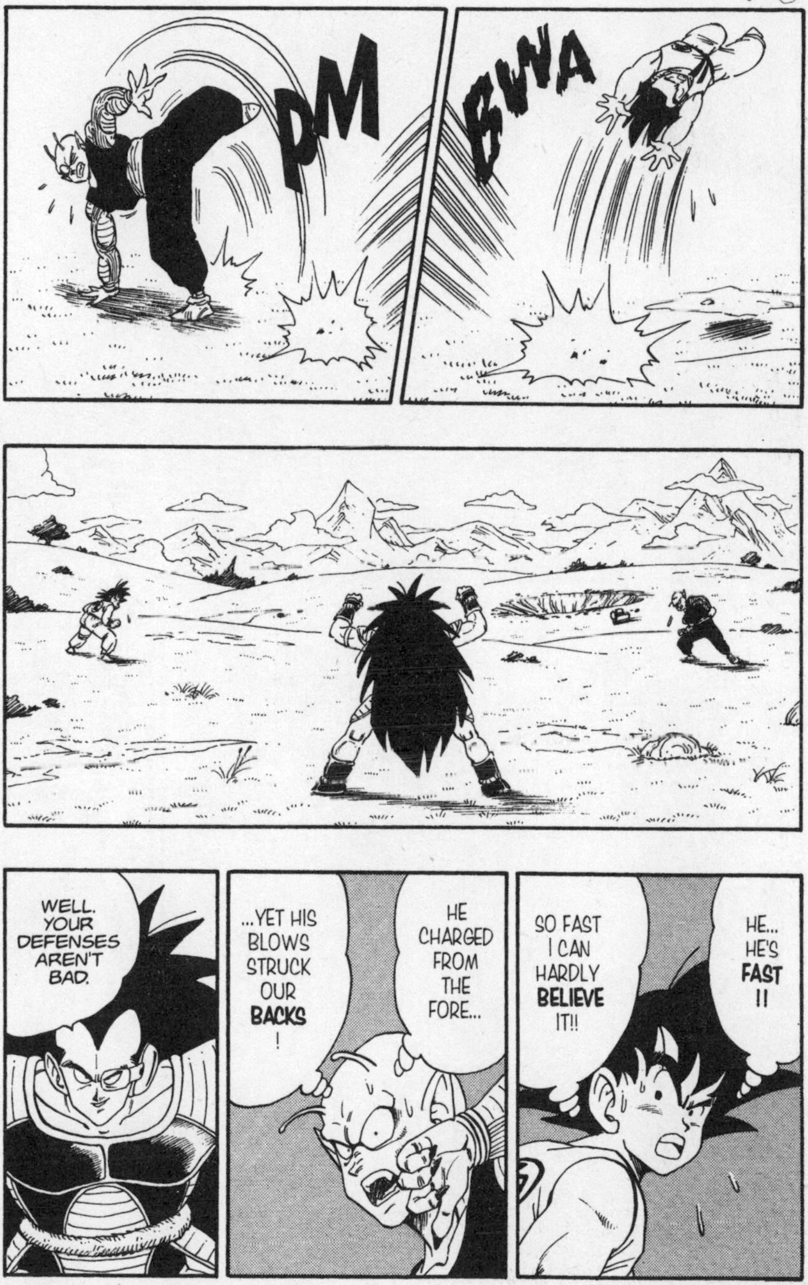
BWA
PM
HE... HE'S **FAST** !!
SO FAST I CAN HARDLY **BELIEVE** IT!!
HE CHARGED FROM THE FORE...
...YET HIS BLOWS STRUCK OUR **BACKS** !
WELL. YOUR DEFENSES AREN'T BAD.

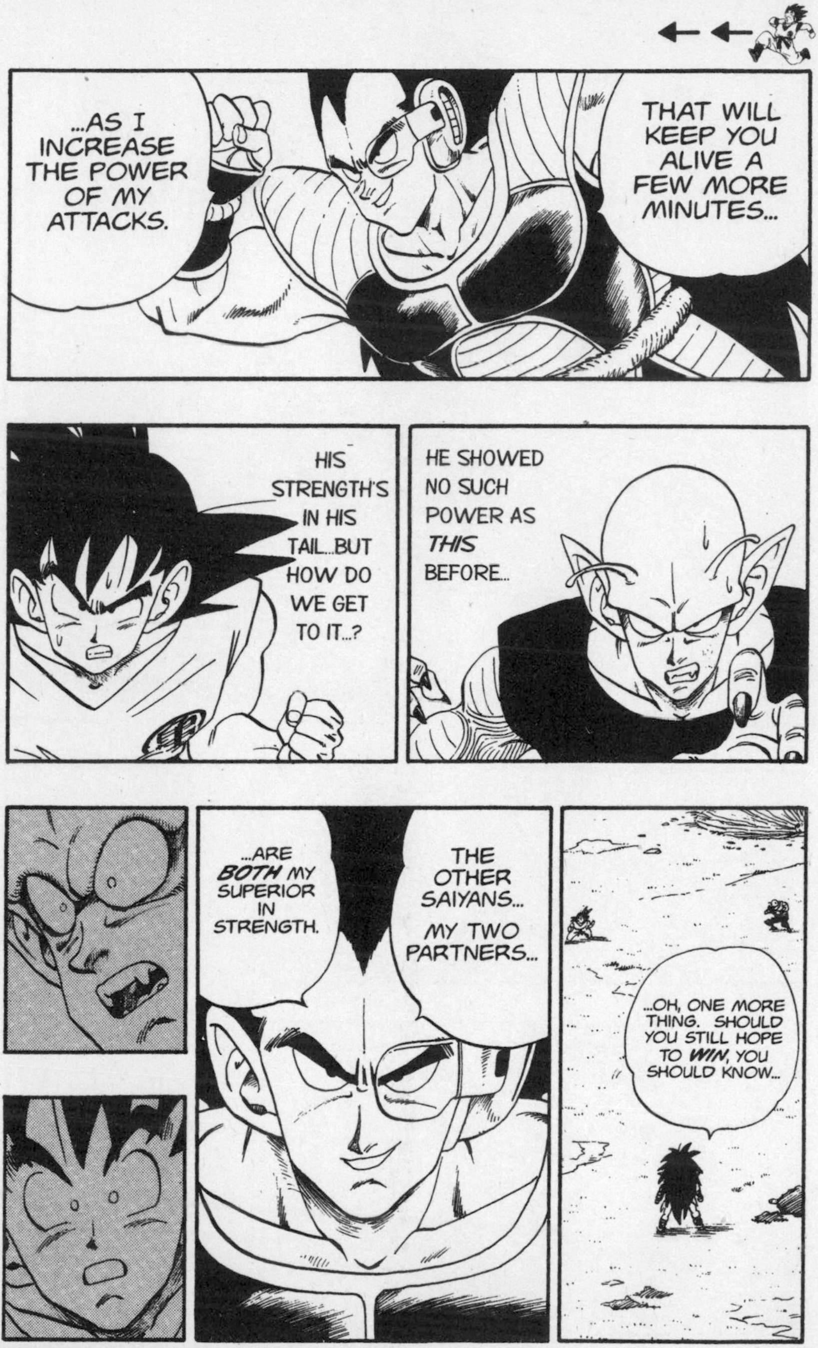
THAT WILL KEEP YOU ALIVE A FEW MORE MINUTES...
...AS I INCREASE THE POWER OF MY ATTACKS.
HE SHOWED NO SUCH POWER AS *THIS* BEFORE...
HIS STRENGTH'S IN HIS TAIL...BUT HOW DO WE GET TO IT...?
...OH, ONE MORE THING. SHOULD YOU STILL HOPE TO *WIN*, YOU SHOULD KNOW...
THE OTHER SAIYANS... MY TWO PARTNERS...
...ARE *BOTH* MY SUPERIOR IN STRENGTH.

NEXT: A NEW KIND OF FEAR!

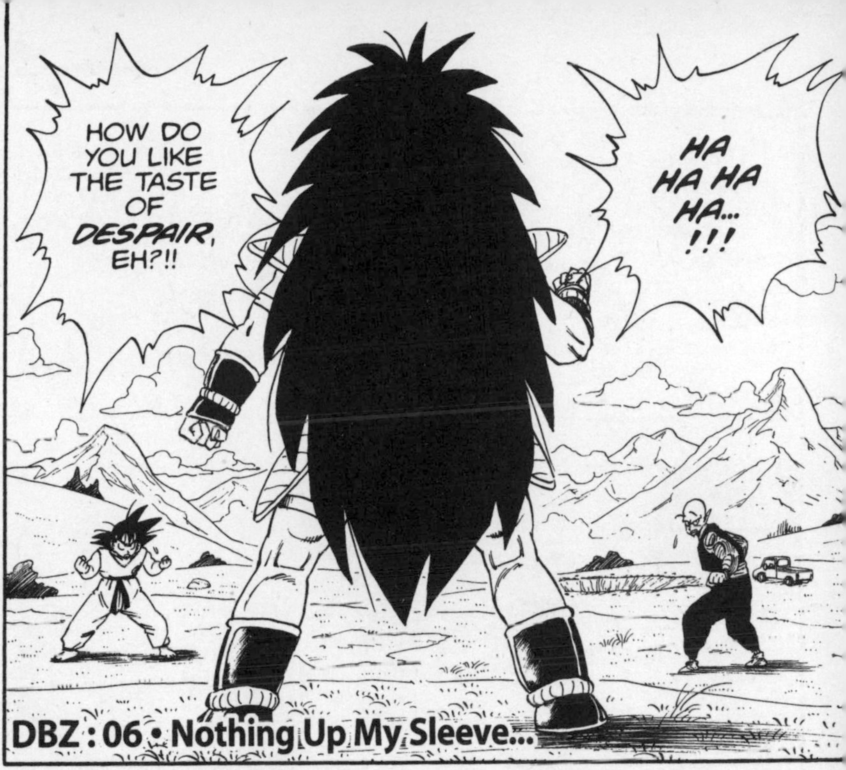
HA HA HA HA...!!!
HOW DO YOU LIKE THE TASTE OF DESPAIR, EH?!!

DBZ : 06 • Nothing Up My Sleeve...

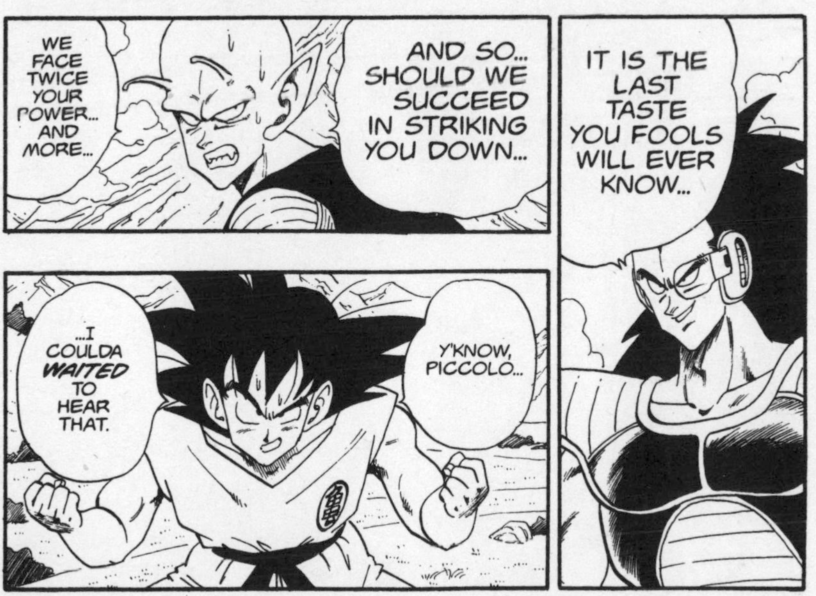
IT IS THE LAST TASTE YOU FOOLS WILL EVER KNOW...
AND SO... SHOULD WE SUCCEED IN STRIKING YOU DOWN...
WE FACE TWICE YOUR POWER... AND MORE...
Y'KNOW, PICCOLO...
...I COULDA WAITED TO HEAR THAT.

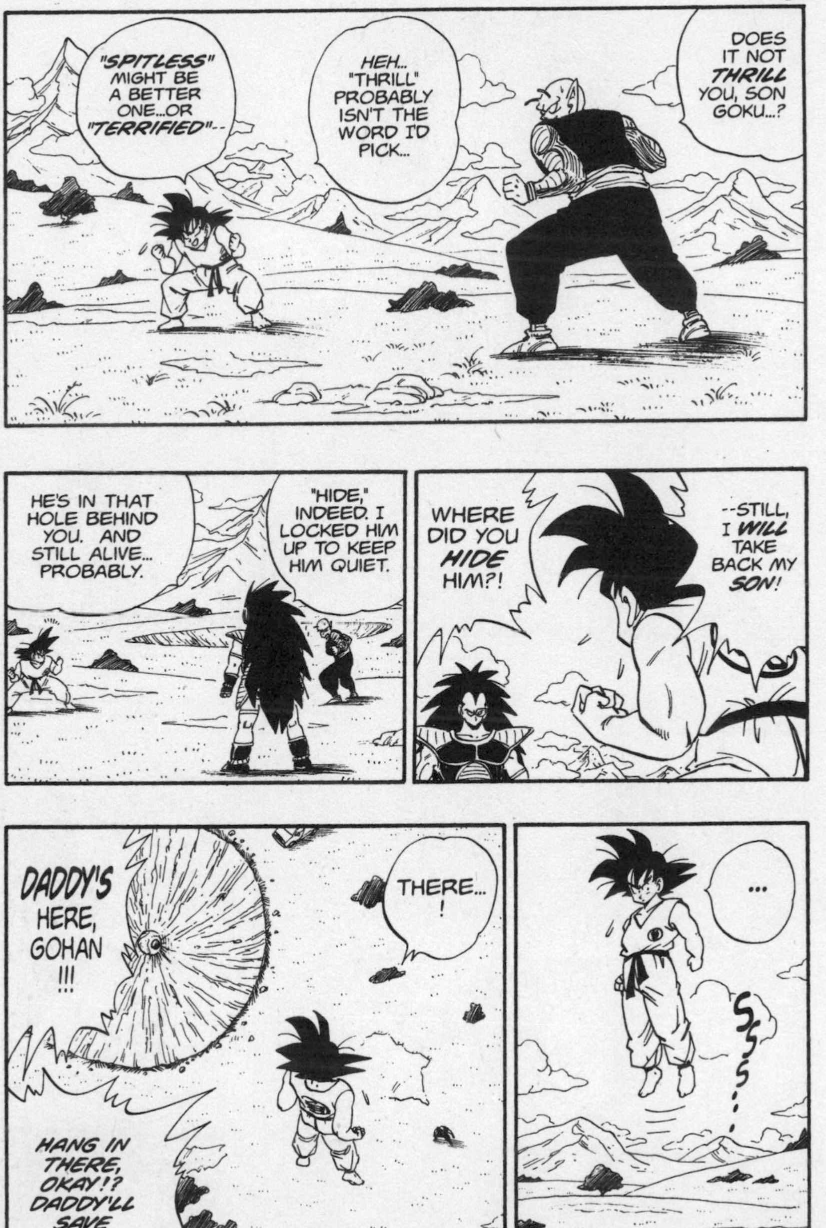
DOES IT NOT THRILL YOU, SON GOKU...?
HEH... "THRILL" PROBABLY ISN'T THE WORD I'D PICK...
"SPITLESS" MIGHT BE A BETTER ONE...OR "TERRIFIED"--
--STILL, I WILL TAKE BACK MY SON!
WHERE DID YOU HIDE HIM?!
"HIDE," INDEED. I LOCKED HIM UP TO KEEP HIM QUIET.
HE'S IN THAT HOLE BEHIND YOU. AND STILL ALIVE... PROBABLY.
...
SSS...
THERE... !
DADDY'S HERE, GOHAN !!!
HANG IN THERE, OKAY!? DADDY'LL SAVE YOU!!

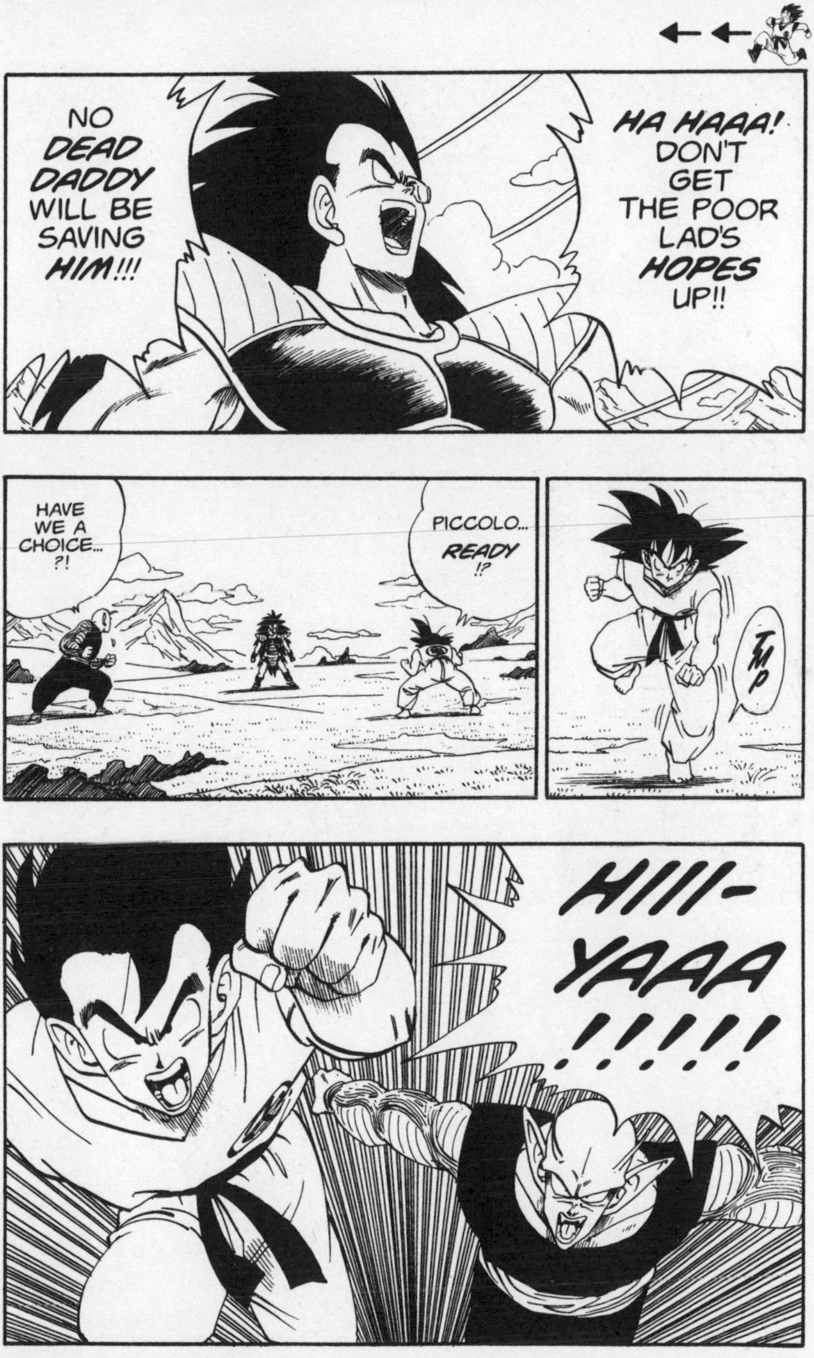
HA HAAA! DON'T GET THE POOR LAD'S HOPES UP!!
NO DEAD DADDY WILL BE SAVING HIM!!!
TMP
PICCOLO... READY!?
HAVE WE A CHOICE...?!
HIII-YAAA!!!!!

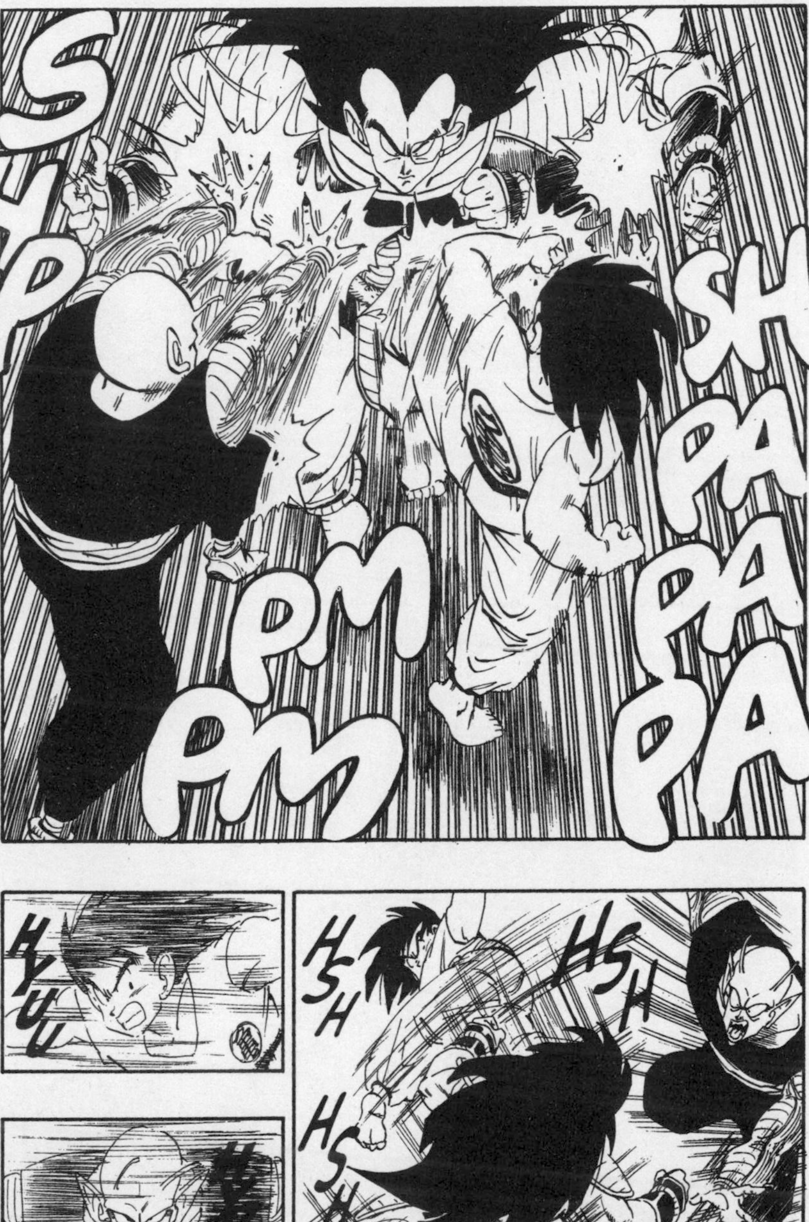
SH
PA
PA
PA
PM
PM
SHP
HSH
HSH
HSH
HYUU

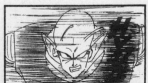

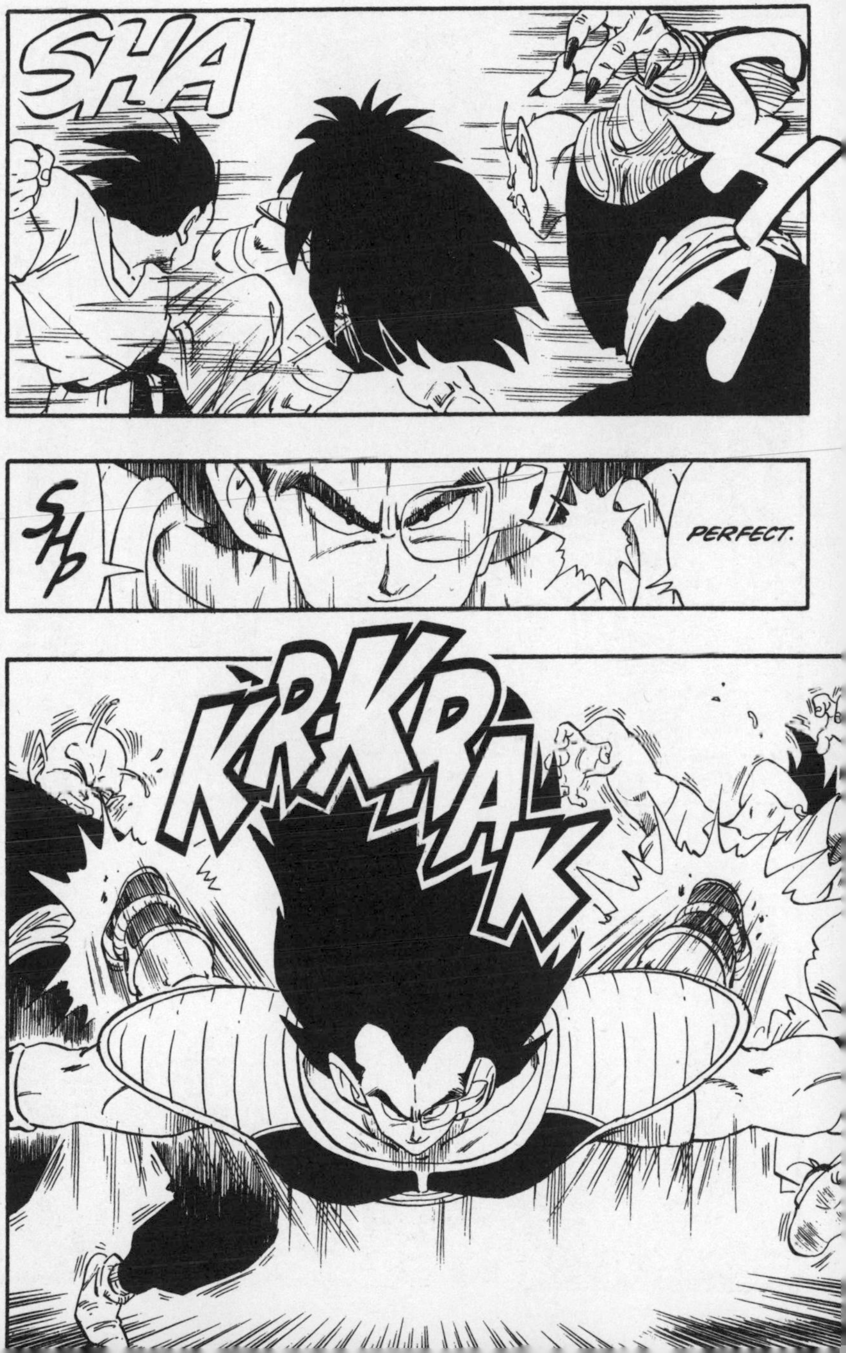
SHA
SHA
PERFECT.
SHP
KR-KRAK

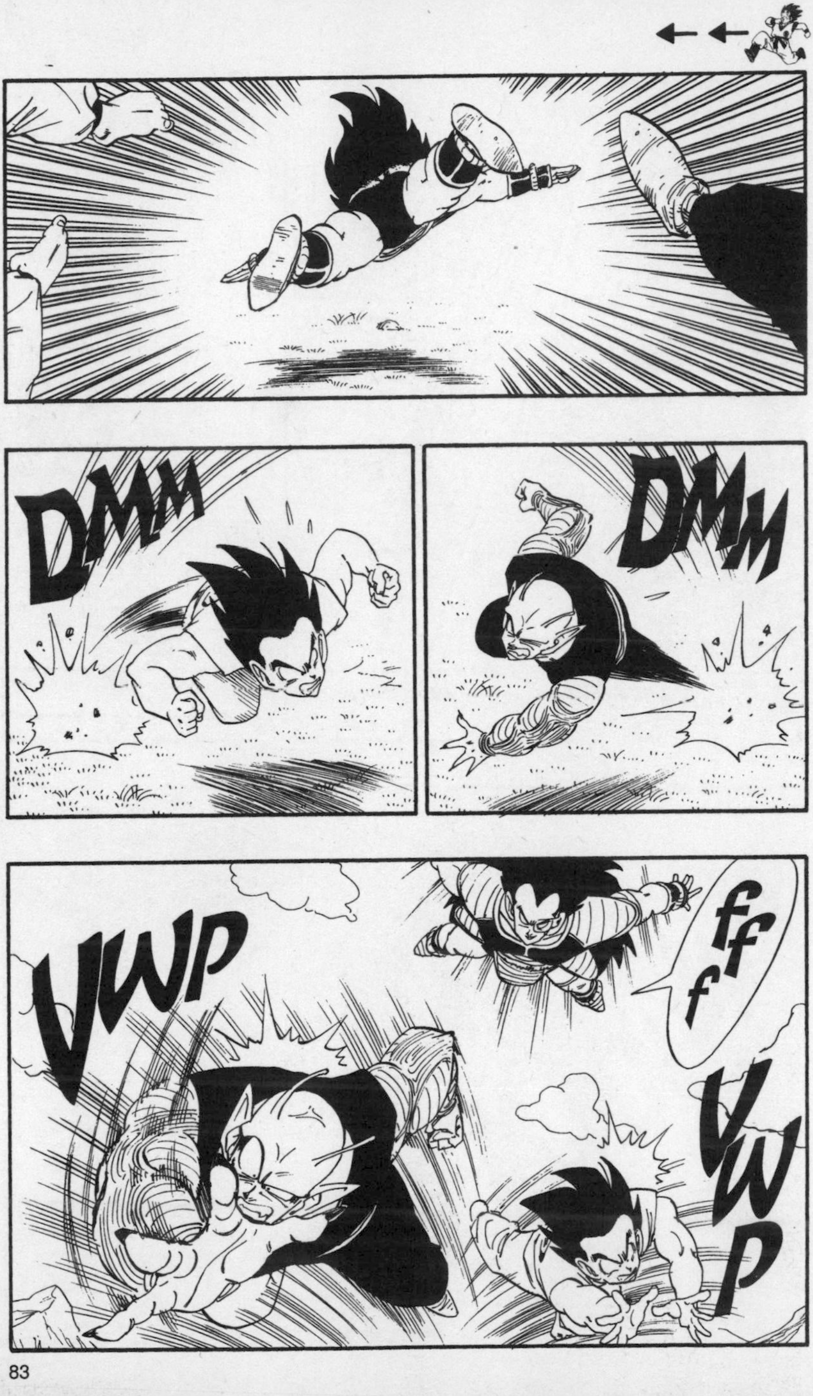
DMM
DMM
fff
VWP
VWP

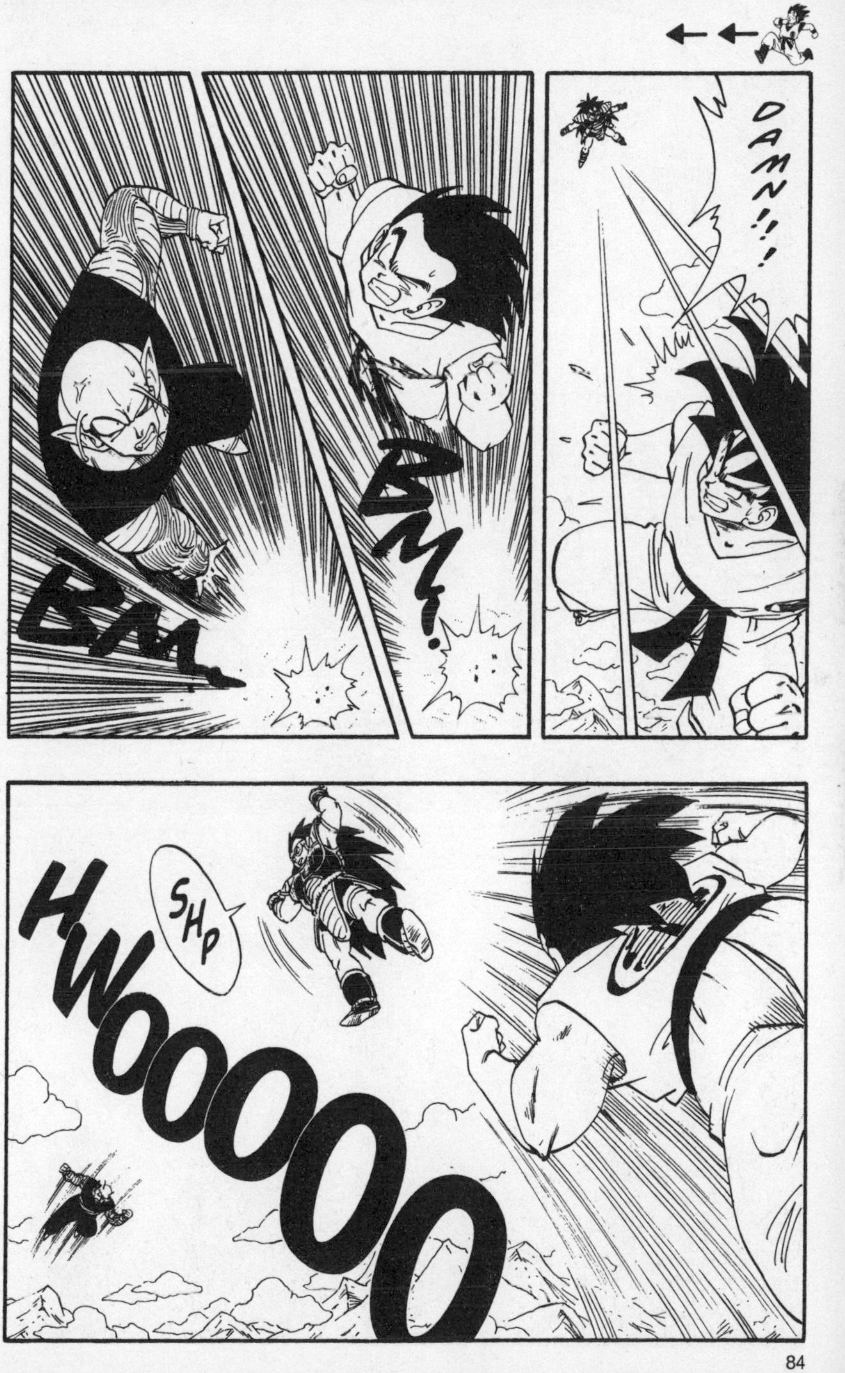
DAMN!!!
BAM!
BAM
SHP
HWOOOOOO

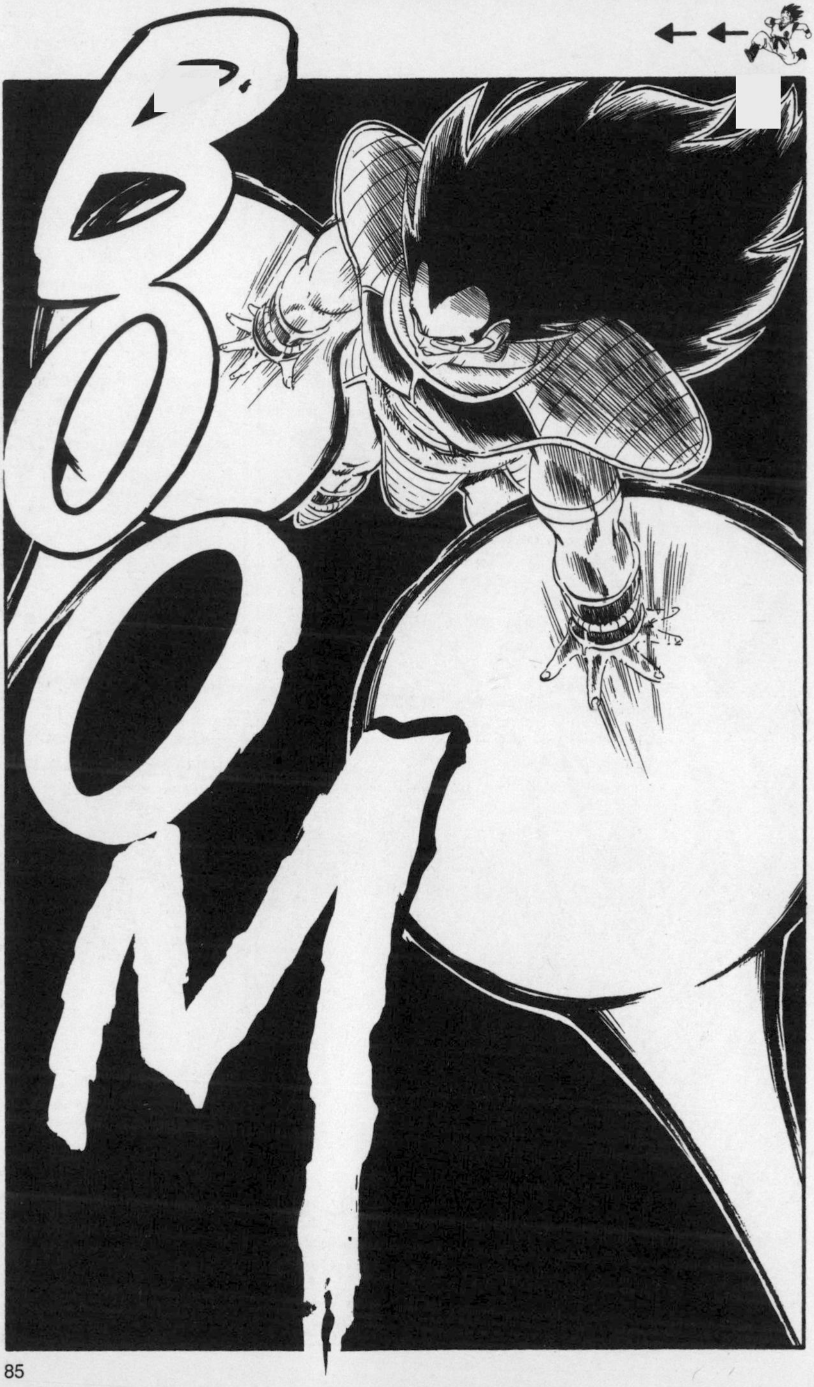
BOOM

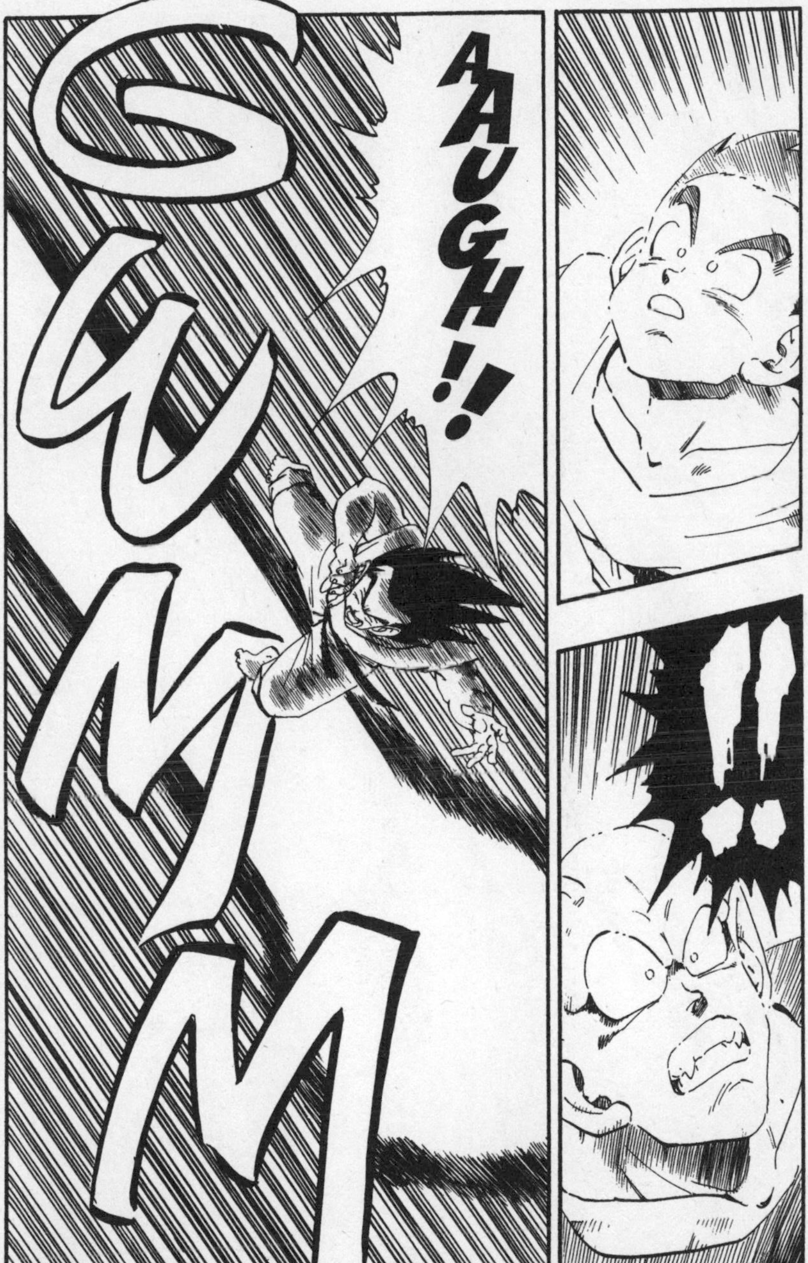
!!
AAUGH!!
GWMM

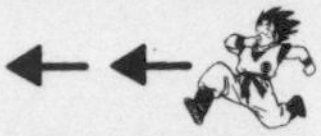

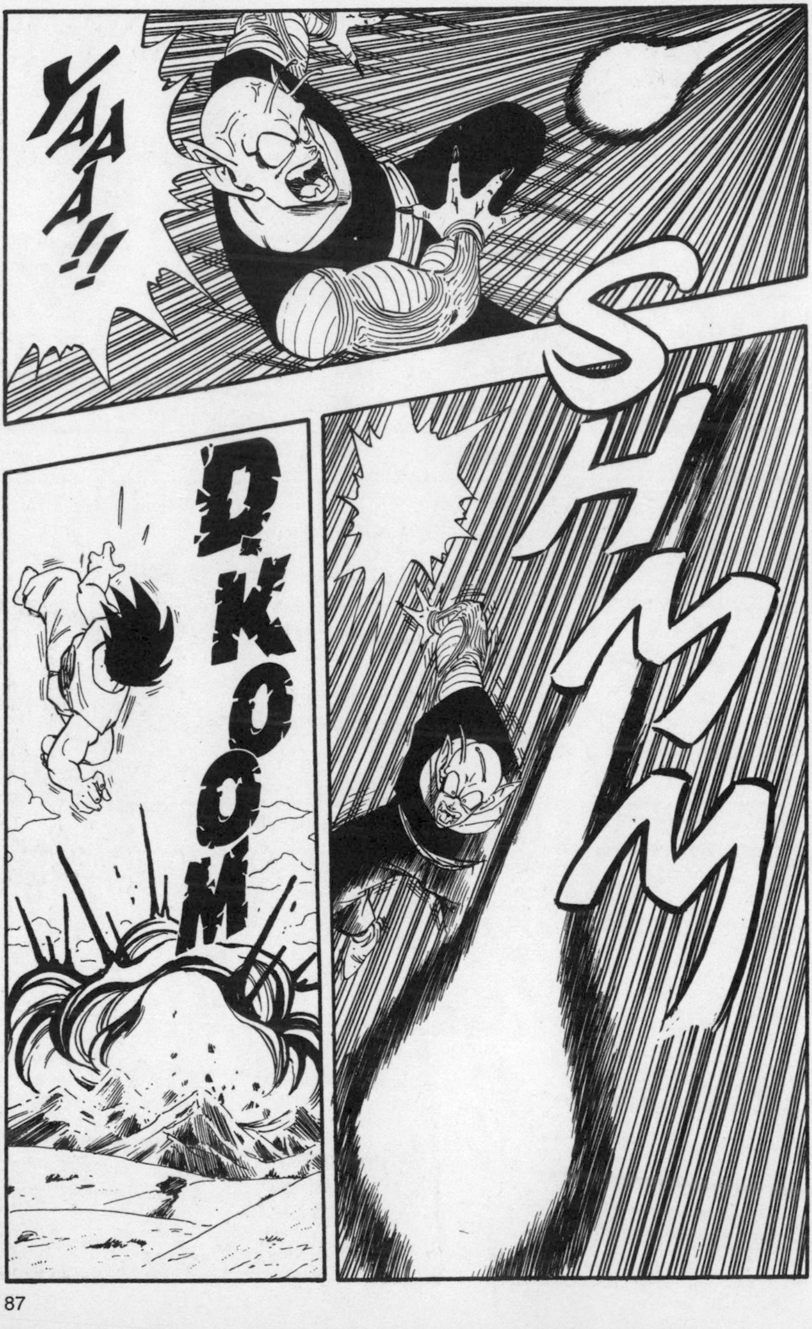
YAAA!!
SHMMM
DKOOM

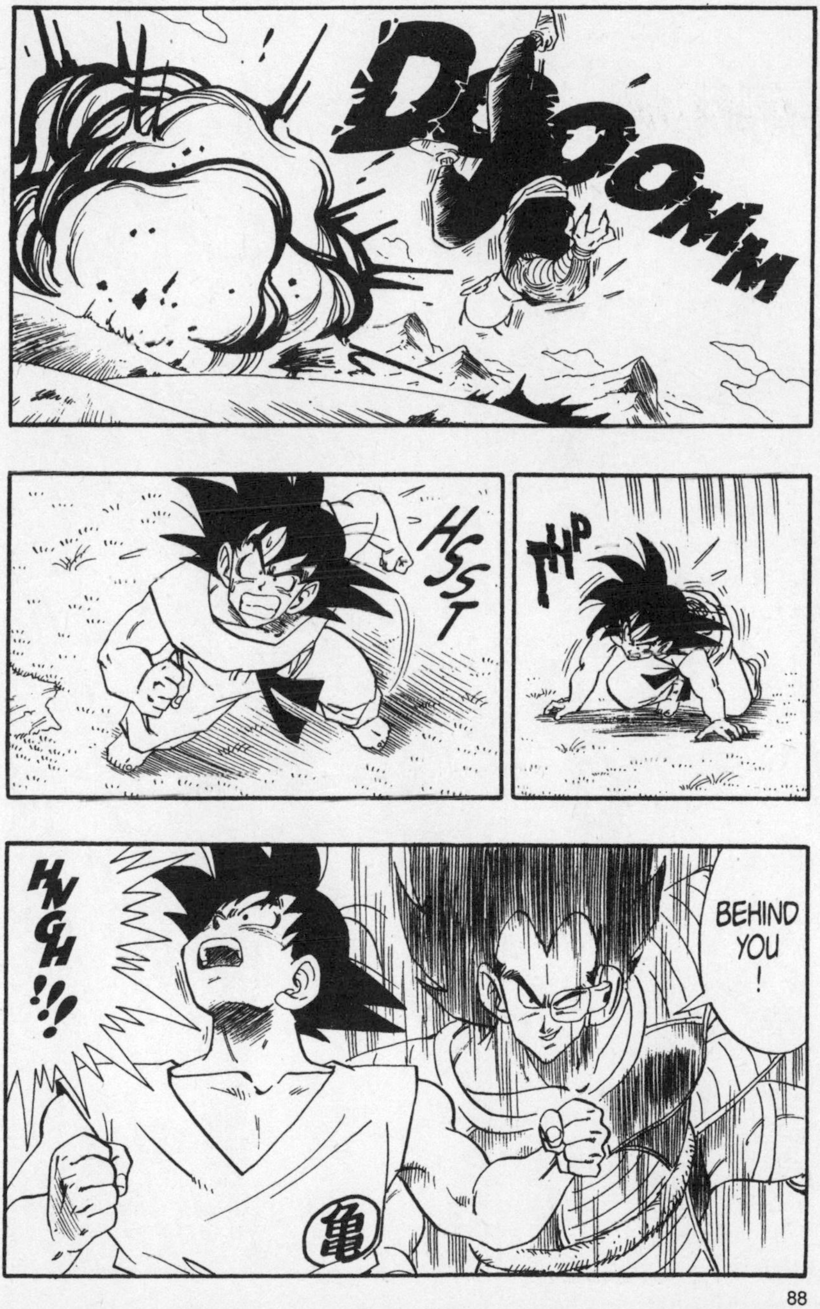
DOOMM
THP
HSST
BEHIND YOU!
HNGH!!!

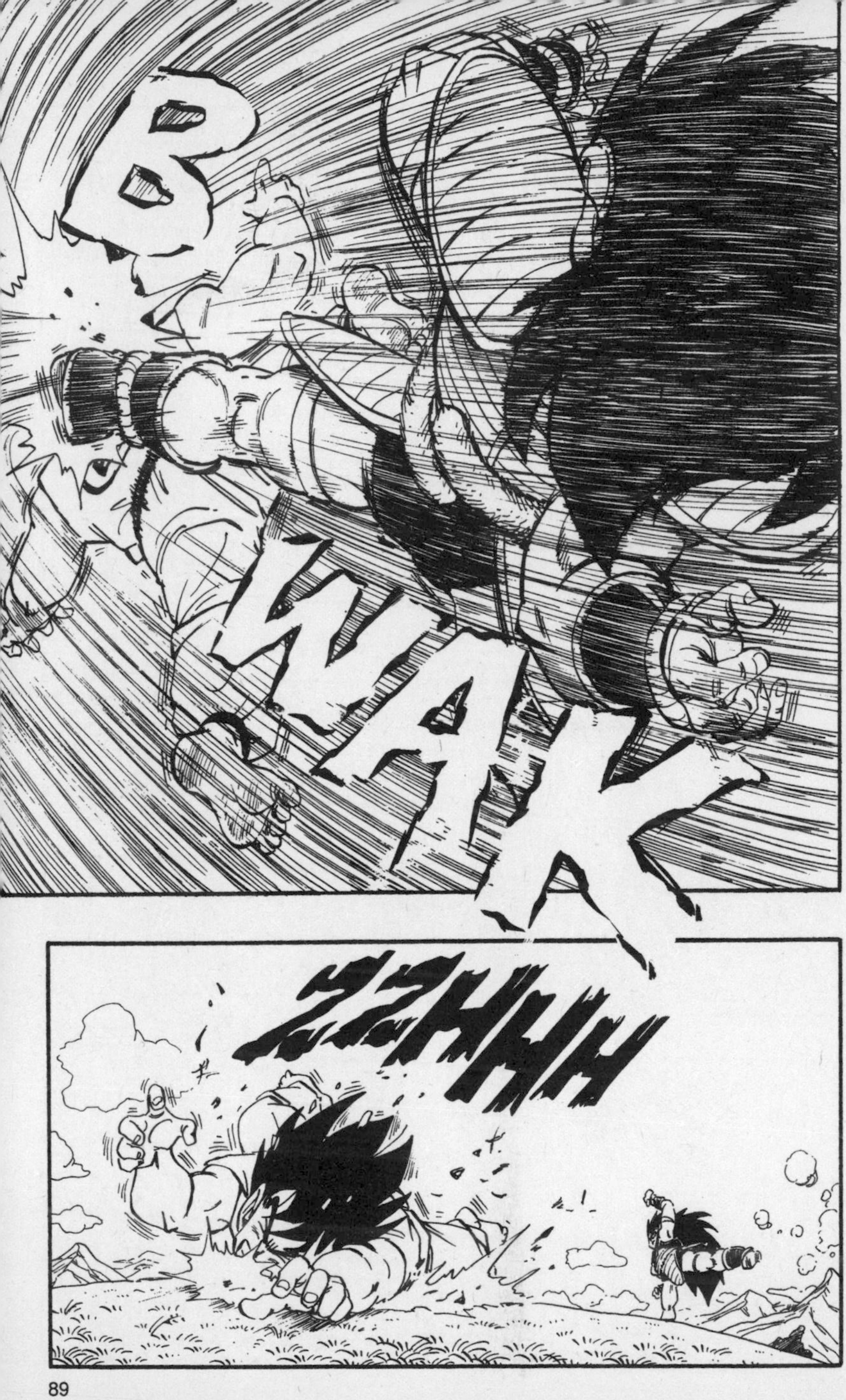
BWAK
ZZHHH

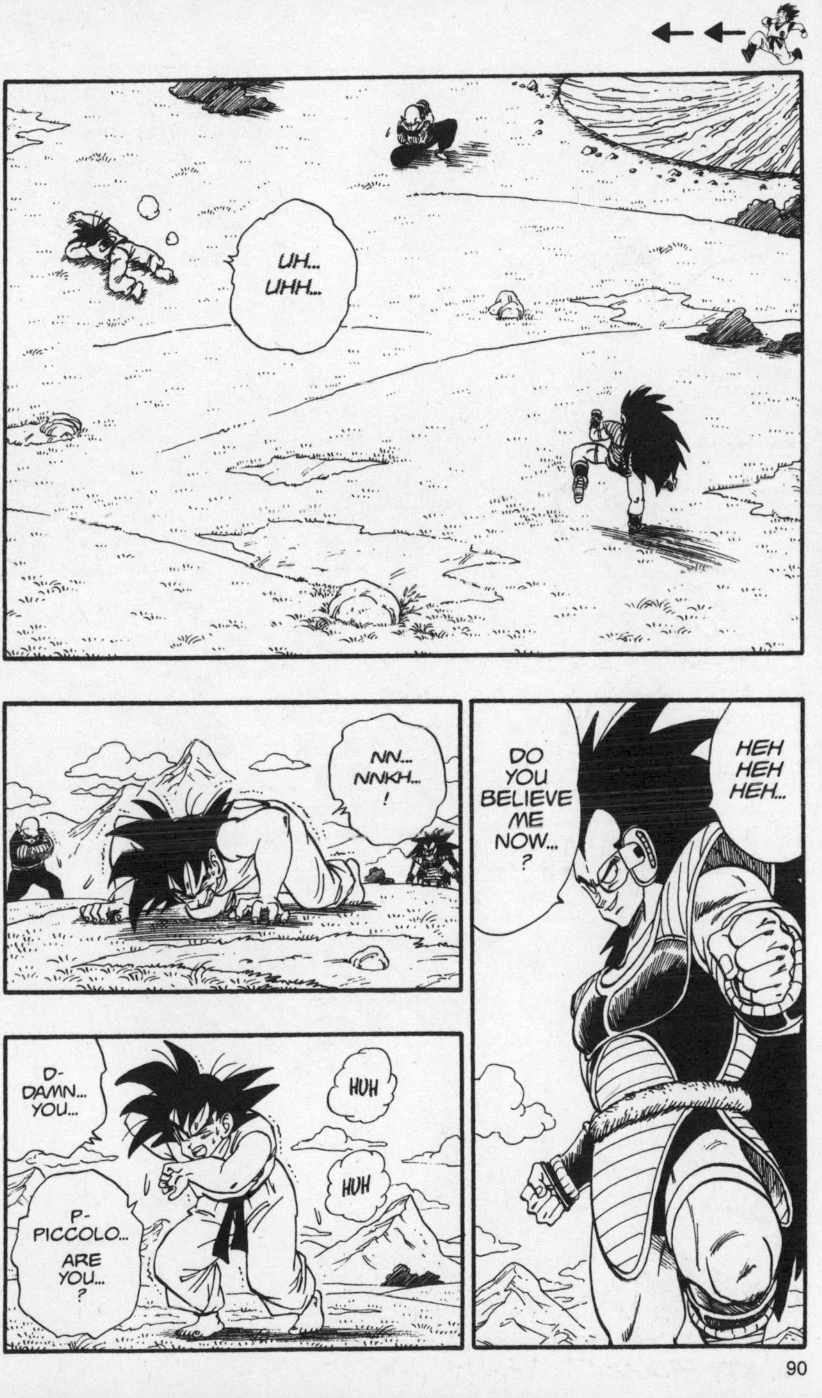
UH... UHH...
HEH HEH HEH...
DO YOU BELIEVE ME NOW... ?
NN... NNKH... !
HUH
D-DAMN... YOU...
HUH
P-PICCOLO... ARE YOU... ?

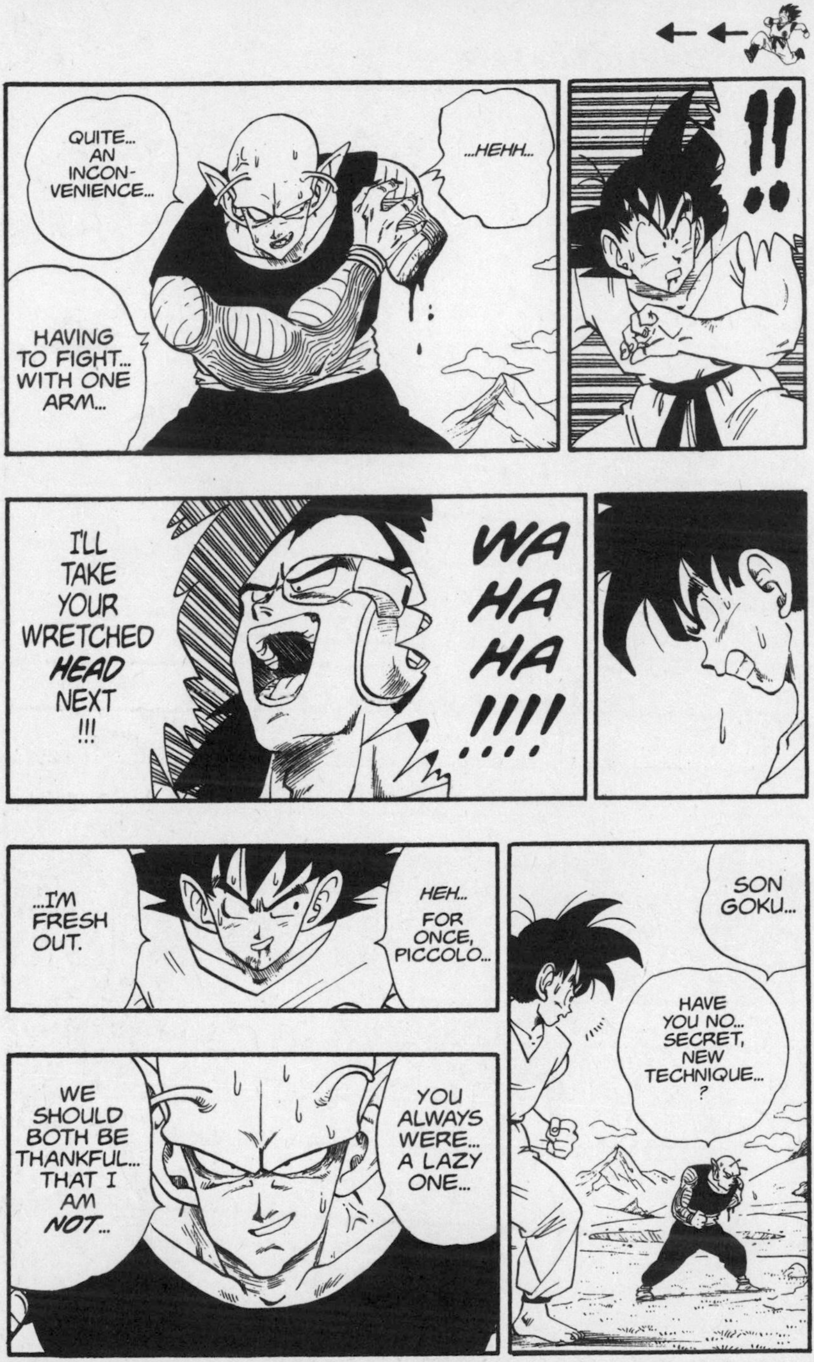
!!
...HEHH...
QUITE... AN INCONVENIENCE...
HAVING TO FIGHT... WITH ONE ARM...
WA HA HA !!!!
I'LL TAKE YOUR WRETCHED HEAD NEXT !!!
SON GOKU...
HAVE YOU NO... SECRET, NEW TECHNIQUE... ?
HEH... FOR ONCE, PICCOLO...
...I'M FRESH OUT.
YOU ALWAYS WERE... A LAZY ONE...
WE SHOULD BOTH BE THANKFUL... THAT I AM NOT...

NEXT: PICCOLO'S TRUMP CARD!

DBZ : 07 • Piccolo's Farewell to Arms!?

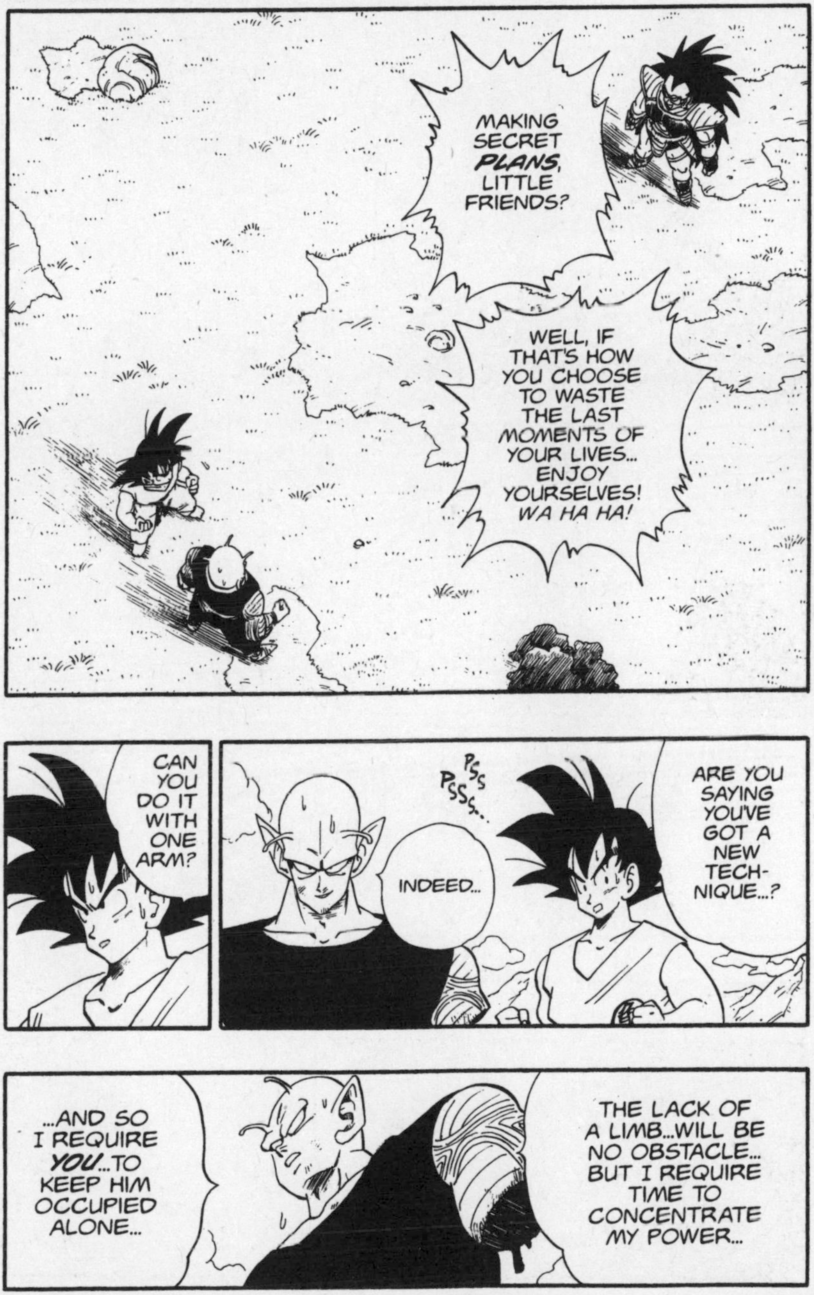
MAKING SECRET *PLANS*, LITTLE FRIENDS?
WELL, IF THAT'S HOW YOU CHOOSE TO WASTE THE LAST MOMENTS OF YOUR LIVES... ENJOY YOURSELVES! *WA HA HA!*
ARE YOU SAYING YOU'VE GOT A NEW TECH-NIQUE...?
PSSS PSSS...
INDEED...
CAN YOU DO IT WITH ONE ARM?
THE LACK OF A LIMB...WILL BE NO OBSTACLE... BUT I REQUIRE TIME TO CONCENTRATE MY POWER...
...AND SO I REQUIRE *YOU*...TO KEEP HIM OCCUPIED ALONE...

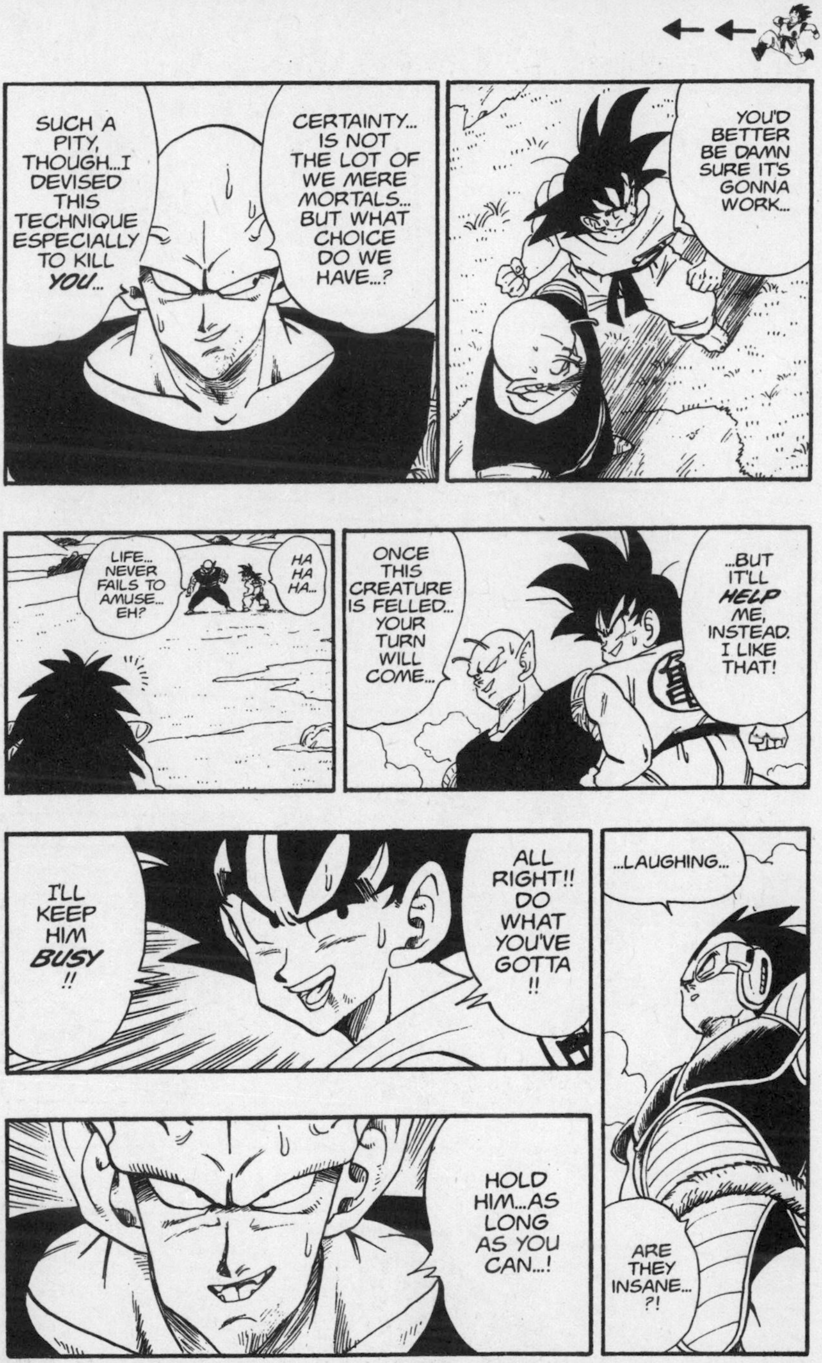
YOU'D BETTER BE DAMN SURE IT'S GONNA WORK...
CERTAINTY... IS NOT THE LOT OF WE MERE MORTALS... BUT WHAT CHOICE DO WE HAVE...?
SUCH A PITY, THOUGH...I DEVISED THIS TECHNIQUE ESPECIALLY TO KILL *YOU*...
...BUT IT'LL *HELP* ME, INSTEAD. I LIKE THAT!
ONCE THIS CREATURE IS FELLED... YOUR TURN WILL COME...
HA HA HA...
LIFE... NEVER FAILS TO AMUSE... EH?
...LAUGHING...
ARE THEY INSANE...?!
ALL RIGHT!! DO WHAT YOU'VE GOTTA!!
I'LL KEEP HIM *BUSY*!!
HOLD HIM...AS LONG AS YOU CAN...!

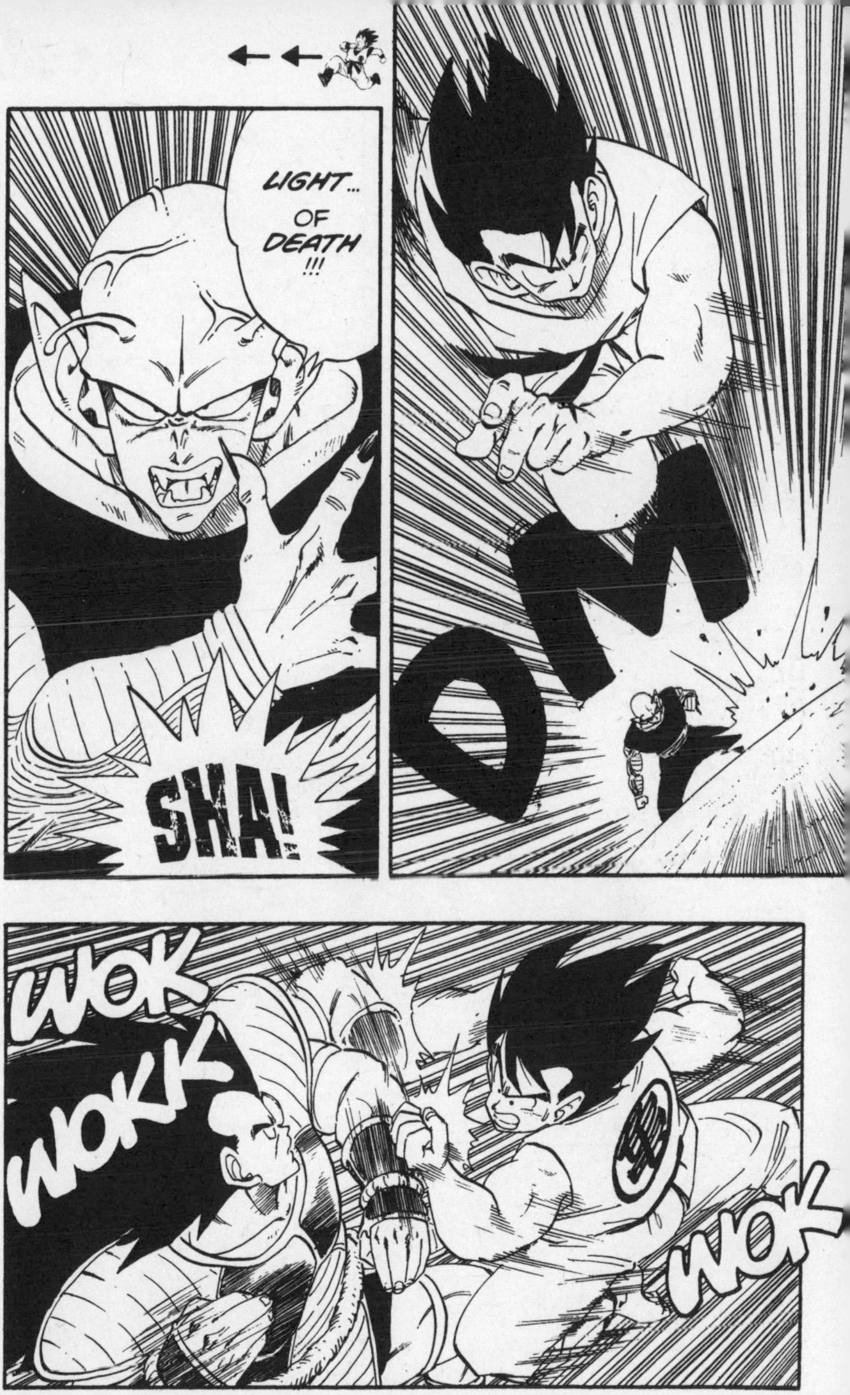
DOM
LIGHT... OF DEATH !!!
SHA!
WOK
WOKK
WOK

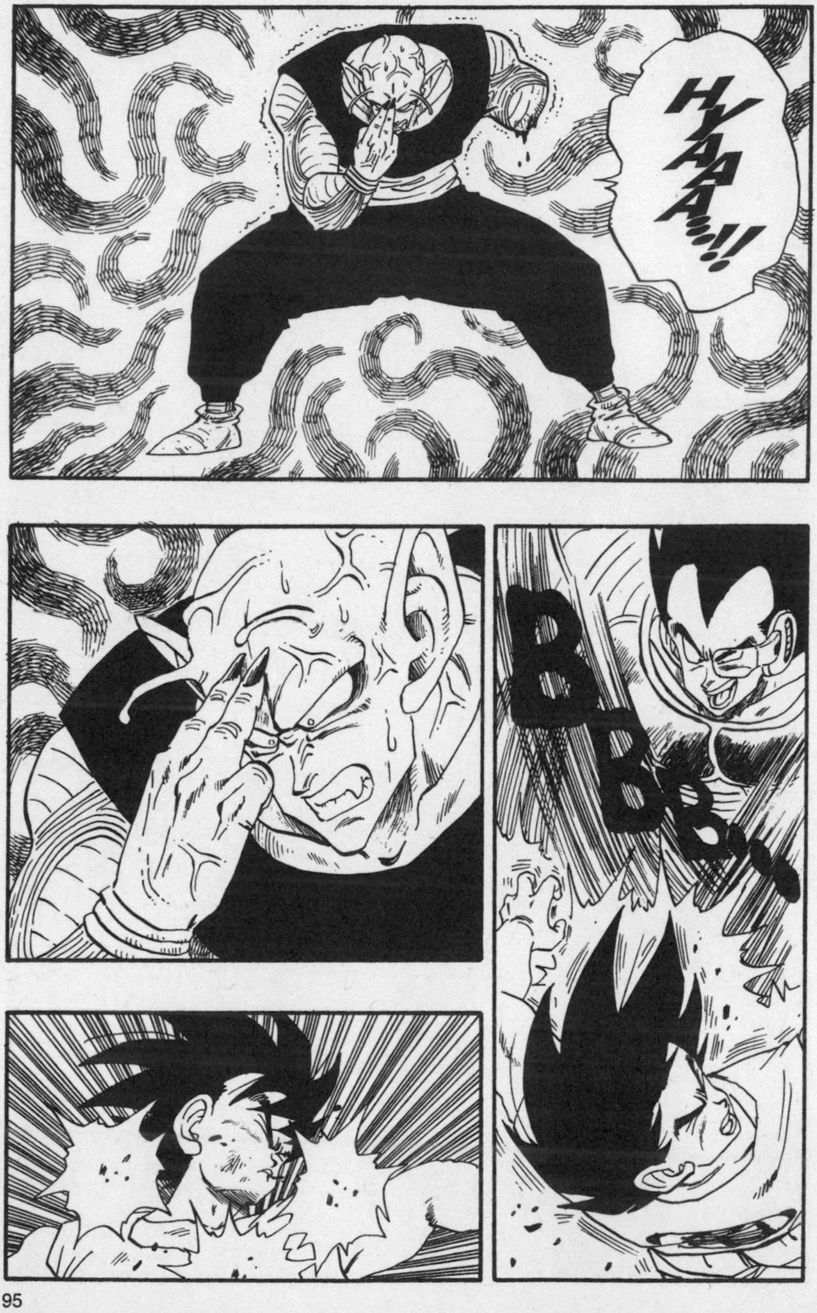
HYAAA...!!
BBBB...

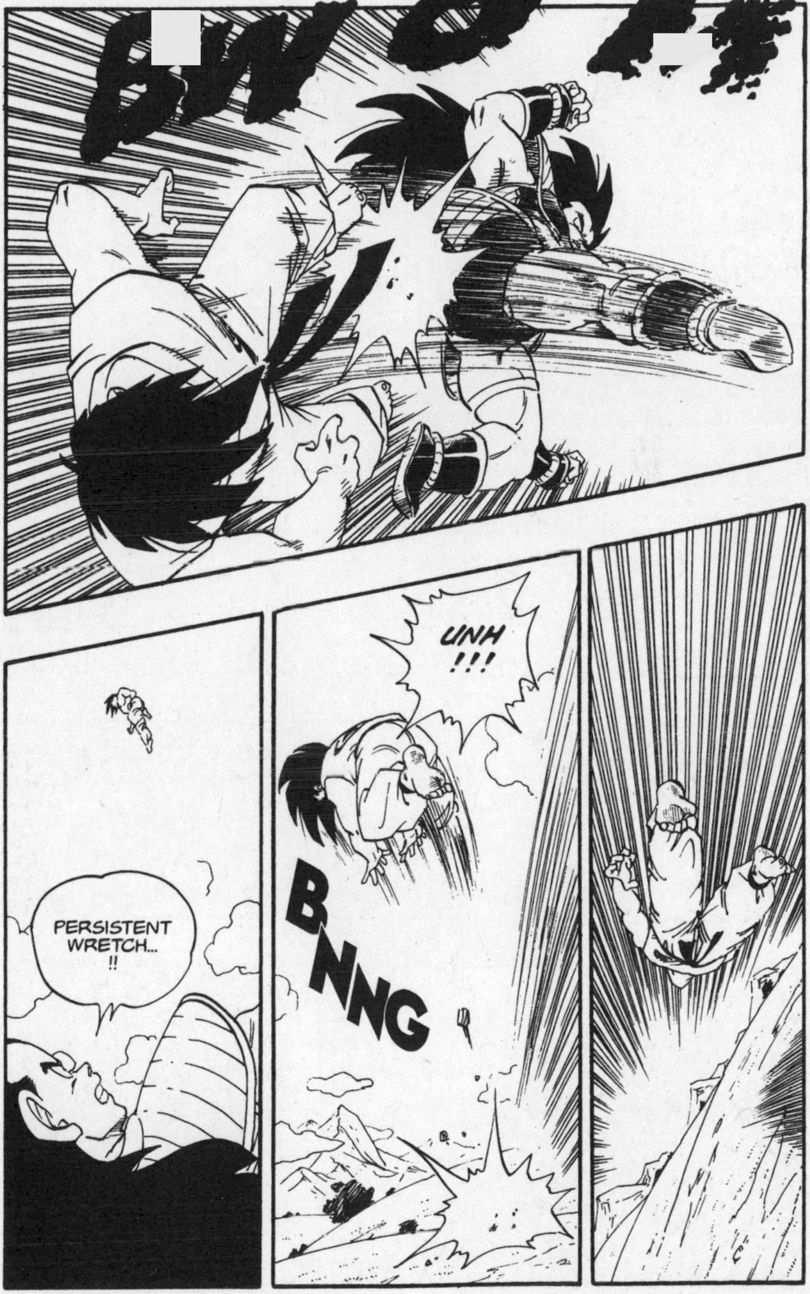
UNH !!!
BNNG
PERSISTENT WRETCH... !!

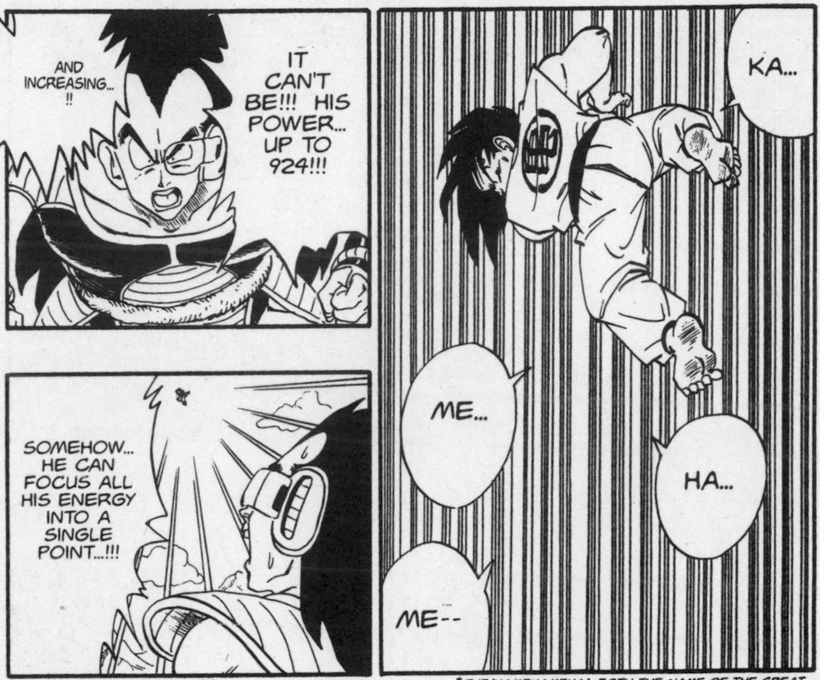
KA...
ME...
HA...
ME--
IT CAN'T BE!!! HIS POWER... UP TO 924!!!
AND INCREASING... !!
SOMEHOW... HE CAN FOCUS ALL HIS ENERGY INTO A SINGLE POINT...!!!

*THE "KAMEHAMEHA," BOTH THE NAME OF THE GREAT HAWAI'IAN KING (1810-19), AND GOKU'S GREAT ***HISSATSU WAZA*** OR "DESPERATION MOVE"...!

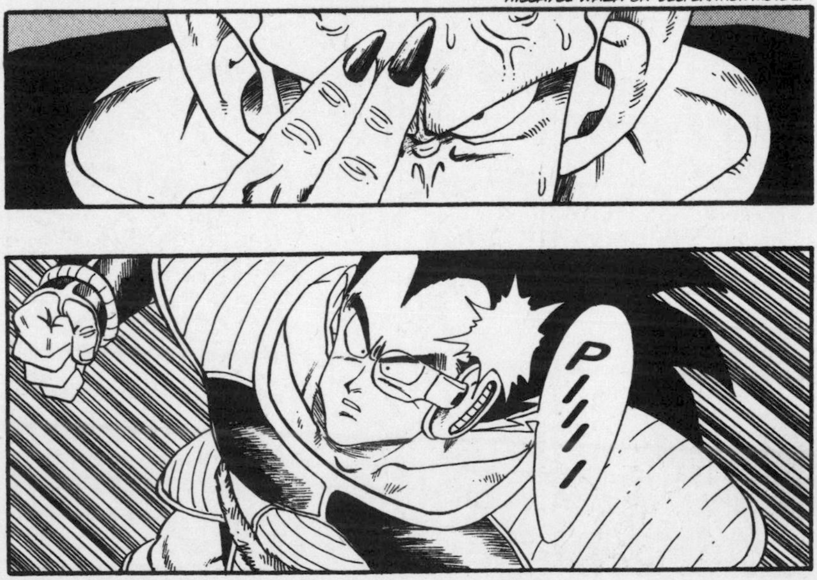
PIIII

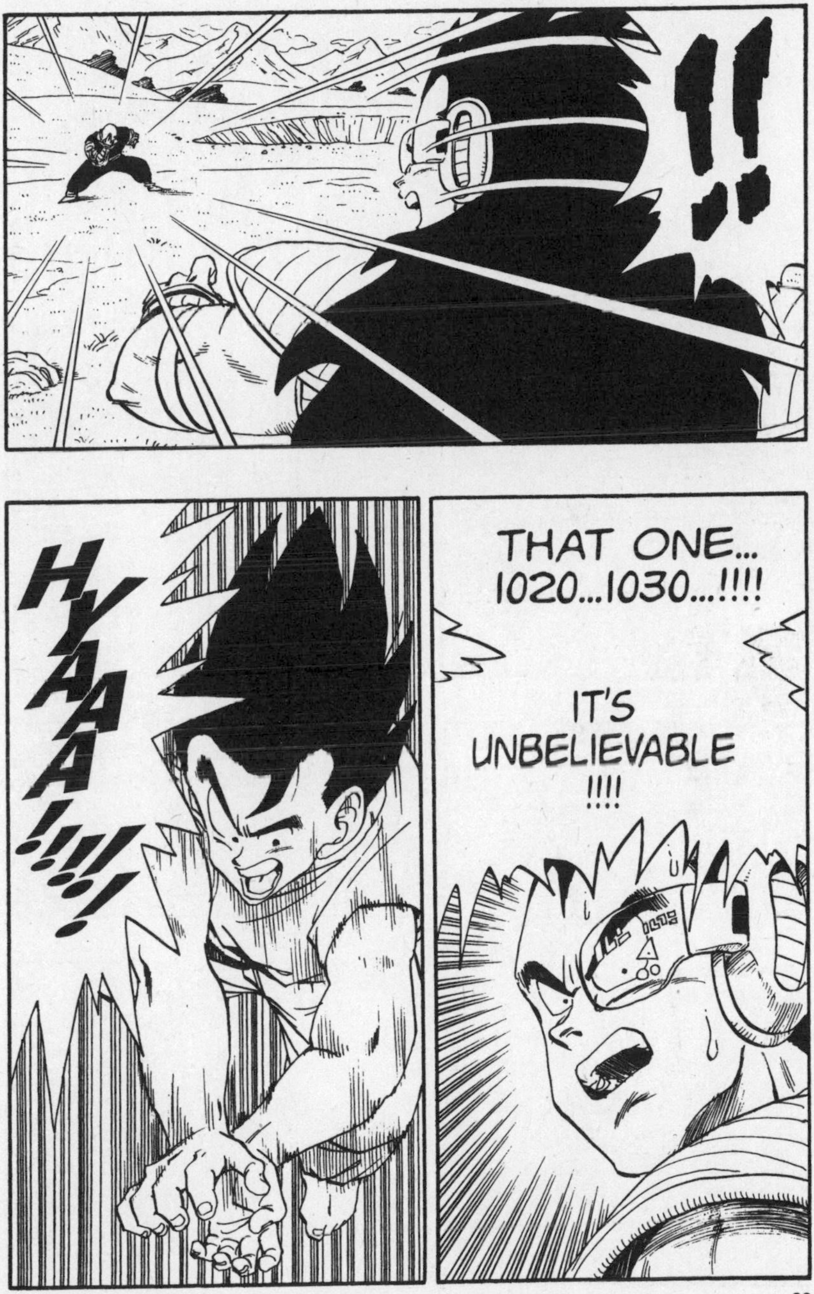
!!
THAT ONE... 1020...1030...!!!!
IT'S UNBELIEVABLE !!!!
HYAAA!!!!!

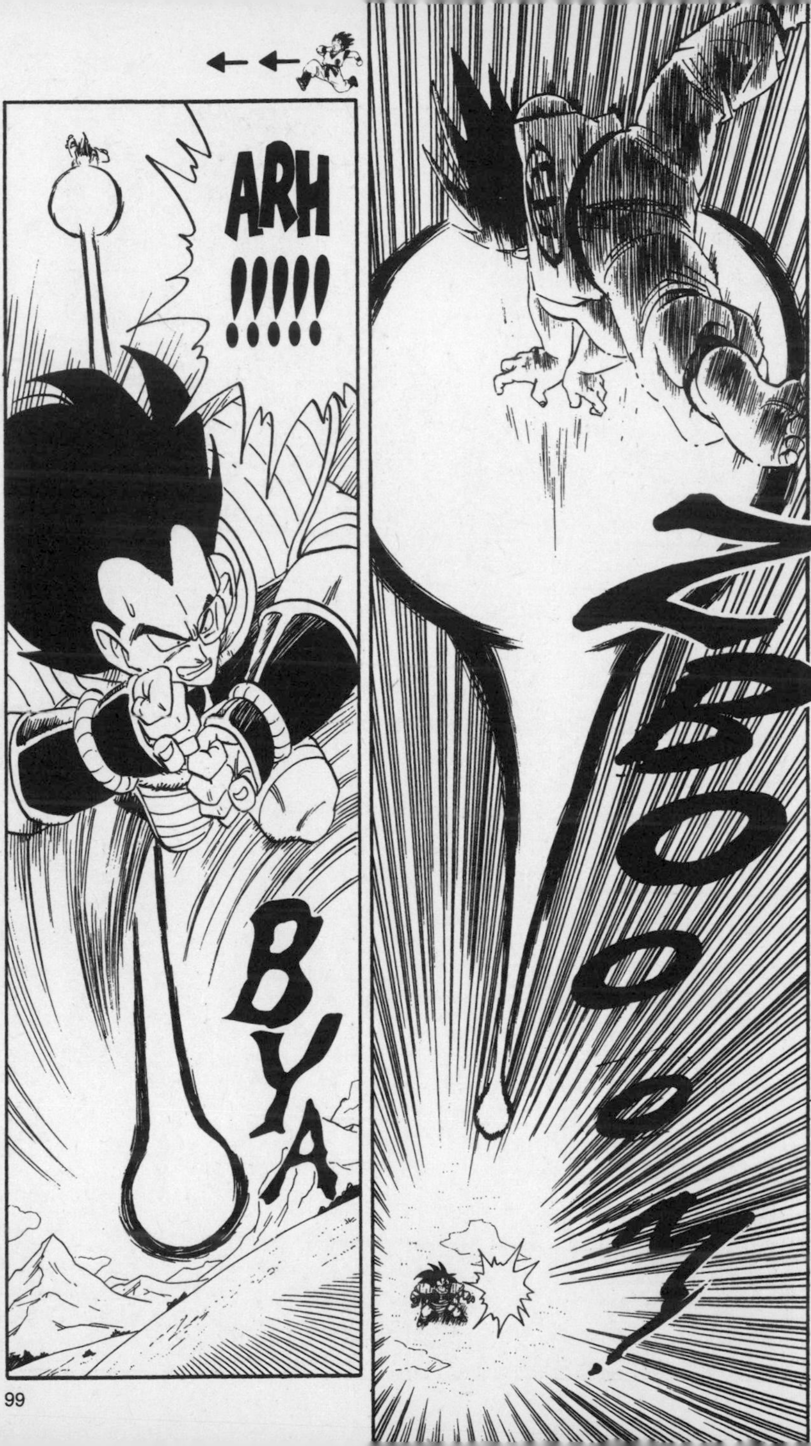
ZBOOOOM!
ARH
!!!!!
BYA

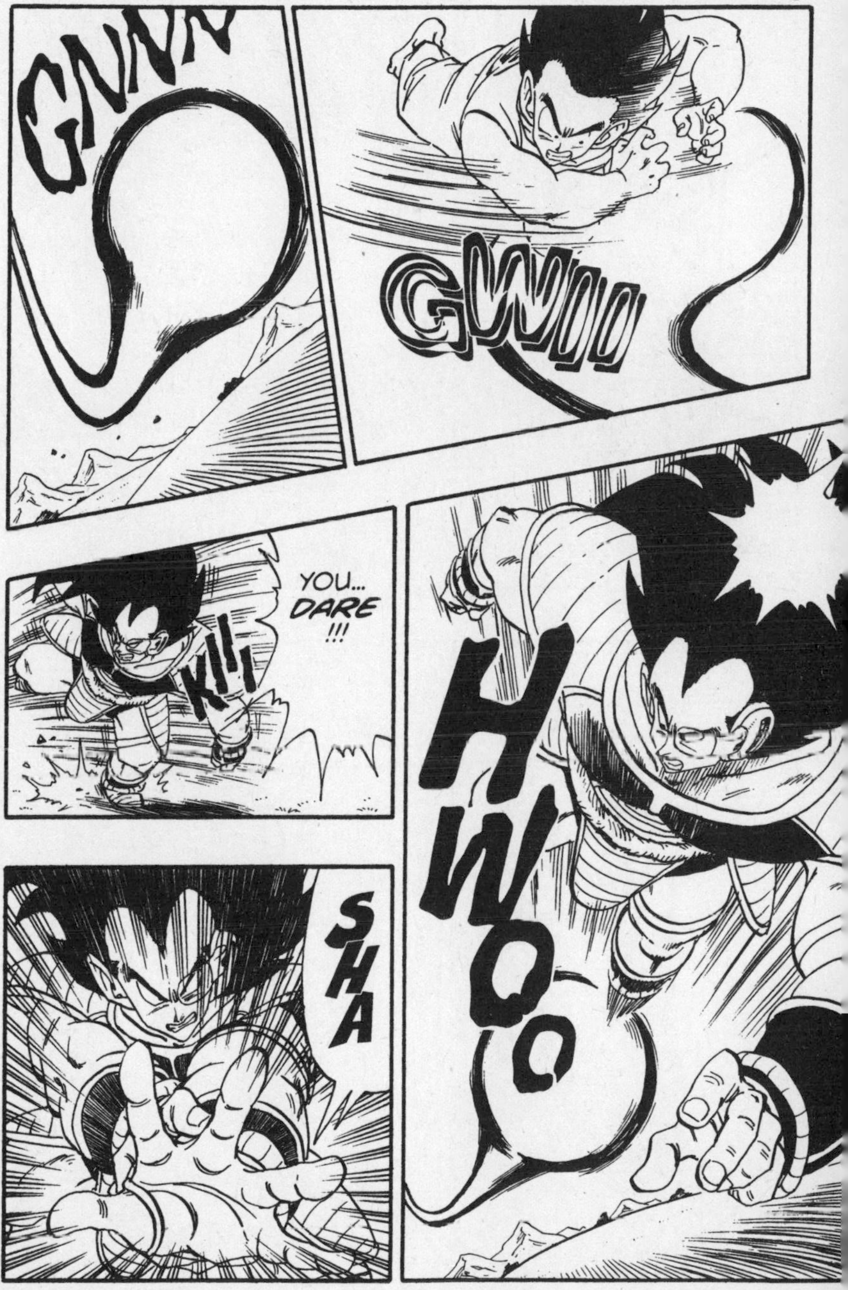
GWIII
GNNN
HWOOO
YOU... DARE!!!
KIII
SHA

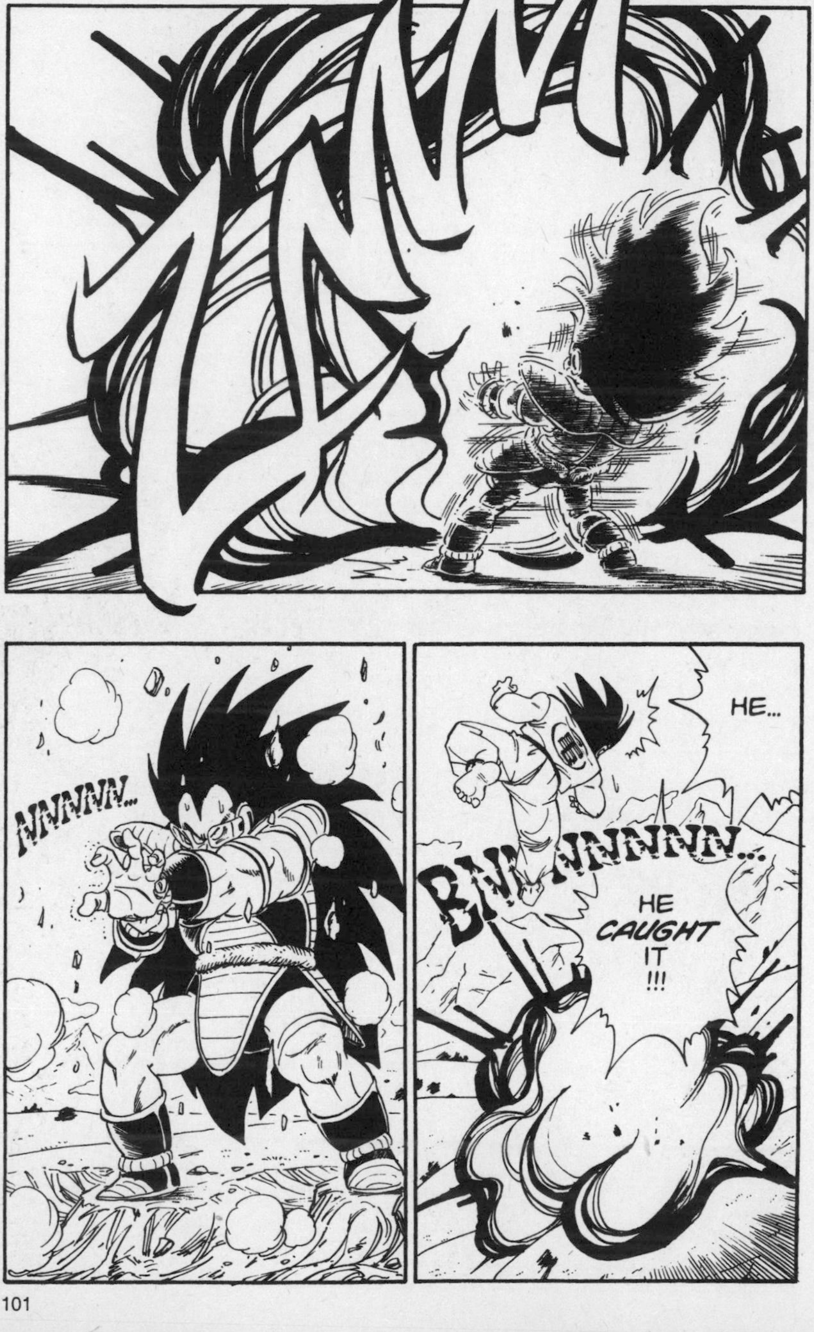
HE...
BNNNNNNNN...
HE CAUGHT IT !!!
NNNNNN...

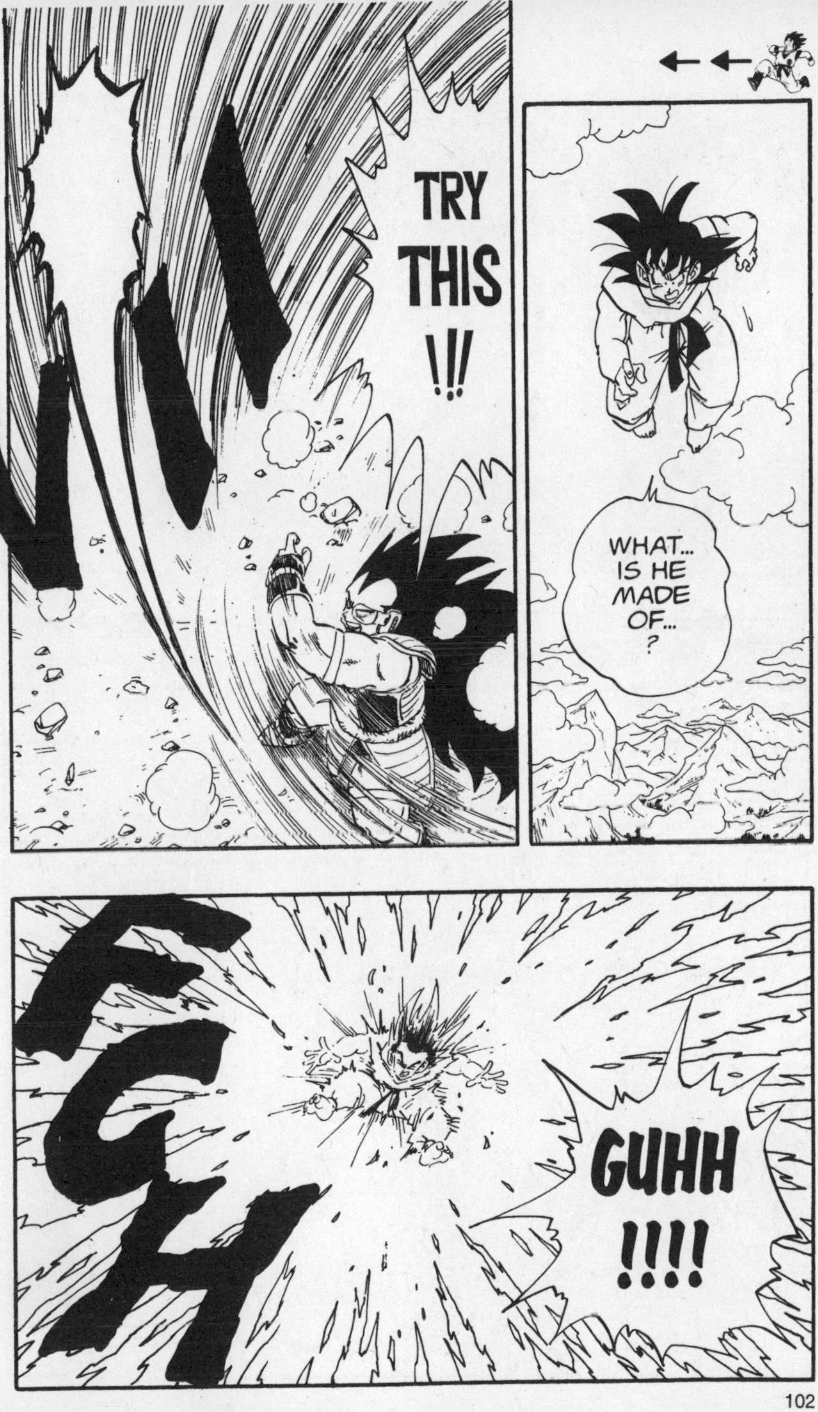
WHAT... IS HE MADE OF... ?
TRY THIS !!!
GUHH !!!!

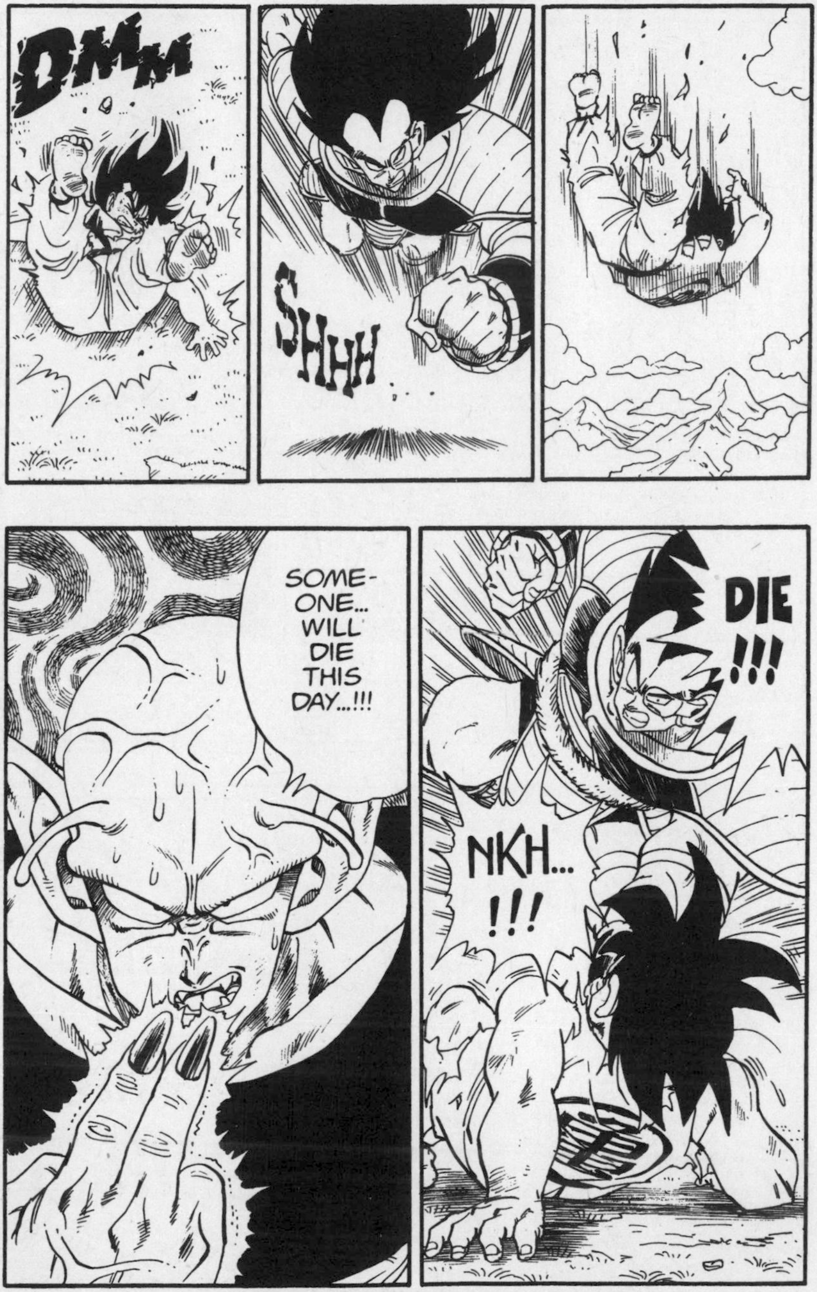
SHHH
DMM
DIE!!!
NKH... !!!
SOME-ONE... WILL DIE THIS DAY...!!!

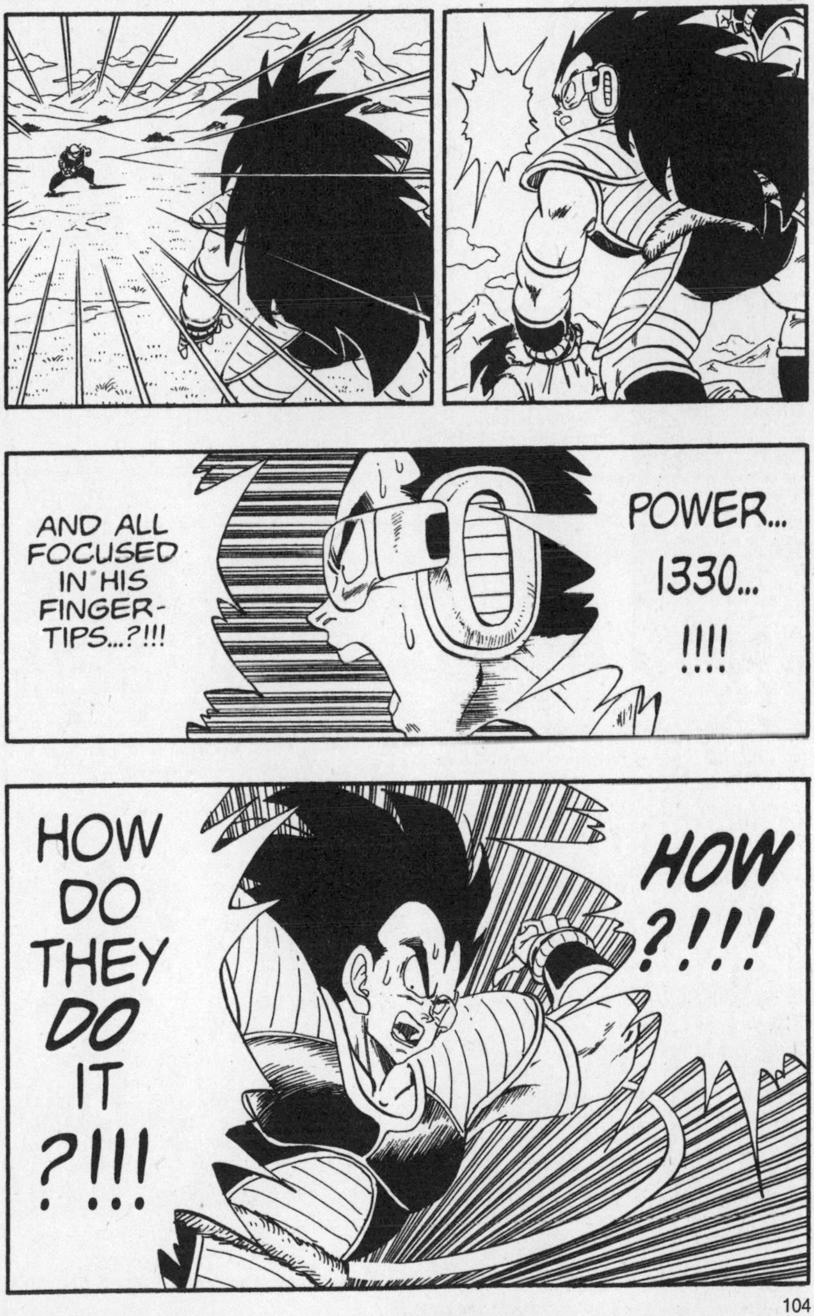
POWER... 1330... !!!!
AND ALL FOCUSED IN HIS FINGER-TIPS...?!!!
HOW ?!!!
HOW DO THEY DO IT ?!!!

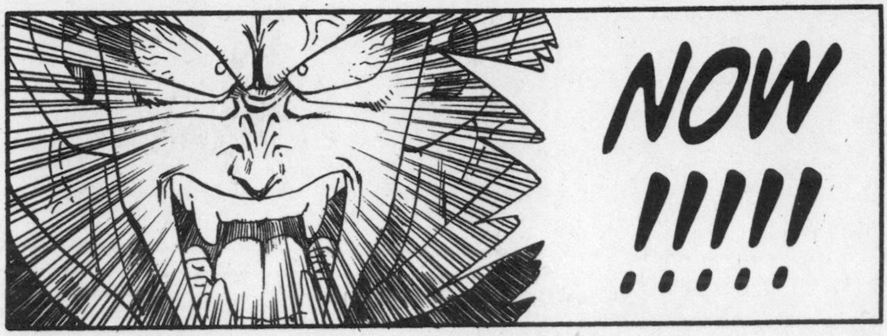
NOW
!!!!!

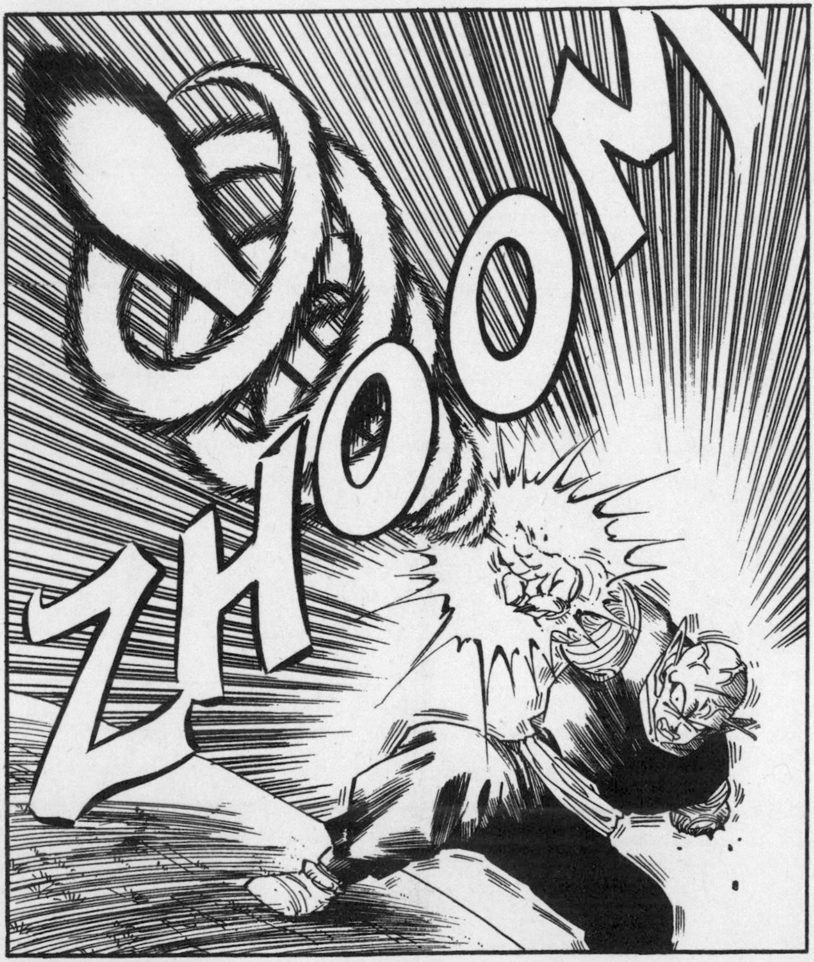
ZHOOOM

NEXT: THE LIGHT OF DEATH!

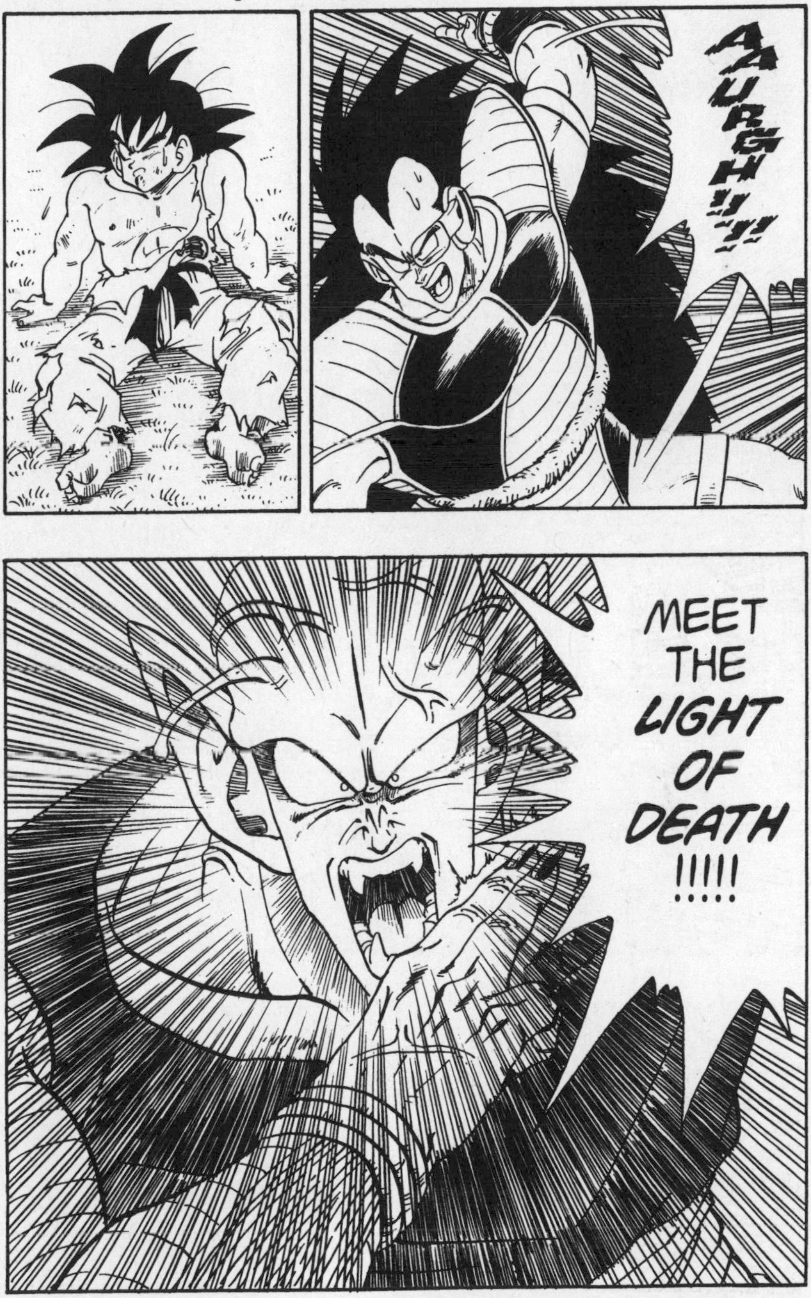
AAURGH!!!!
MEET THE LIGHT OF DEATH !!!!!

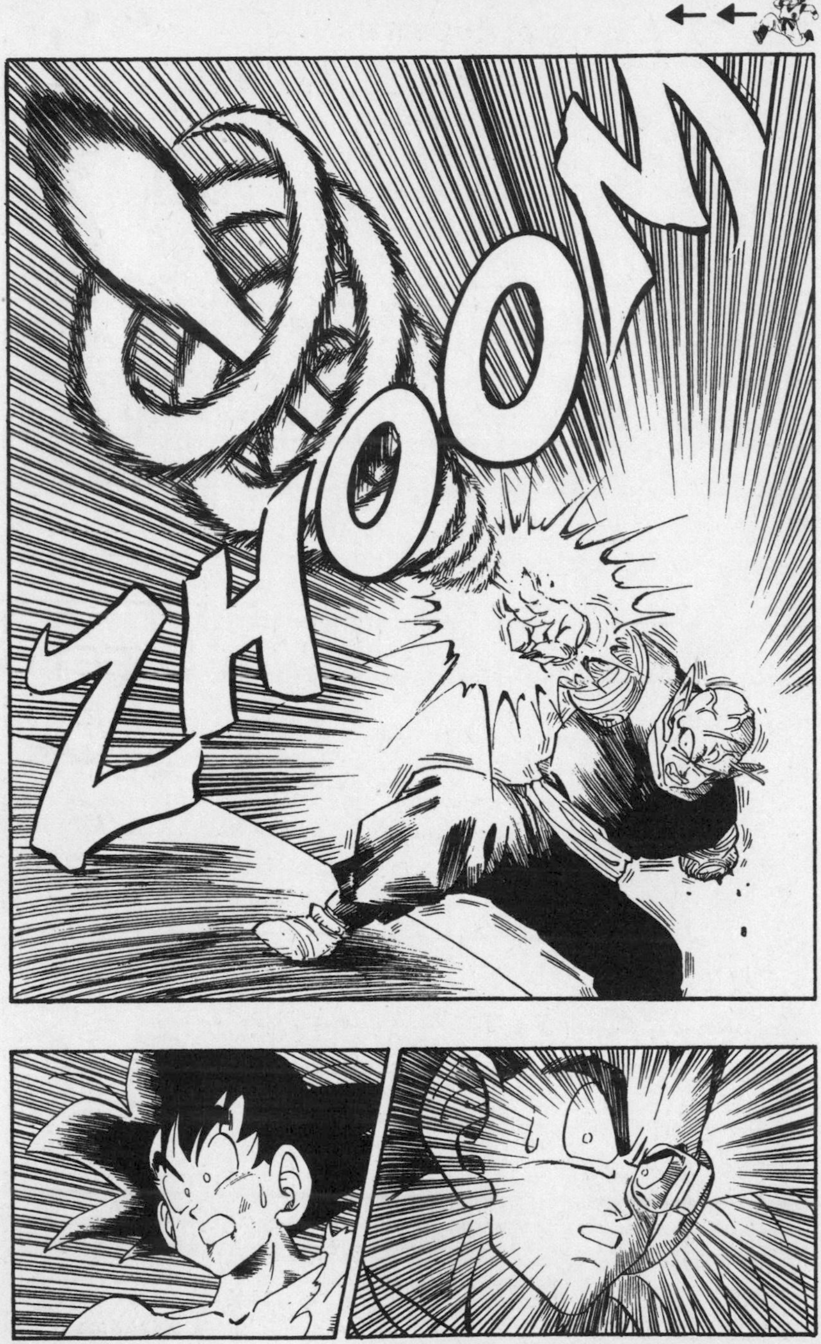
ZHOOOM

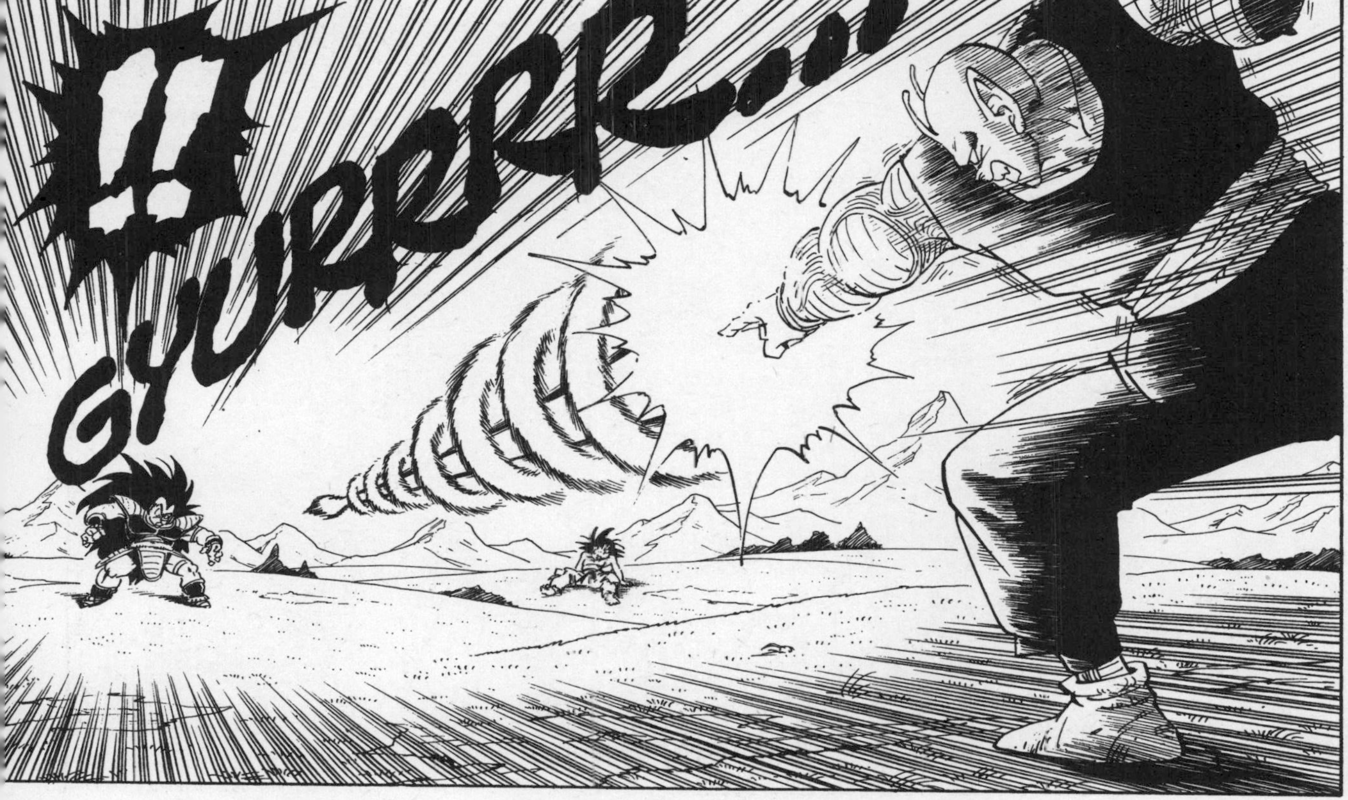
GYURRR...!!

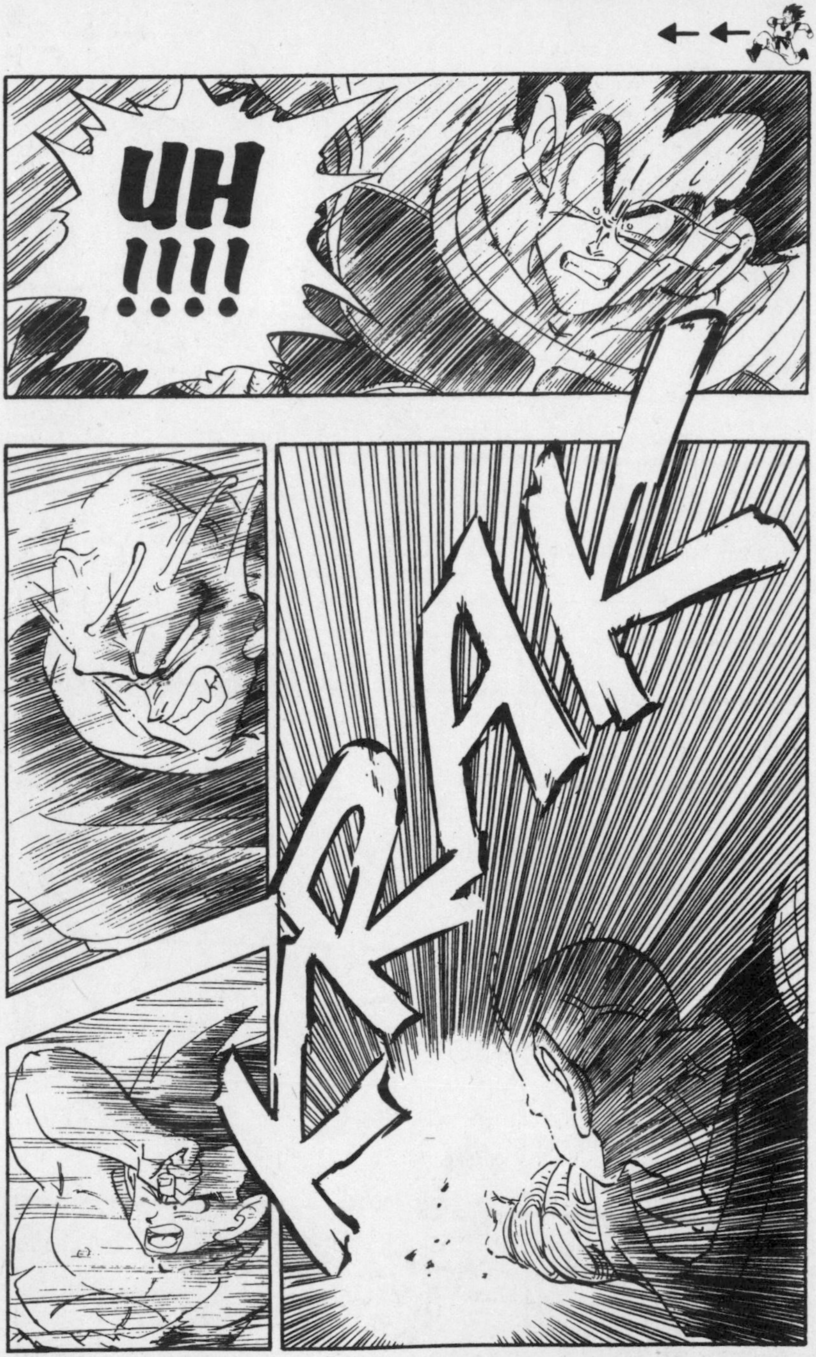
UH
!!!!
KRAK

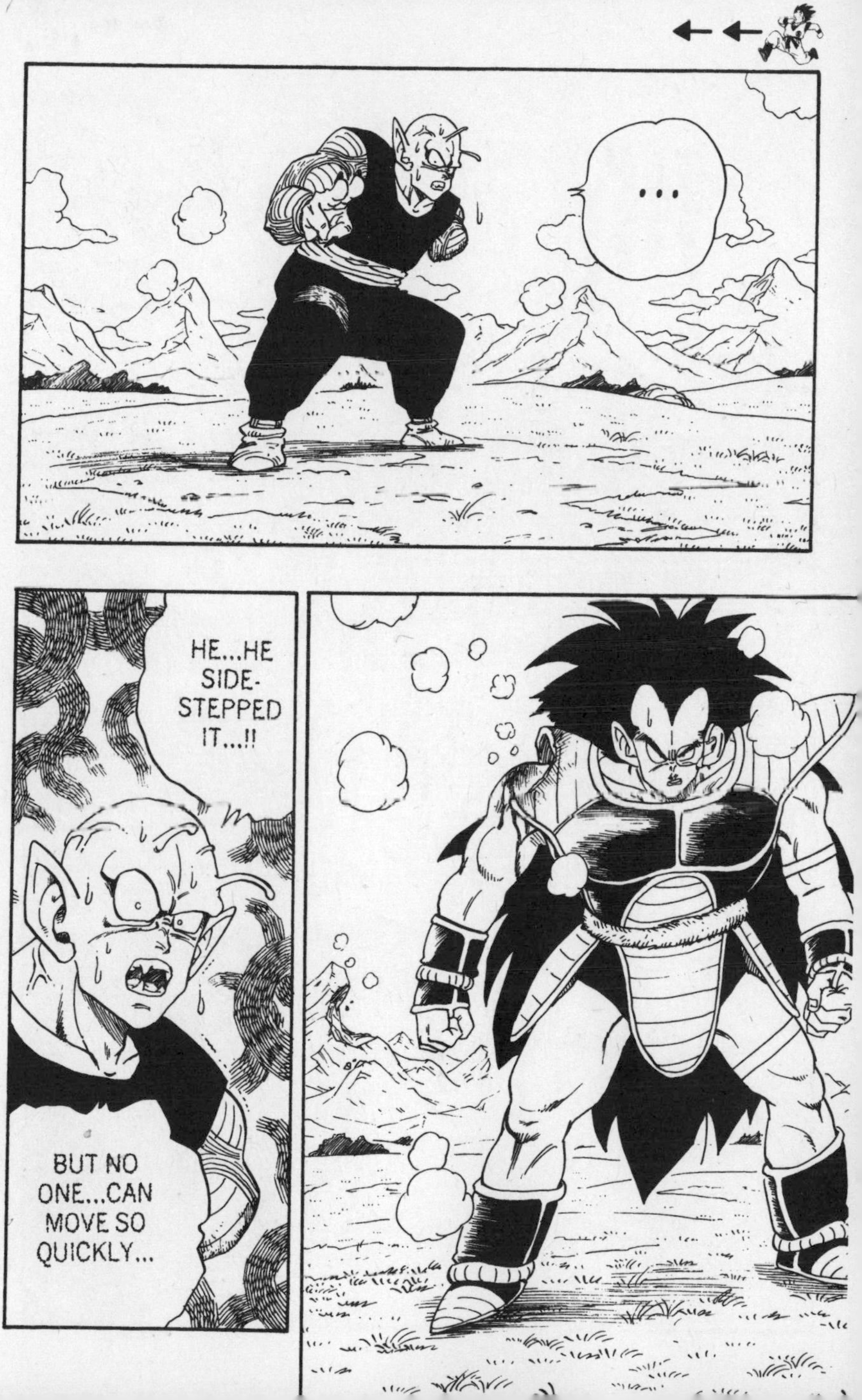
...
HE...HE SIDE-STEPPED IT...!!
BUT NO ONE...CAN MOVE SO QUICKLY...

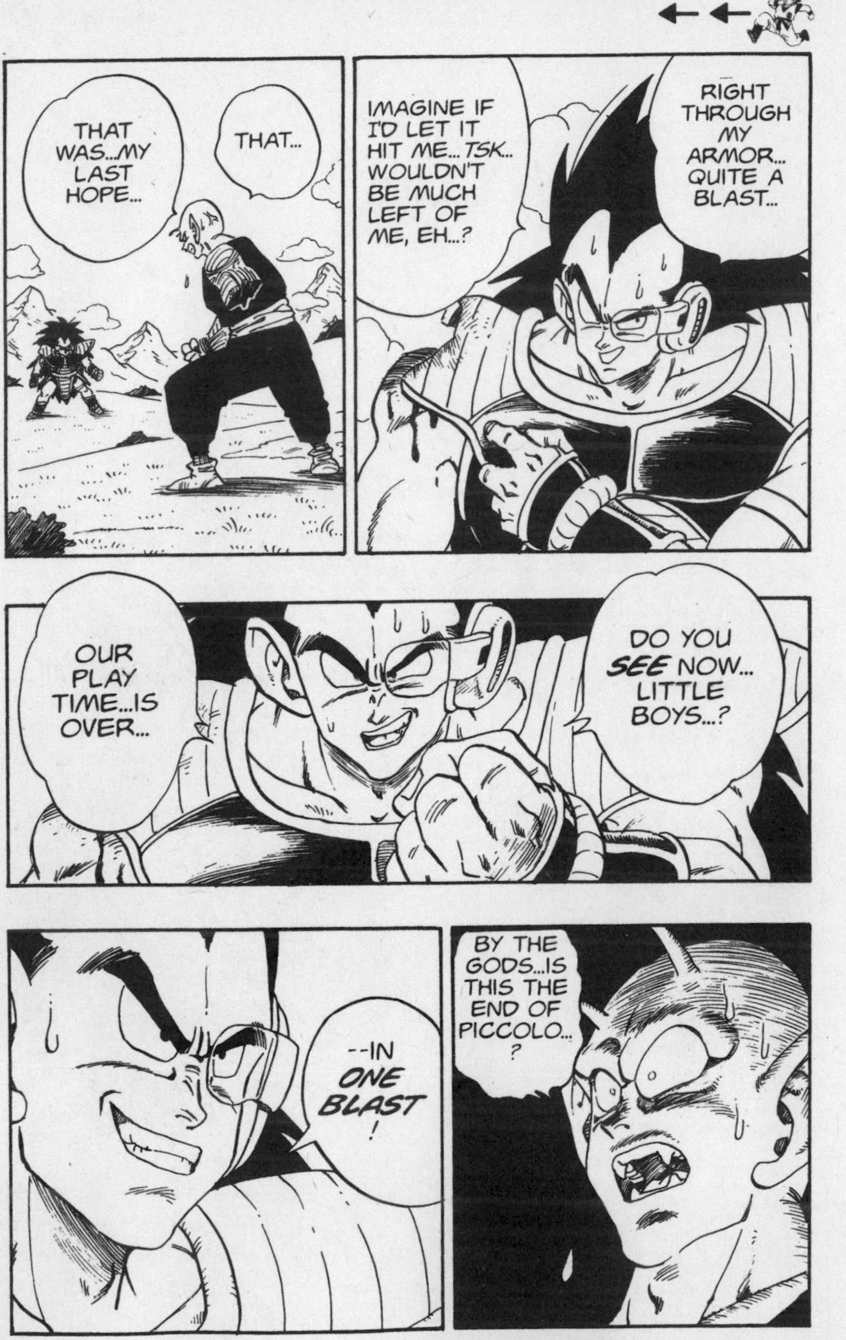
RIGHT THROUGH MY ARMOR... QUITE A BLAST...
IMAGINE IF I'D LET IT HIT ME... *TSK*... WOULDN'T BE MUCH LEFT OF ME, EH...?
THAT...
THAT WAS...MY LAST HOPE...
DO YOU *SEE* NOW... LITTLE BOYS...?
OUR PLAY TIME...IS OVER...
BY THE GODS...IS THIS THE END OF PICCOLO...?
--IN *ONE BLAST*!

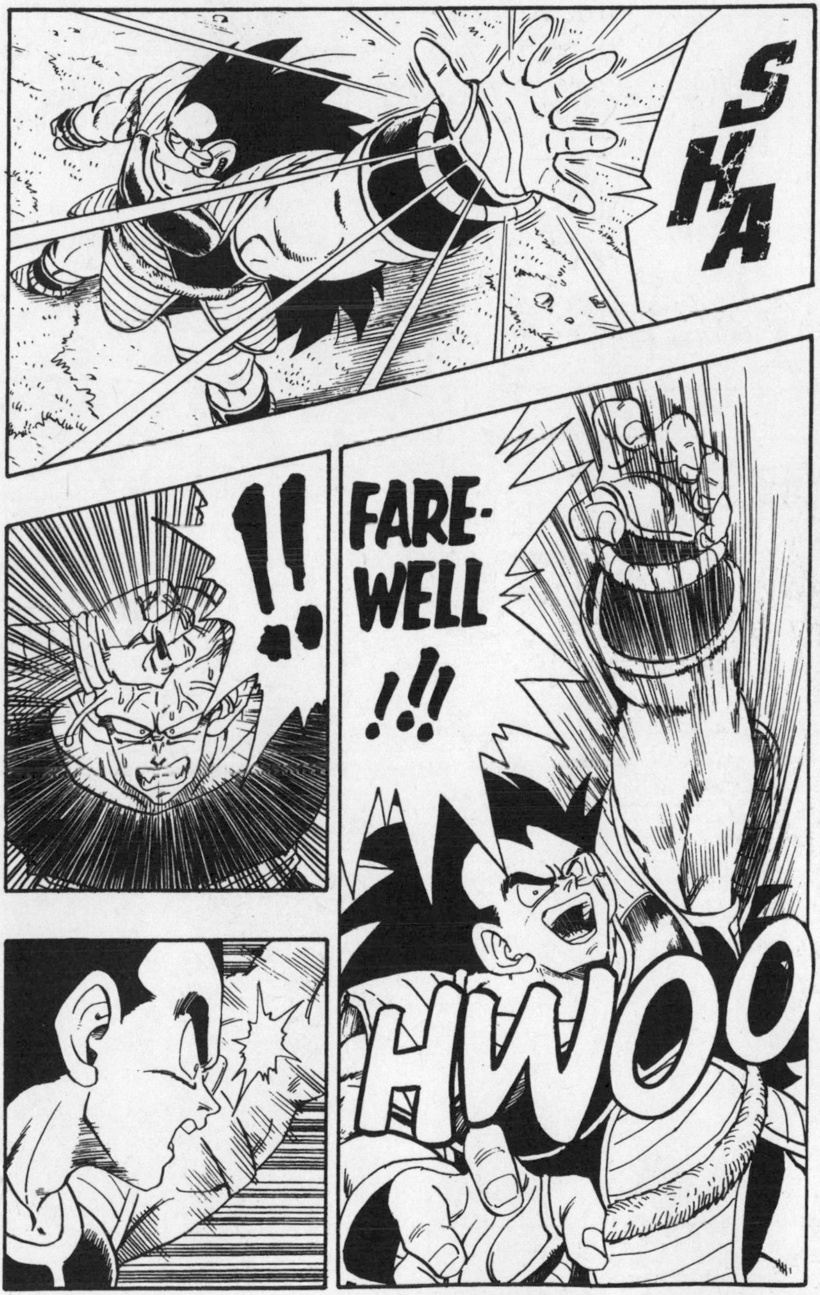
SHA
FARE-WELL !!!
HWOO
!!

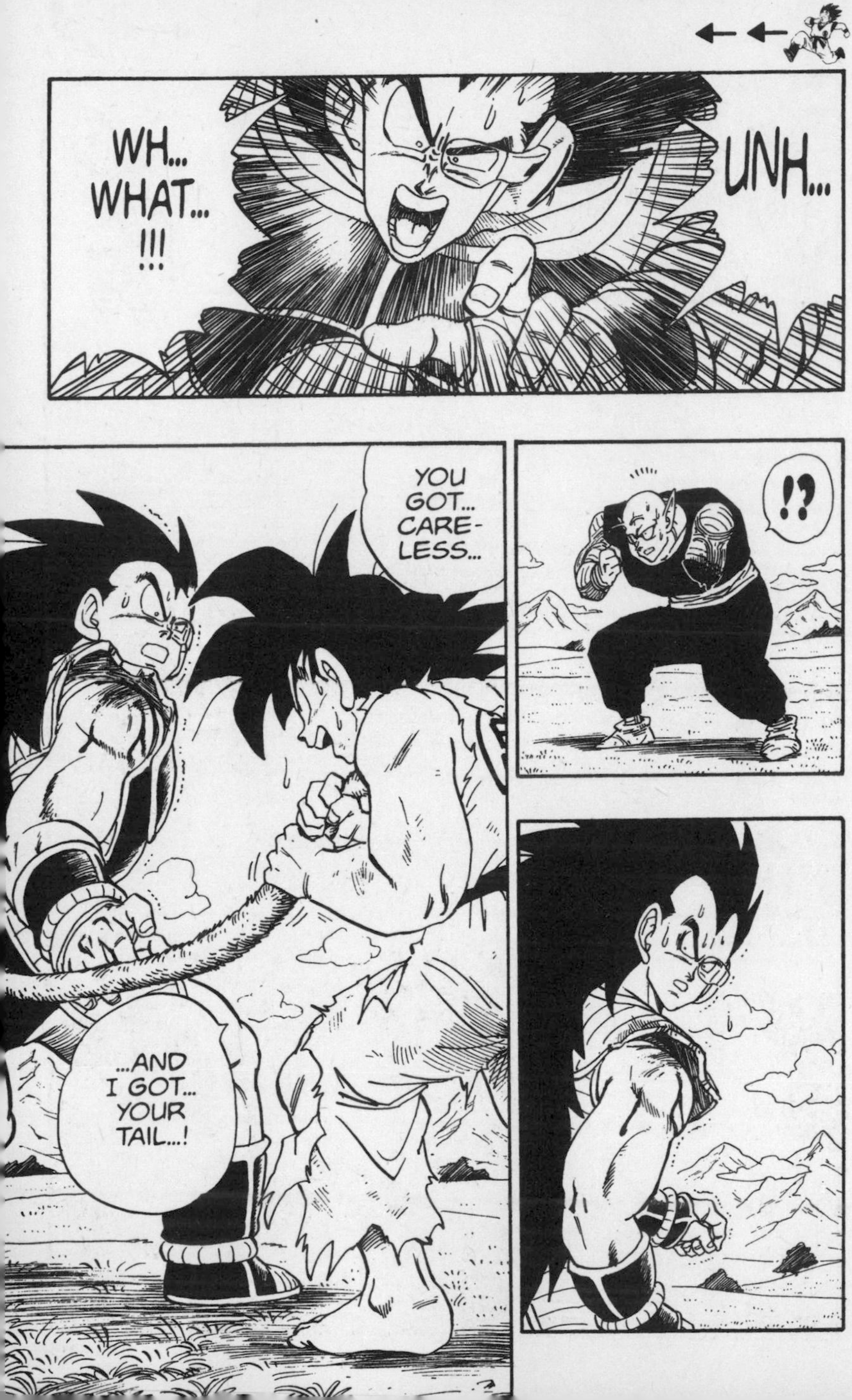
UNH...
WH... WHAT... !!!
!?
YOU GOT... CARE-LESS...
...AND I GOT... YOUR TAIL...!

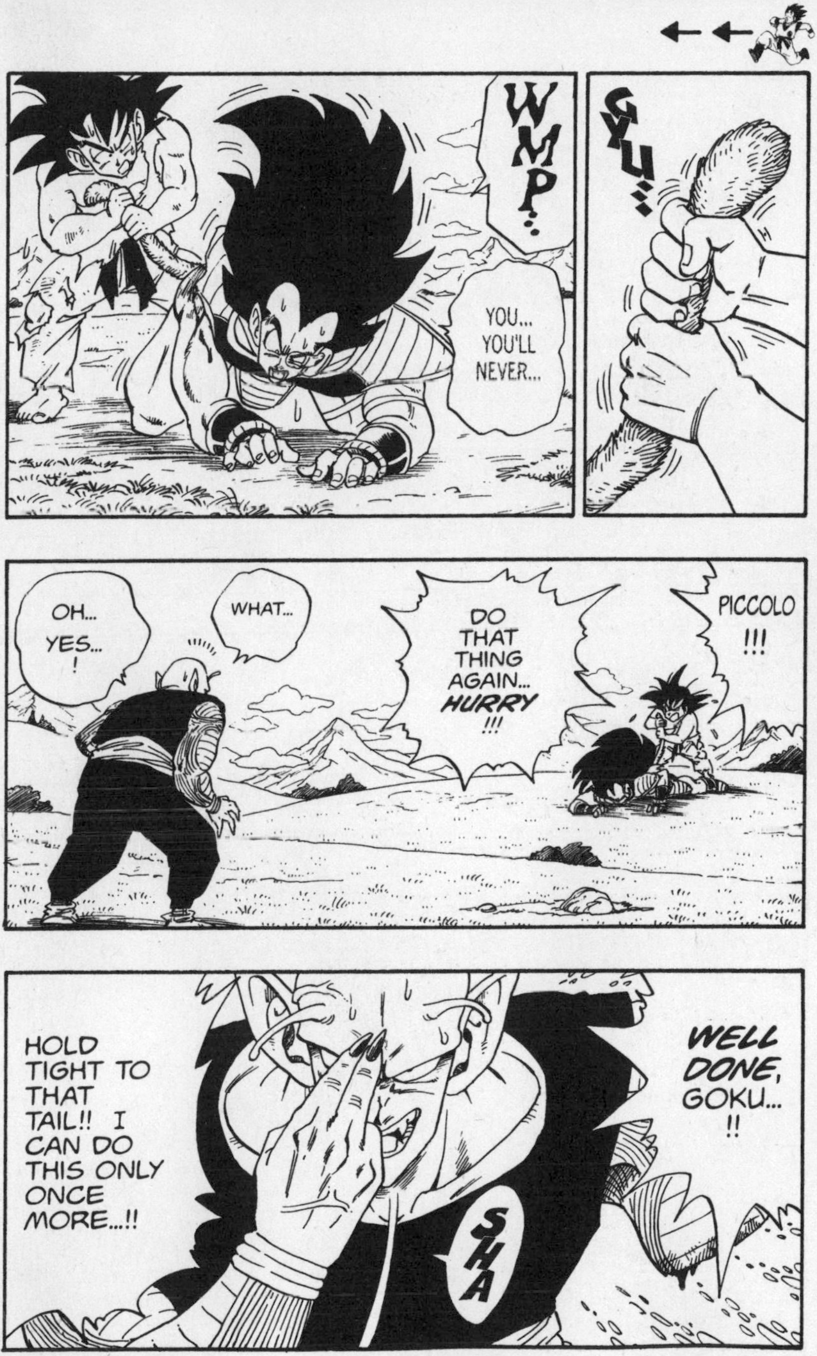
GYU...
WMP...
YOU... YOU'LL NEVER...
PICCOLO!!!
DO THAT THING AGAIN... HURRY!!!
WHAT...
OH... YES...!
WELL DONE, GOKU...!!
SHA
HOLD TIGHT TO THAT TAIL!! I CAN DO THIS ONLY ONCE MORE...!!

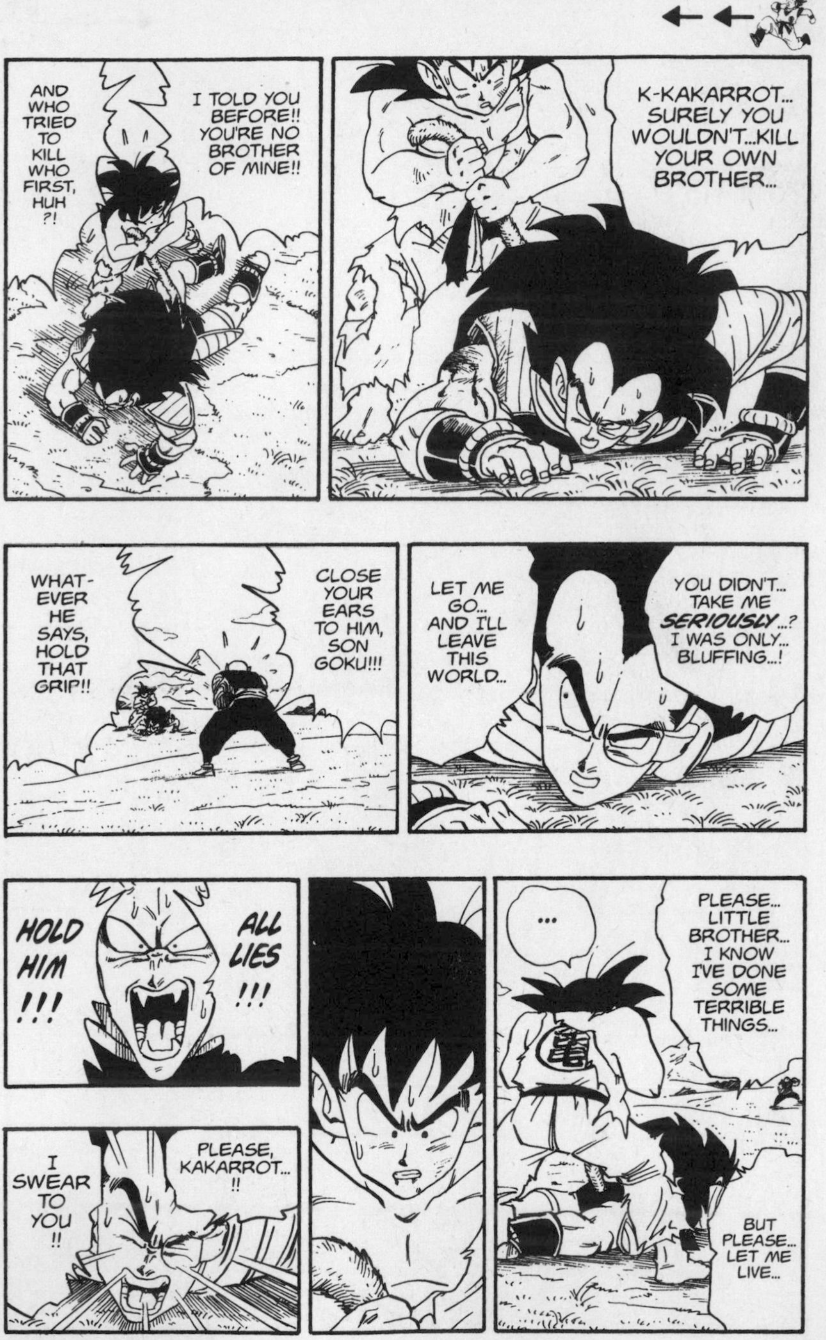
K-KAKARROT... SURELY YOU WOULDN'T...KILL YOUR OWN BROTHER...
I TOLD YOU BEFORE!! YOU'RE NO BROTHER OF MINE!!
AND WHO TRIED TO KILL WHO FIRST, HUH ?!
YOU DIDN'T... TAKE ME SERIOUSLY...? I WAS ONLY... BLUFFING...!
LET ME GO... AND I'LL LEAVE THIS WORLD...
CLOSE YOUR EARS TO HIM, SON GOKU!!!
WHAT-EVER HE SAYS, HOLD THAT GRIP!!
PLEASE... LITTLE BROTHER... I KNOW I'VE DONE SOME TERRIBLE THINGS...
...
BUT PLEASE... LET ME LIVE...
ALL LIES !!!
HOLD HIM !!!
PLEASE, KAKARROT... !!
I SWEAR TO YOU !!

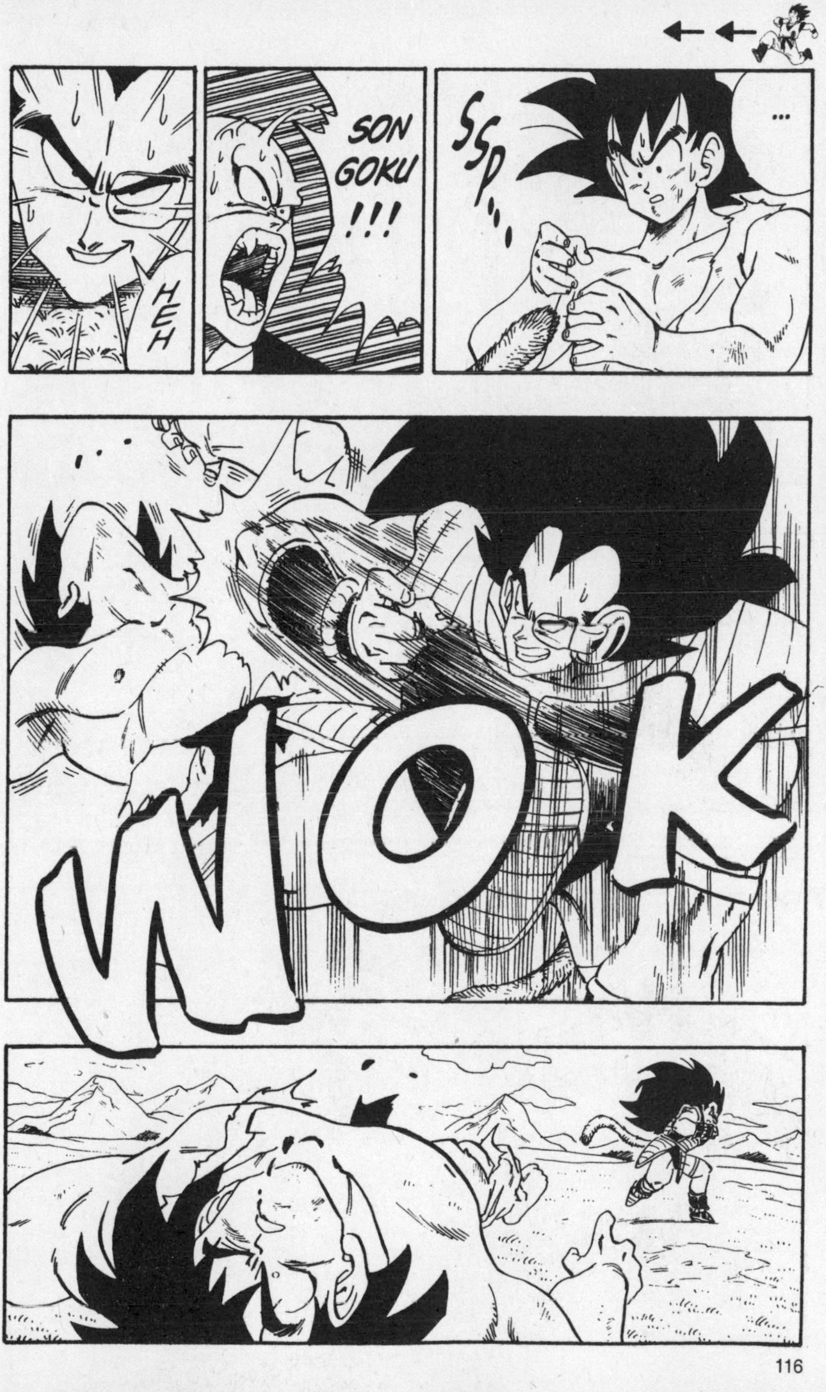
...
SSP...
SON GOKU !!!
HEH
...
WOK
...

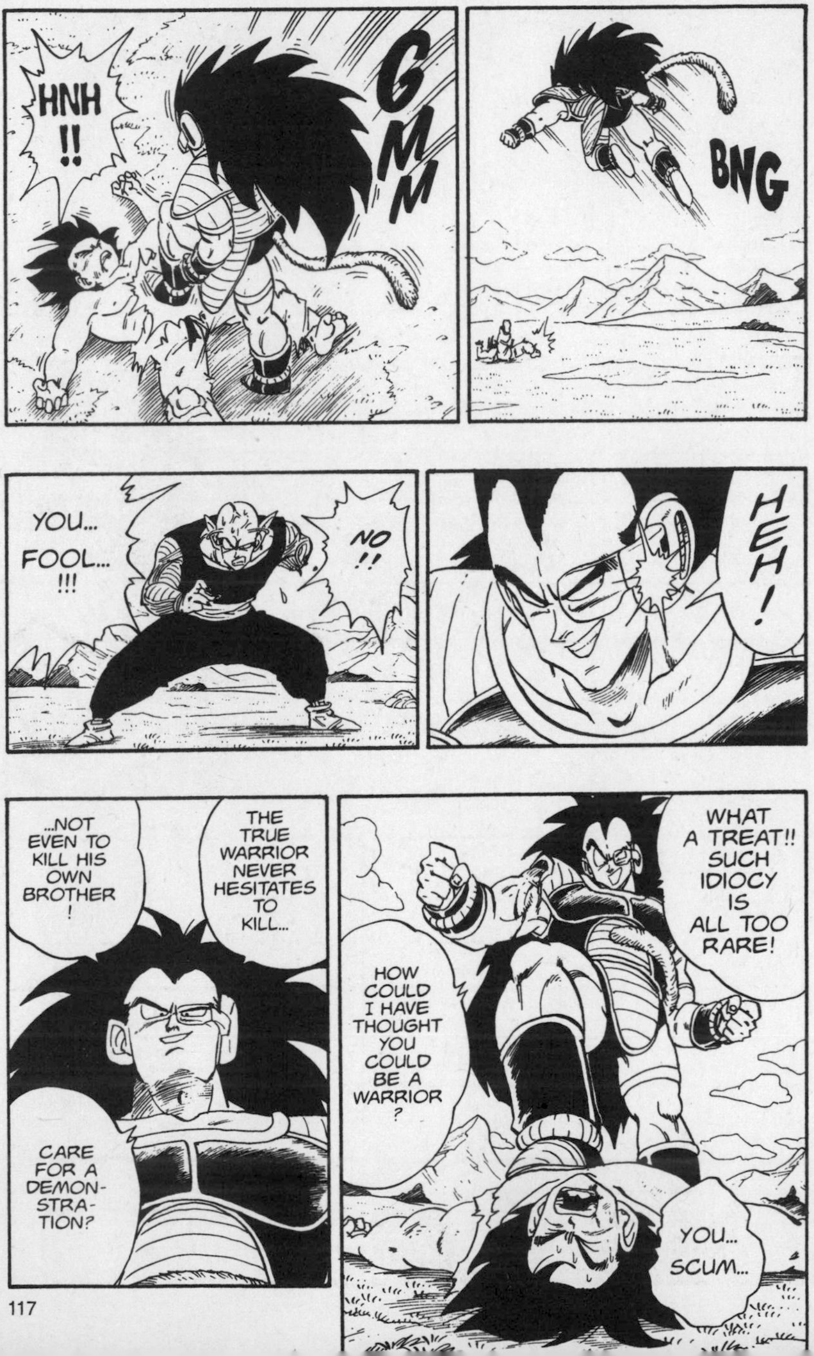
BNG
HNH !!
GMM
HEH!
NO !!
YOU... FOOL... !!!
WHAT A TREAT!! SUCH IDIOCY IS ALL TOO RARE!
HOW COULD I HAVE THOUGHT YOU COULD BE A WARRIOR ?
YOU... SCUM...
THE TRUE WARRIOR NEVER HESITATES TO KILL...
...NOT EVEN TO KILL HIS OWN BROTHER !
CARE FOR A DEMON-STRA-TION?

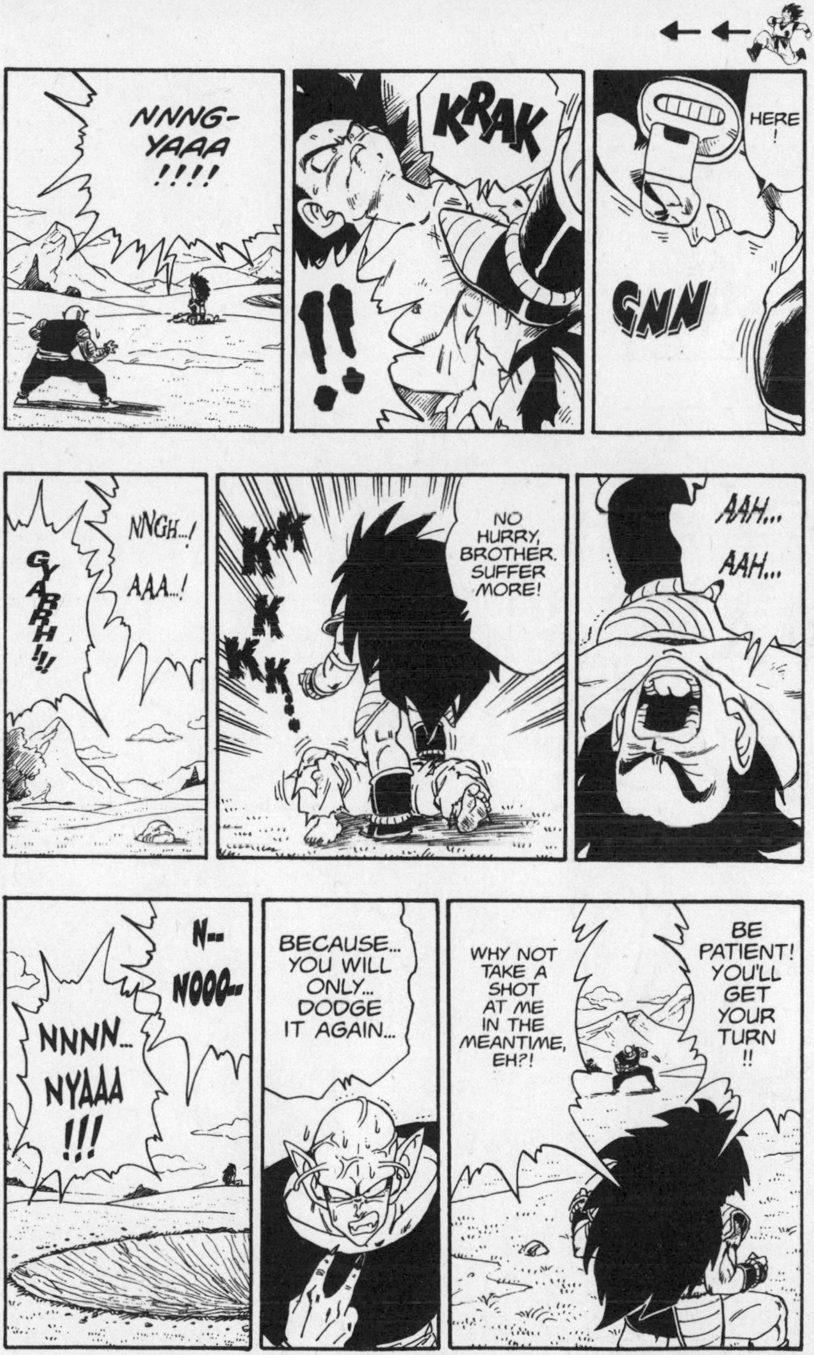
HERE!
GNN
KRAK
!!
NNNG-YAAA!!!!
AAH... AAH...
NO HURRY, BROTHER. SUFFER MORE!
KKKKK...
NNGH...! AAA...!
GYARRH!!!
BE PATIENT! YOU'LL GET YOUR TURN!!
WHY NOT TAKE A SHOT AT ME IN THE MEANTIME, EH?!
BECAUSE... YOU WILL ONLY... DODGE IT AGAIN...
N-- NOOO--
NNNN... NYAAA!!!

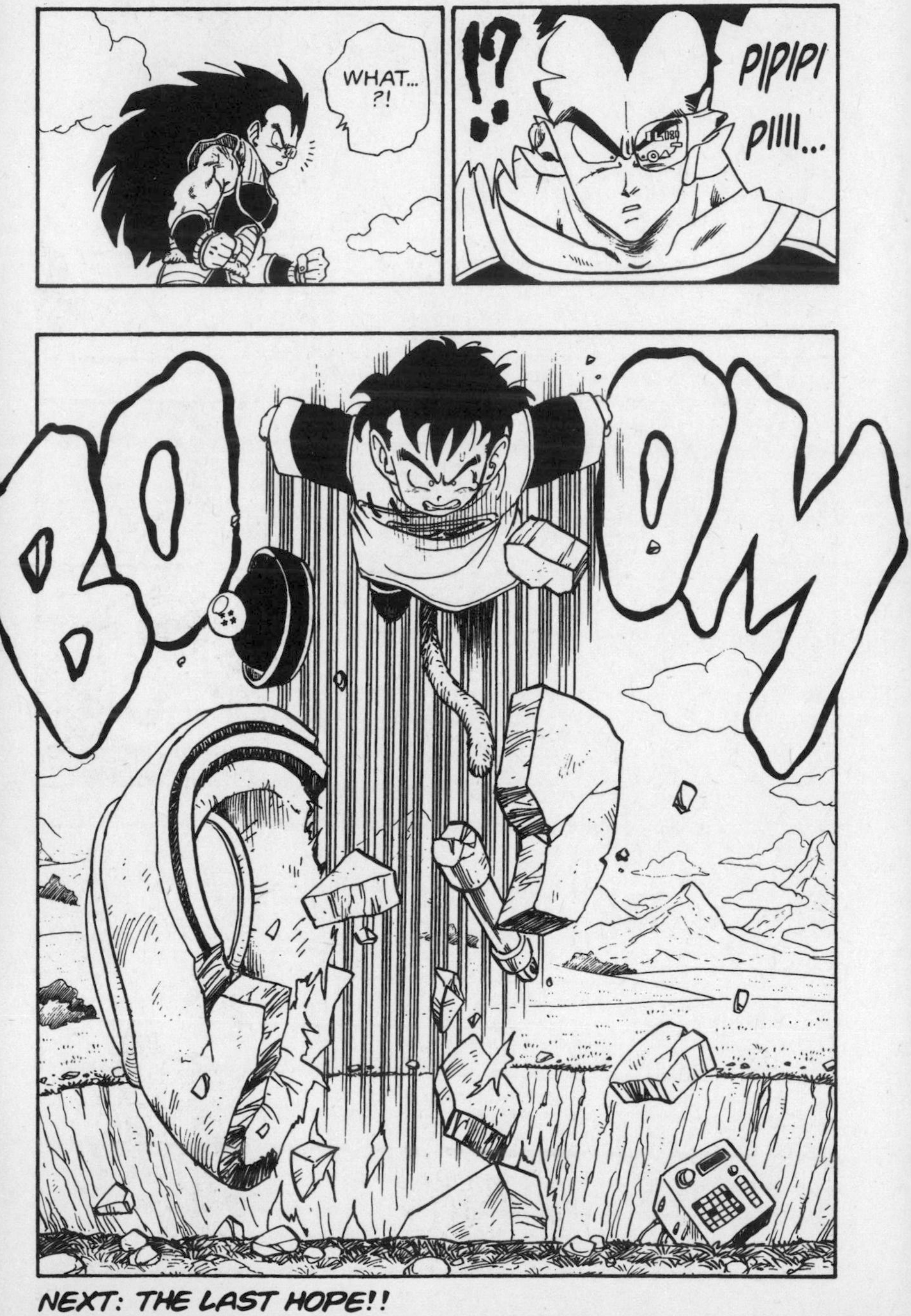
!?
PIPIPI
PIIII...
WHAT... ?!
BOOM

NEXT: THE LAST HOPE!!

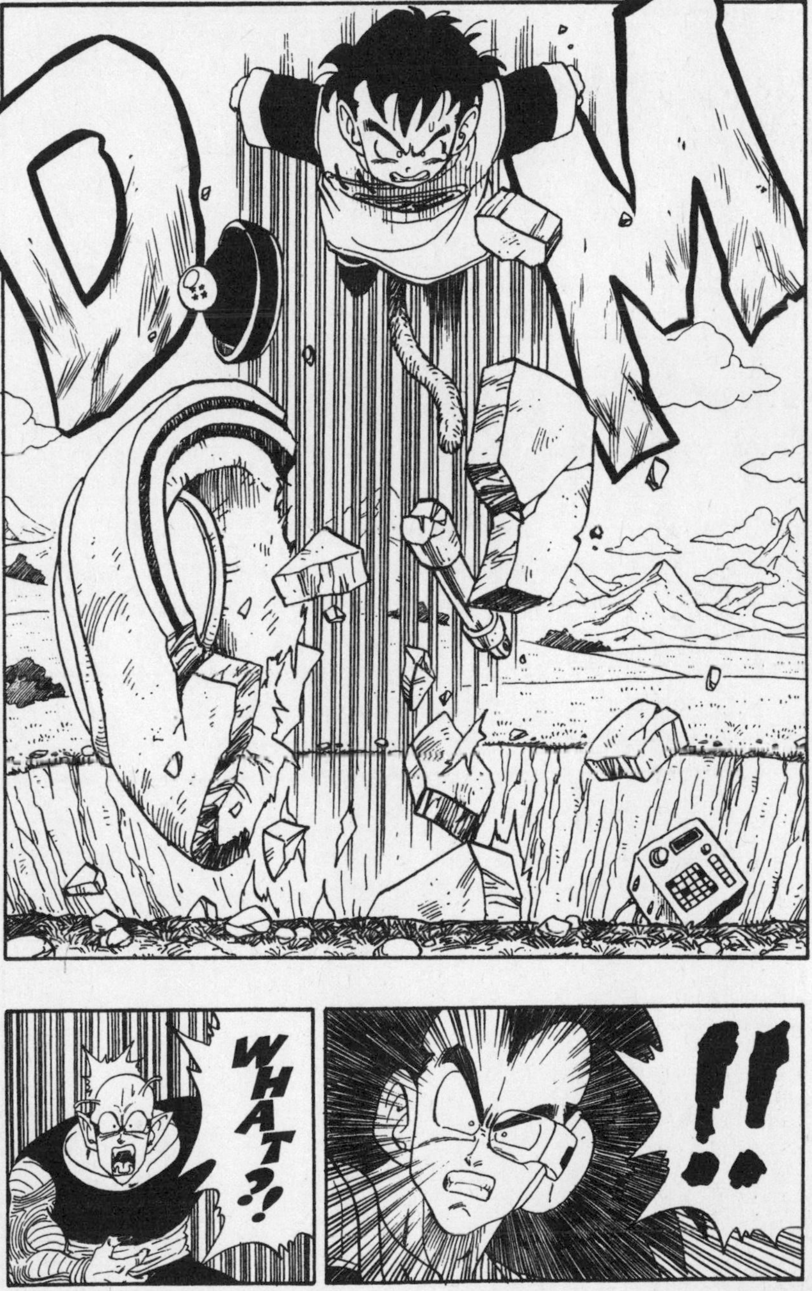
!!
WHAT?!

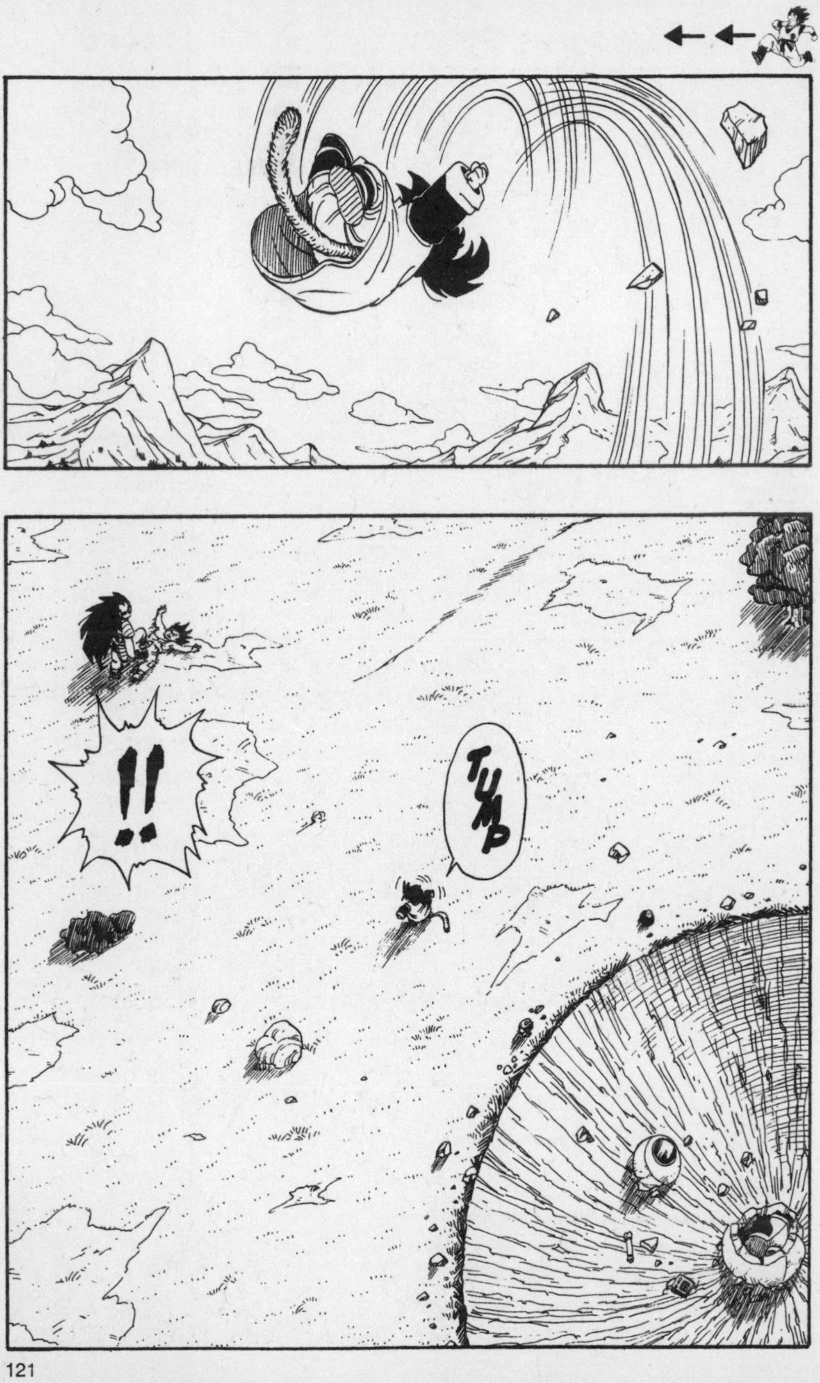
TUMP
!!

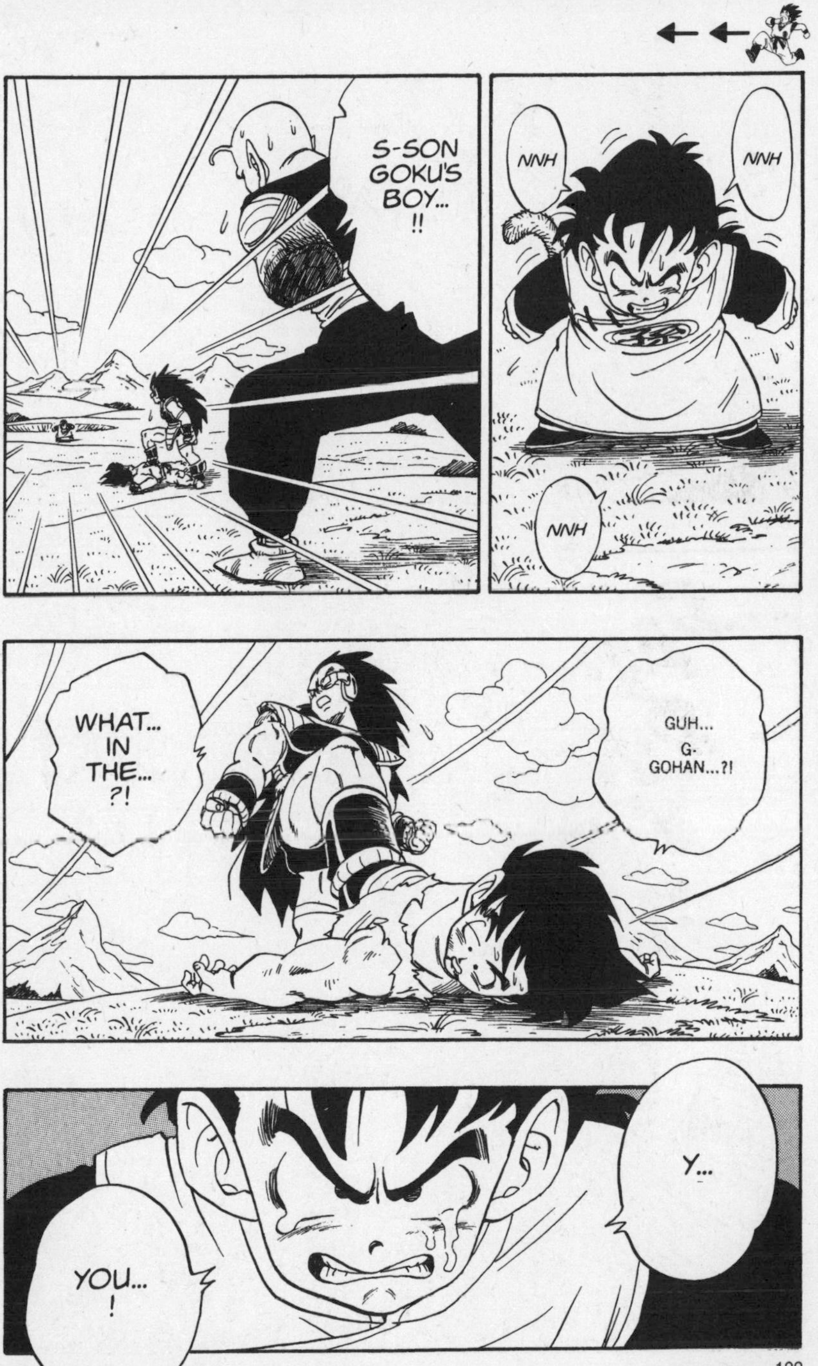
NNH
NNH
NNH
S-SON GOKU'S BOY... !!
GUH... G-GOHAN...?!
WHAT... IN THE... ?!
Y...
YOU... !

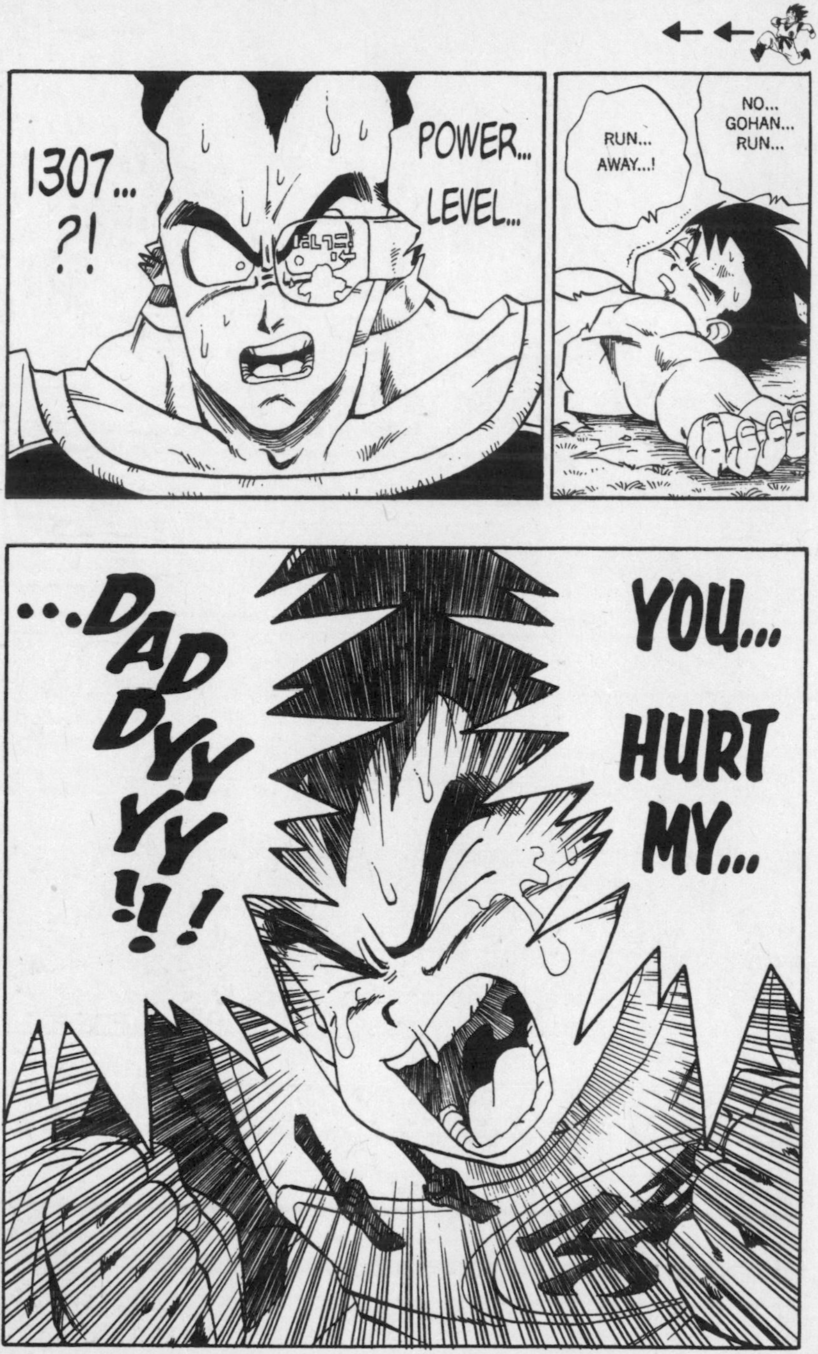
NO... GOHAN... RUN...
RUN... AWAY...!
POWER... LEVEL...
1307... ?!
YOU... HURT MY...
...DADDYYY!!!

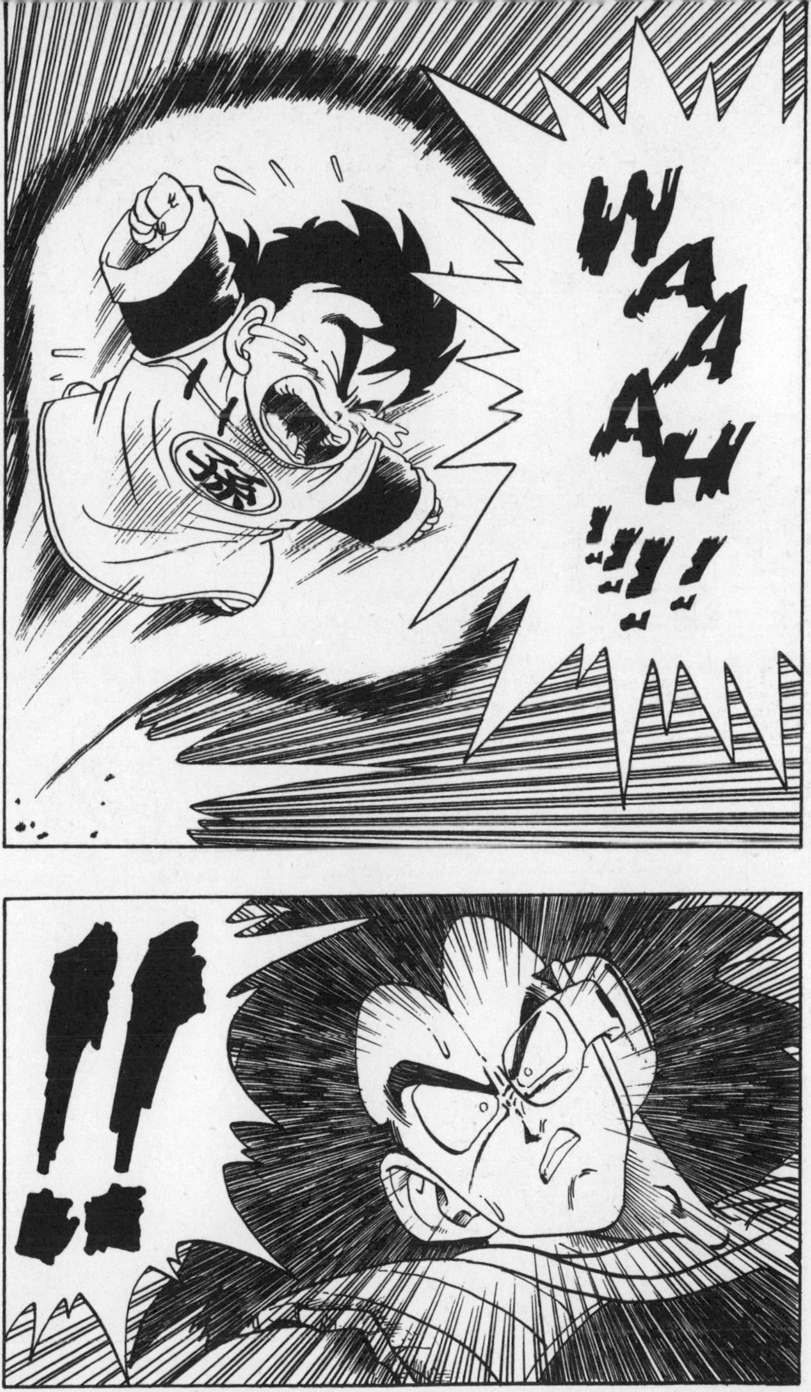
WAAAH!!!
孫
!!

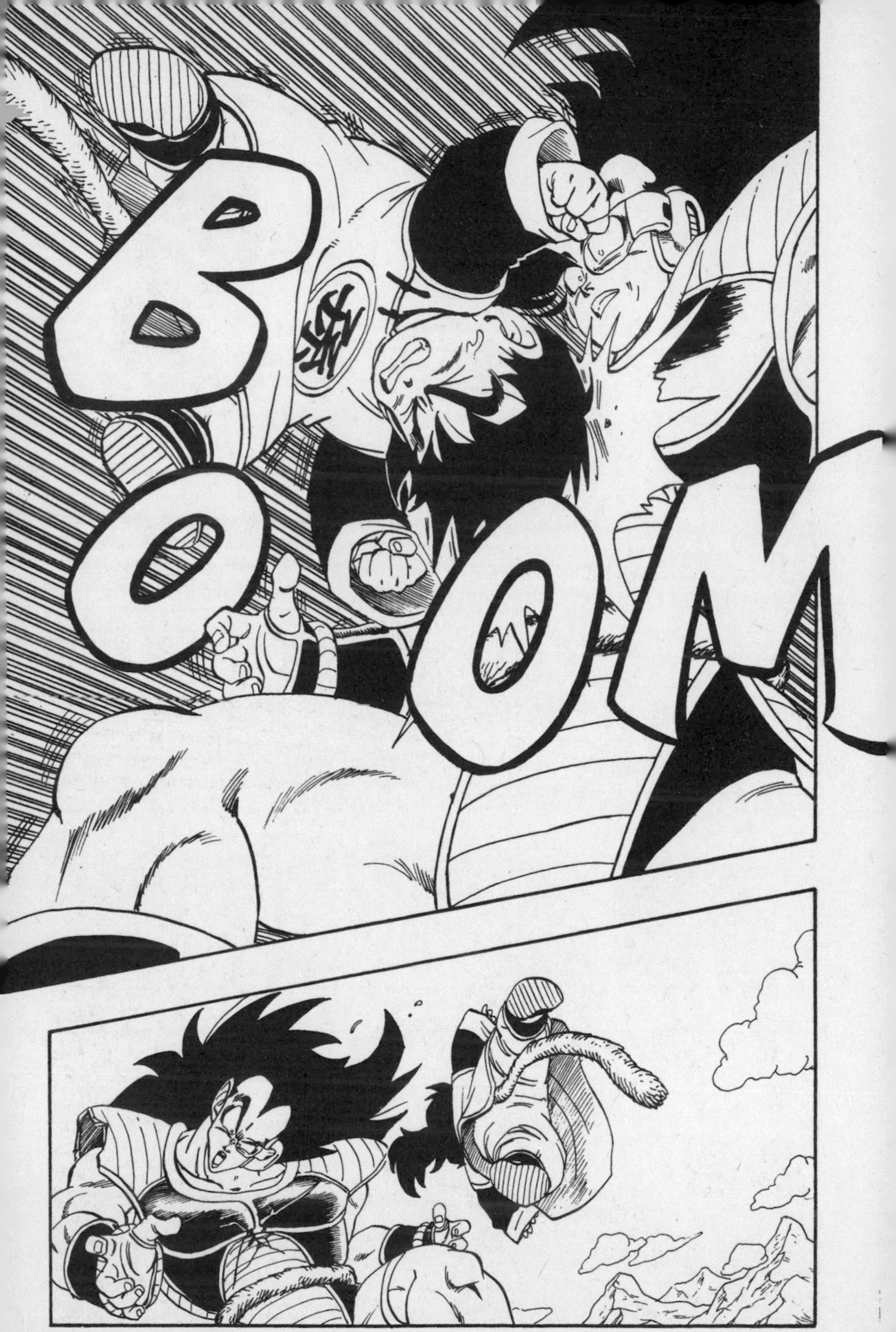
BOOM

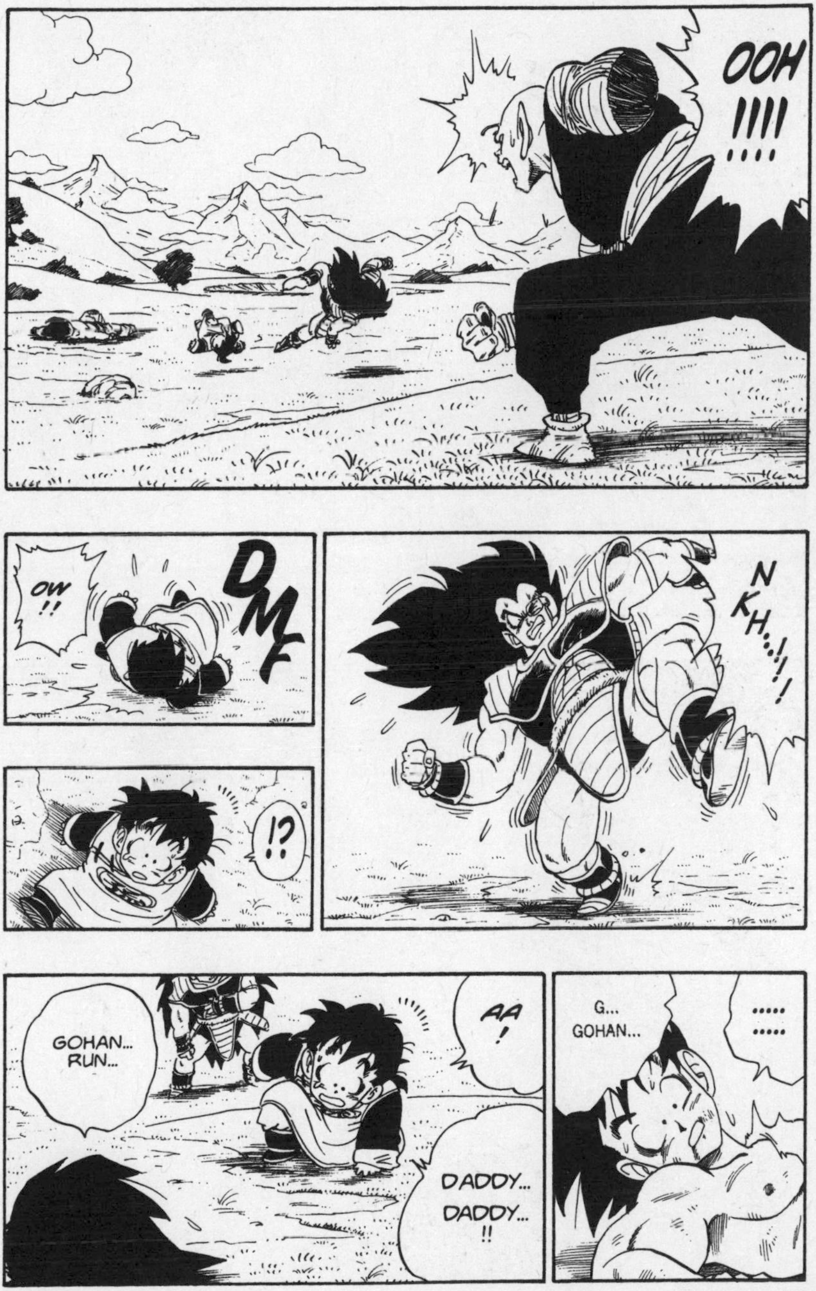
OOH
!!!!
!!!!
NKH...!!!
OW
!!
DMF
!?
.....
.....
G...
GOHAN...
AA
!
GOHAN...
RUN...
DADDY...
DADDY...
!!

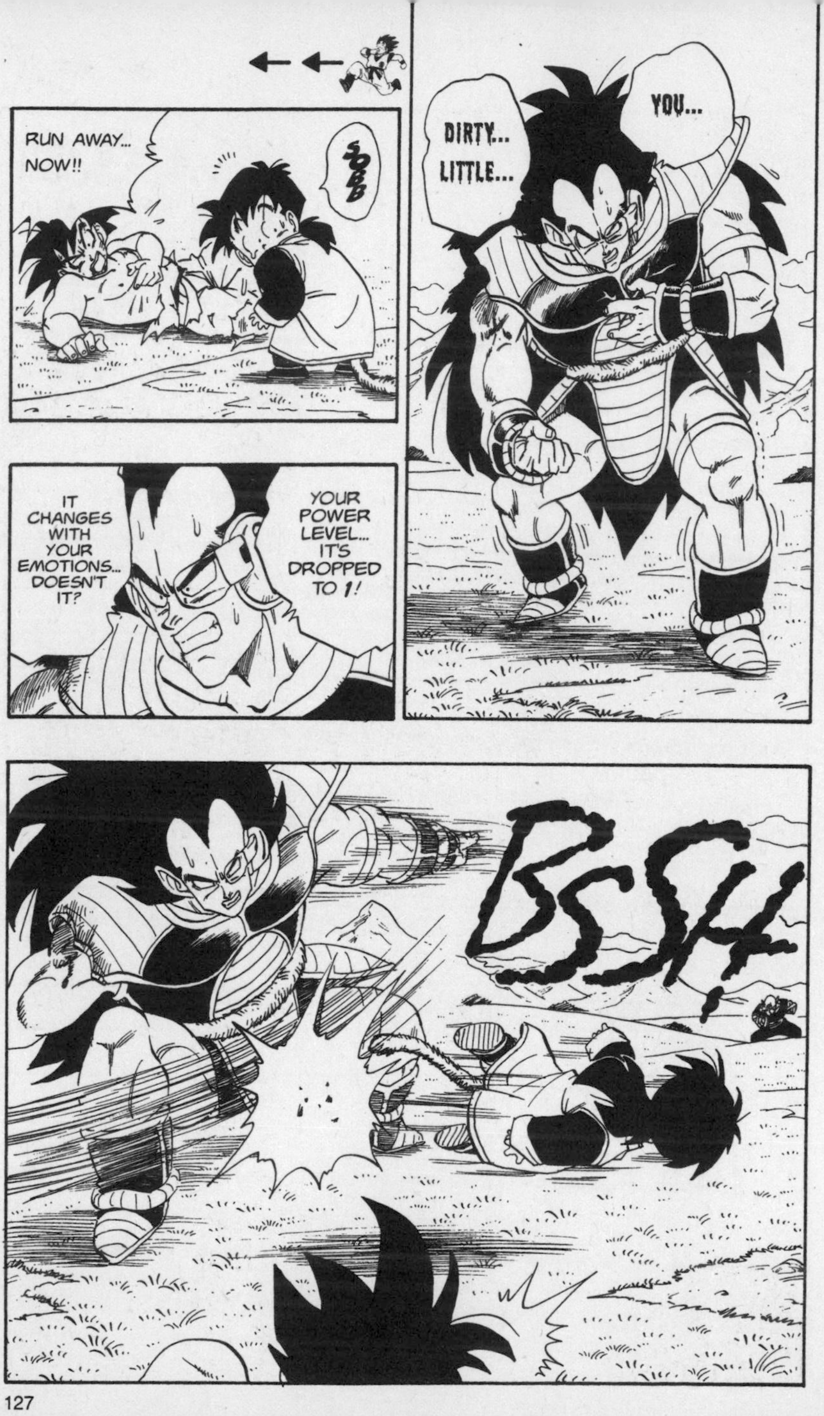
YOU...
DIRTY... LITTLE...
SOBB
RUN AWAY... NOW!!
YOUR POWER LEVEL... IT'S DROPPED TO 1!
IT CHANGES WITH YOUR EMOTIONS... DOESN'T IT?
BSSH

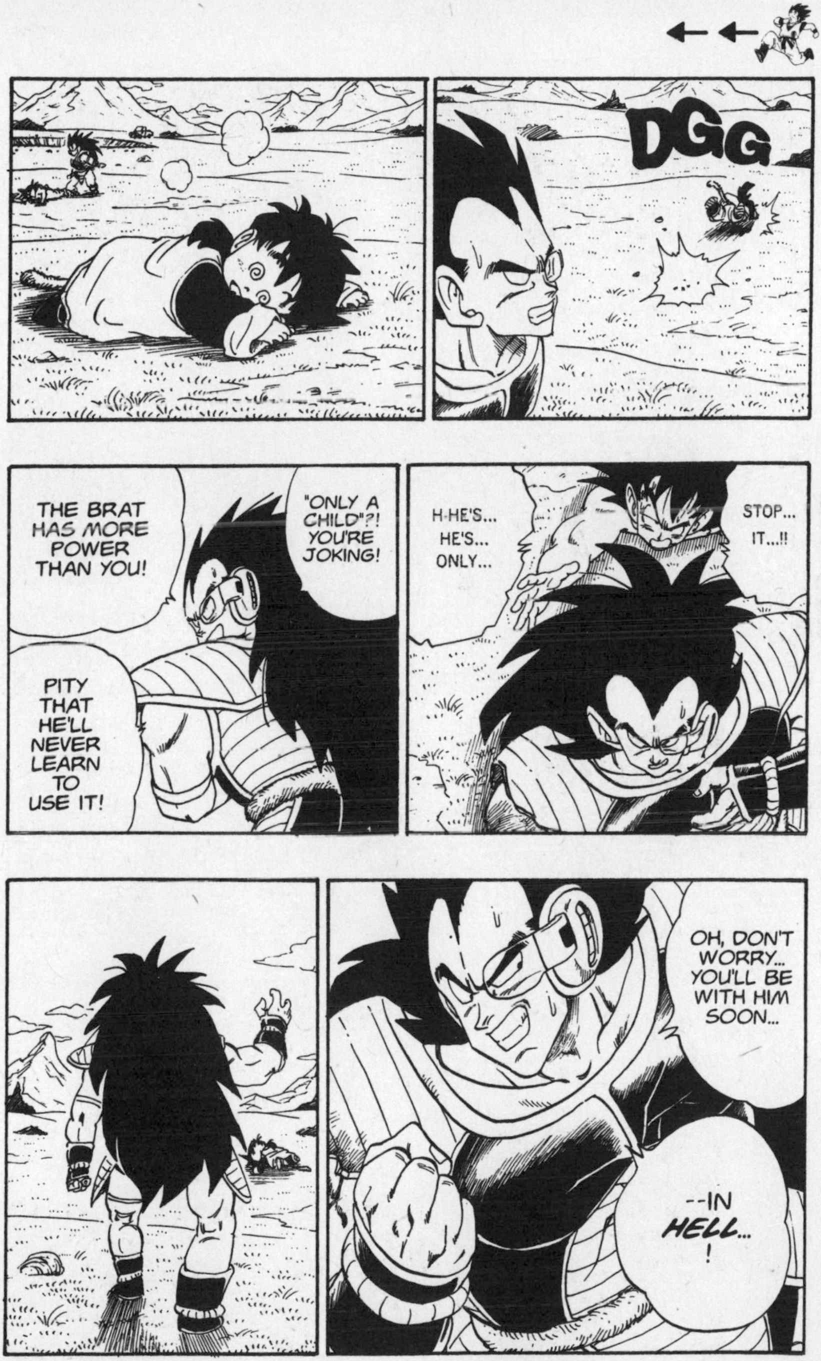
DGG
STOP... IT...!!
H-HE'S... HE'S... ONLY...
"ONLY A CHILD"?! YOU'RE JOKING!
THE BRAT HAS MORE POWER THAN YOU!
PITY THAT HE'LL NEVER LEARN TO USE IT!
OH, DON'T WORRY... YOU'LL BE WITH HIM SOON...
--IN *HELL...* !

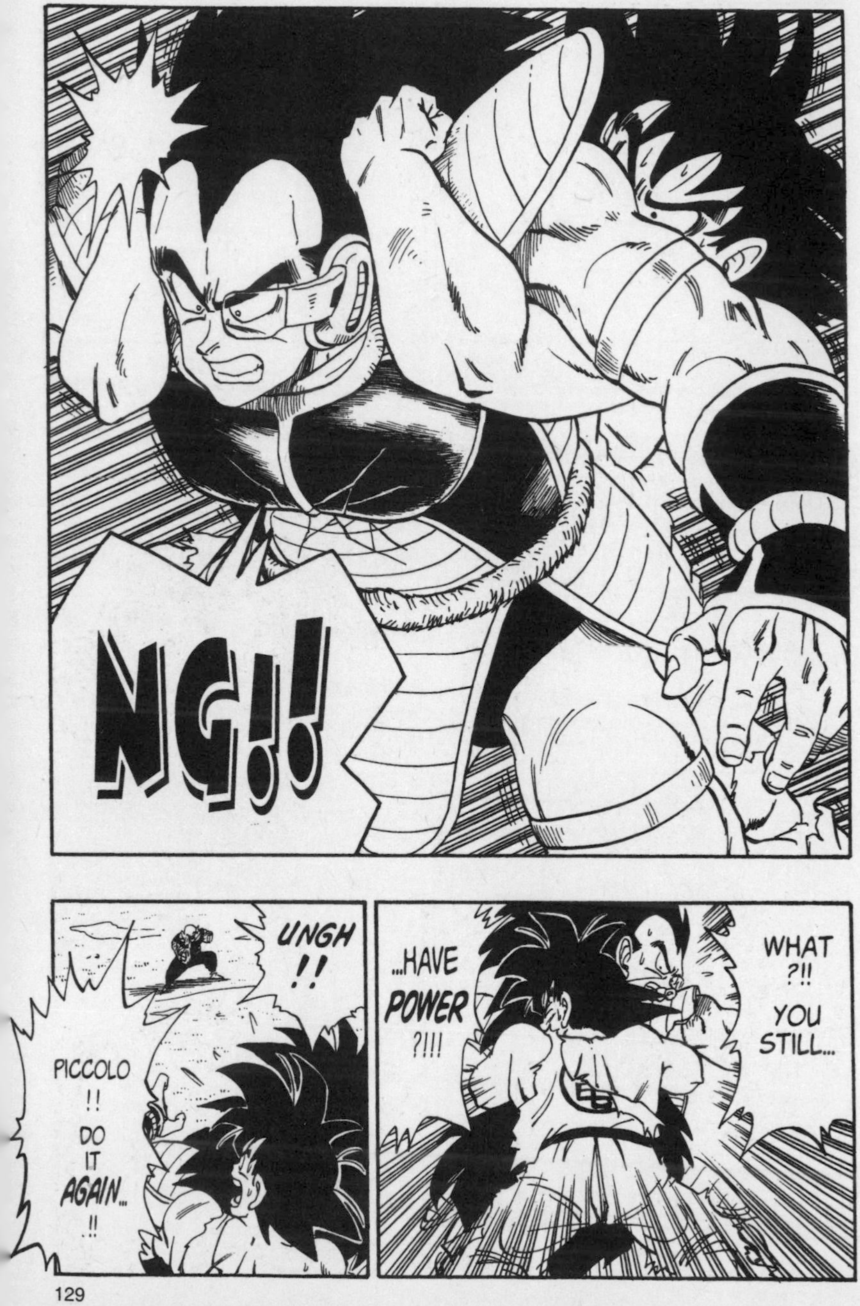
NG!!
WHAT ?!! YOU STILL...
...HAVE POWER ?!!!
UNGH !!
PICCOLO !! DO IT AGAIN... !!

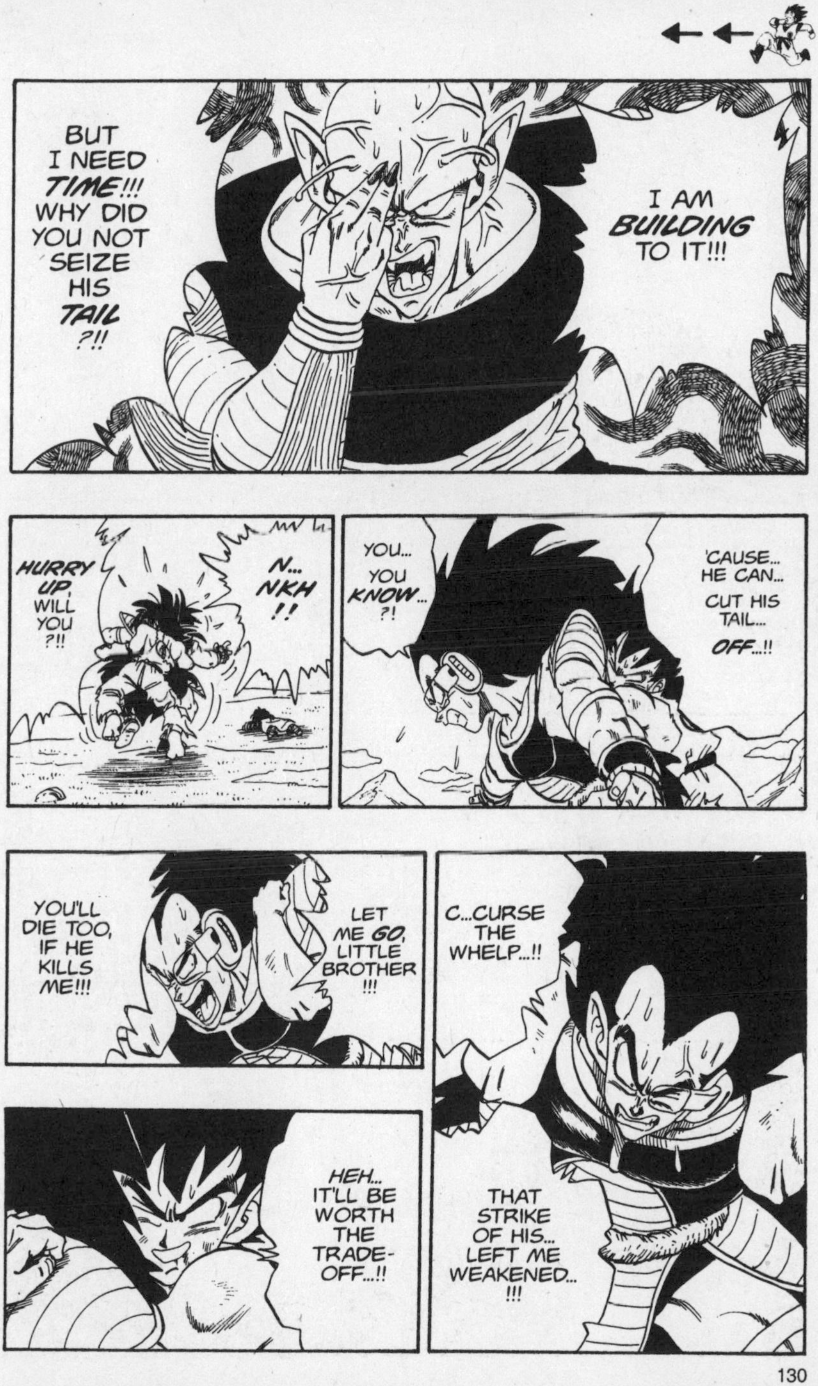
I AM BUILDING TO IT!!!
BUT I NEED TIME!!! WHY DID YOU NOT SEIZE HIS TAIL?!!
'CAUSE... HE CAN... CUT HIS TAIL... OFF...!!
YOU... YOU KNOW...?!
N... NKH!!
HURRY UP, WILL YOU?!!
C...CURSE THE WHELP...!!
THAT STRIKE OF HIS... LEFT ME WEAKENED...!!!
LET ME GO, LITTLE BROTHER!!!
YOU'LL DIE TOO, IF HE KILLS ME!!!
HEH... IT'LL BE WORTH THE TRADE-OFF...!!

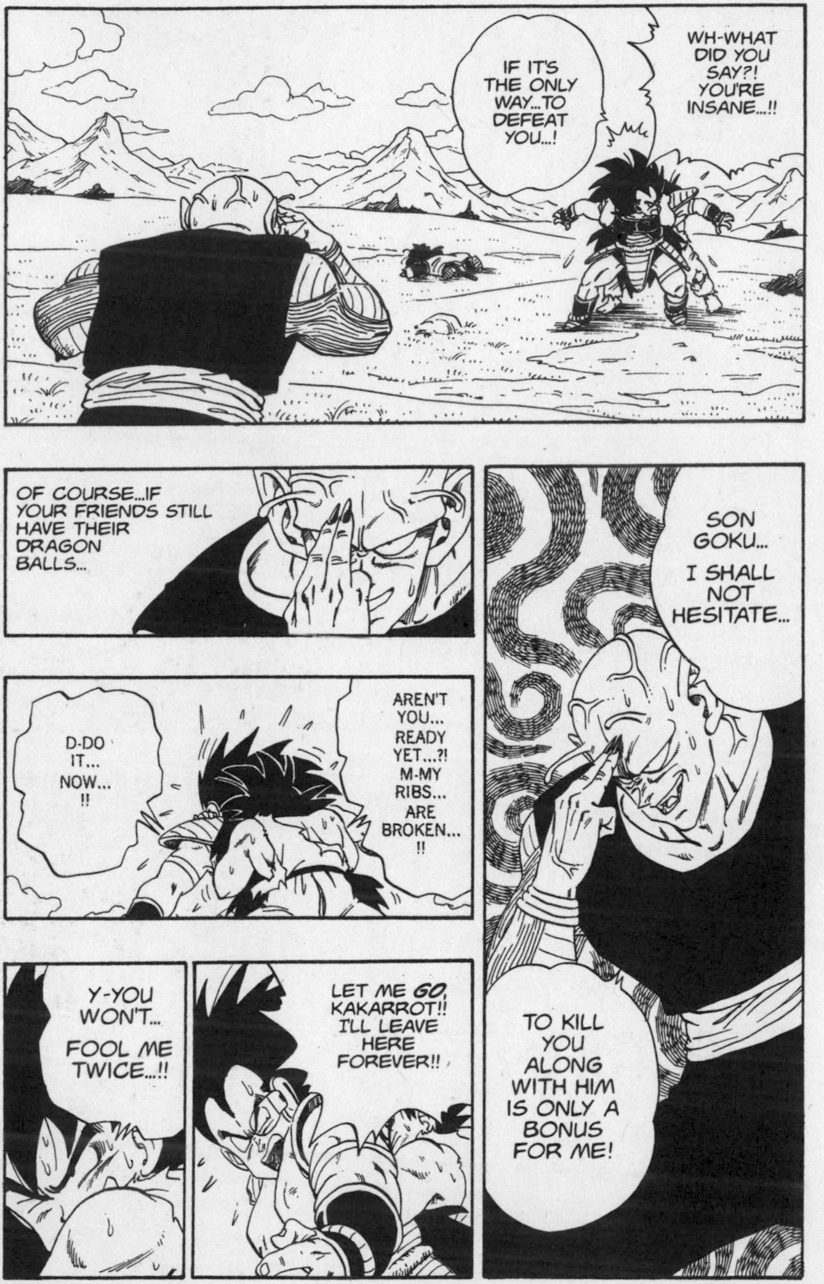
WH-WHAT DID YOU SAY?! YOU'RE INSANE...!!
IF IT'S THE ONLY WAY...TO DEFEAT YOU...!
SON GOKU... I SHALL NOT HESITATE...
TO KILL YOU ALONG WITH HIM IS ONLY A BONUS FOR ME!
OF COURSE...IF YOUR FRIENDS STILL HAVE THEIR DRAGON BALLS...
AREN'T YOU... READY YET...?! M-MY RIBS... ARE BROKEN... !!
D-DO IT... NOW... !!
LET ME GO, KAKARROT!! I'LL LEAVE HERE FOREVER!!
Y-YOU WON'T... FOOL ME TWICE...!!

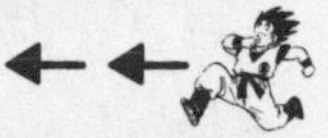

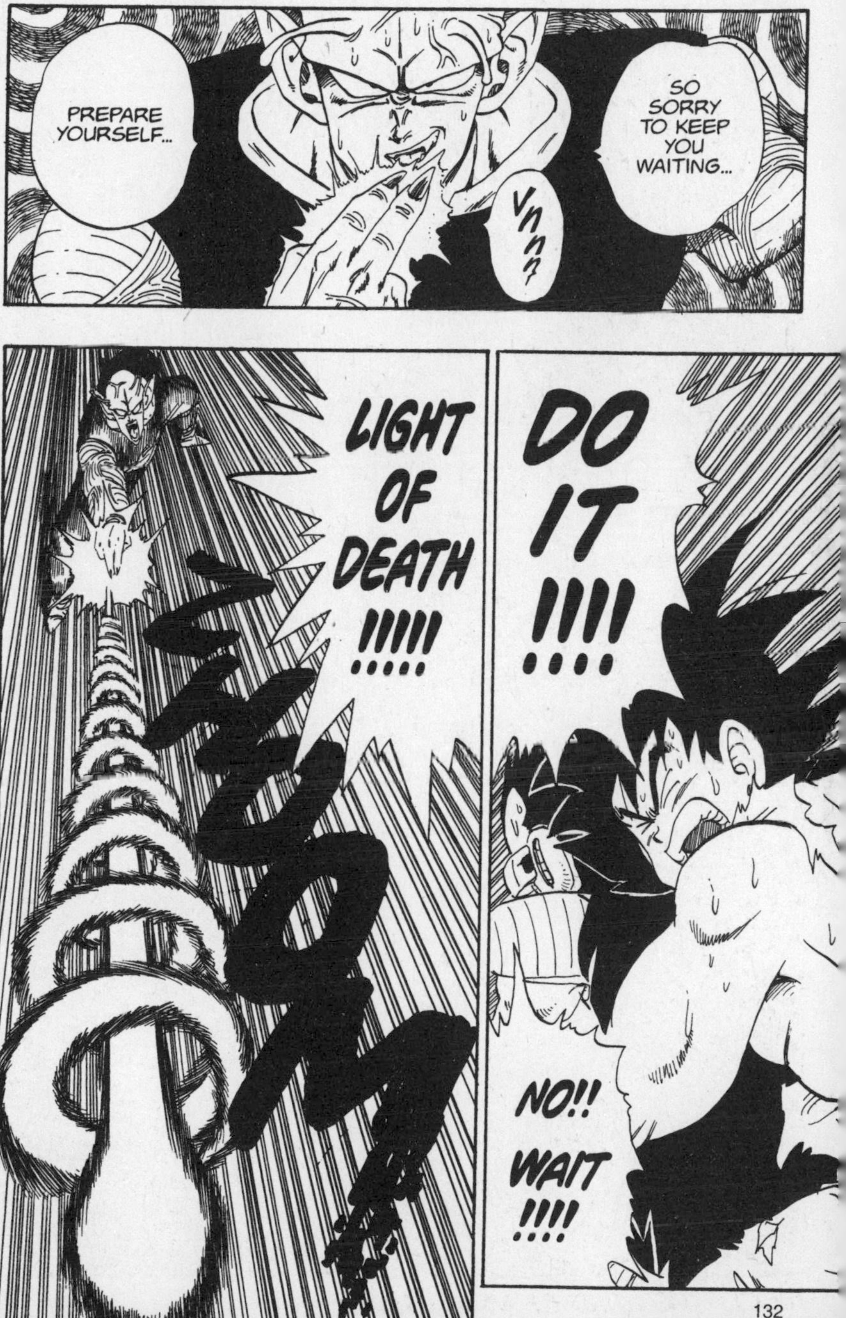
SO SORRY TO KEEP YOU WAITING...
PREPARE YOURSELF...
DO IT!!!!
NO!! WAIT!!!!
LIGHT OF DEATH!!!!!

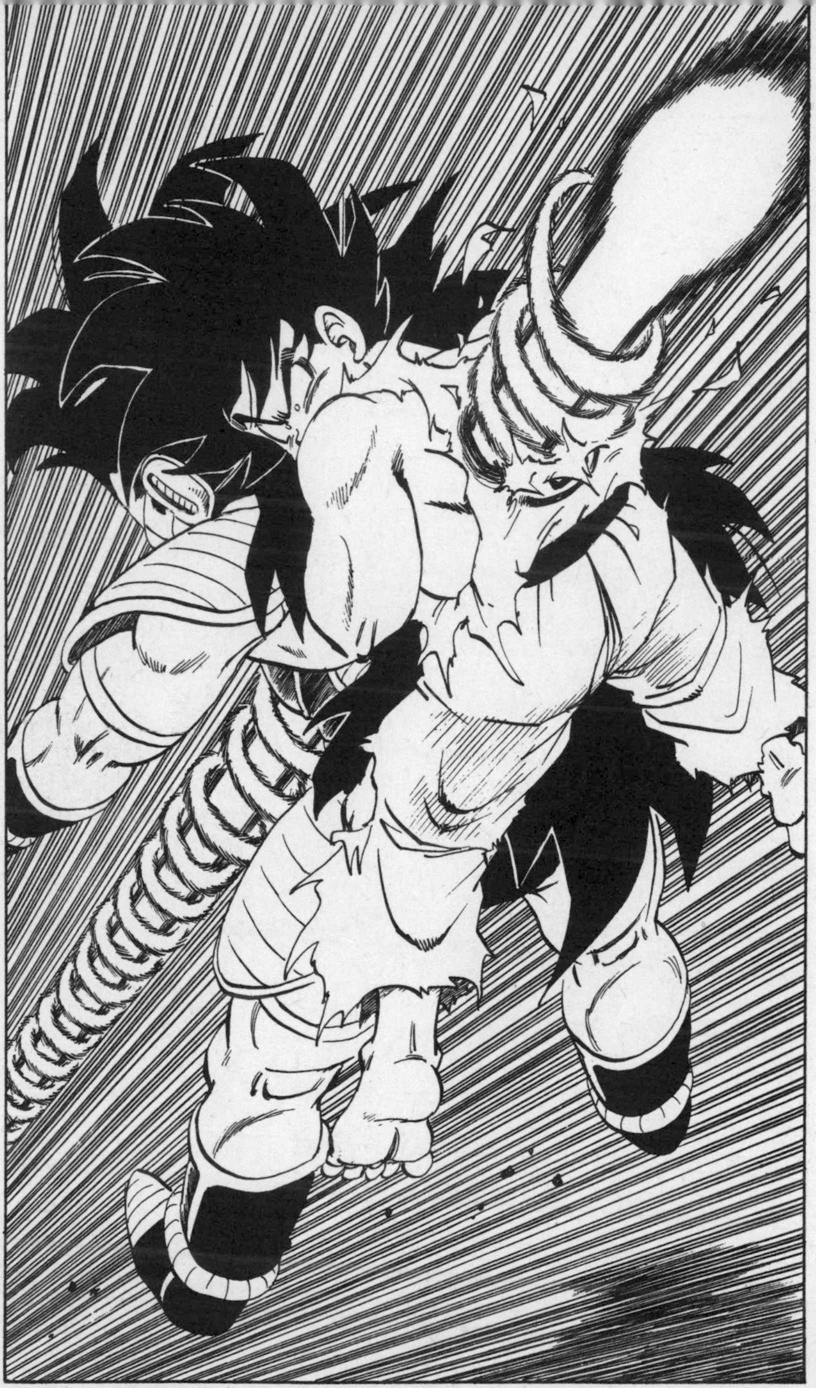

NEXT: THE HAND OF KAMI-SAMA!

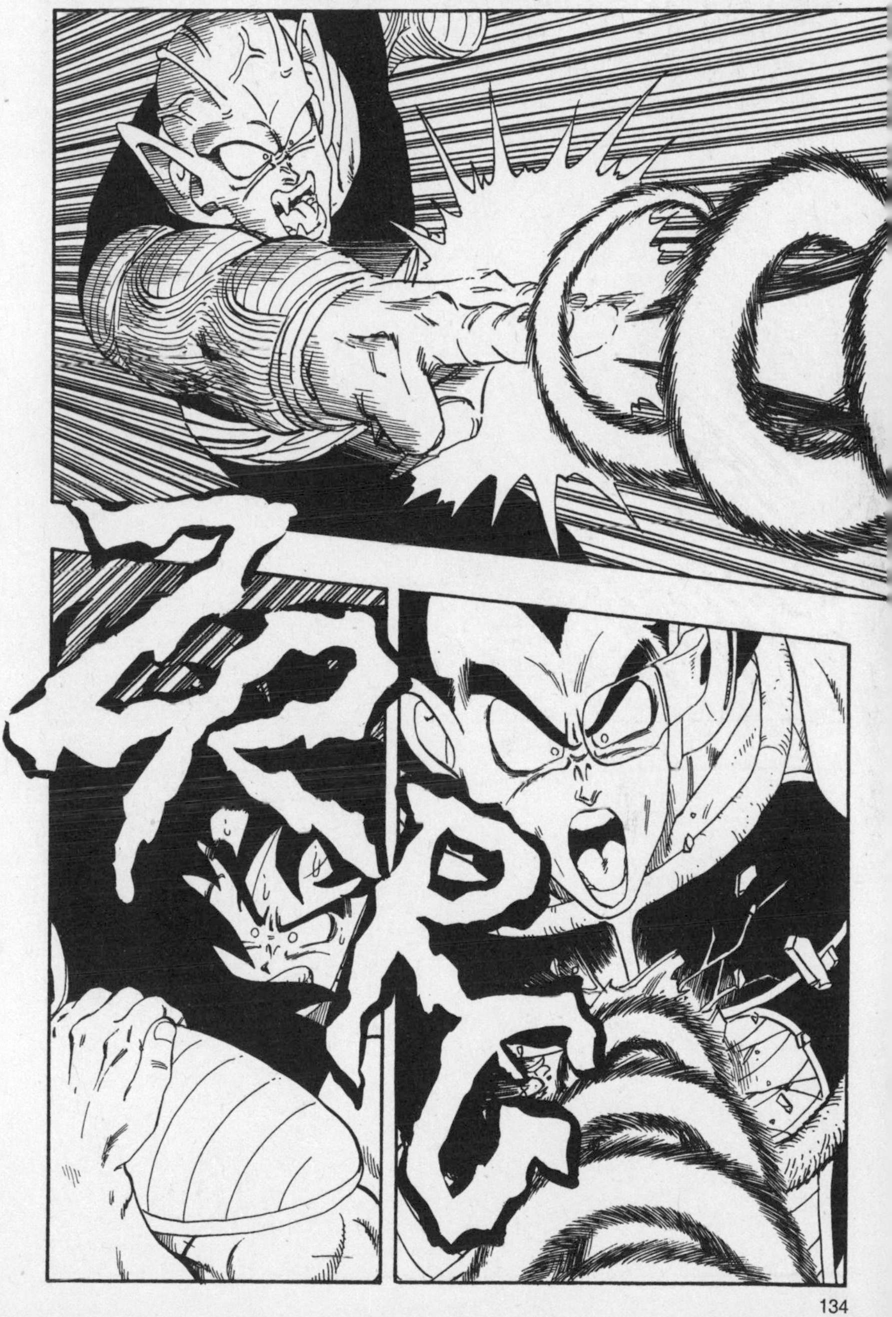

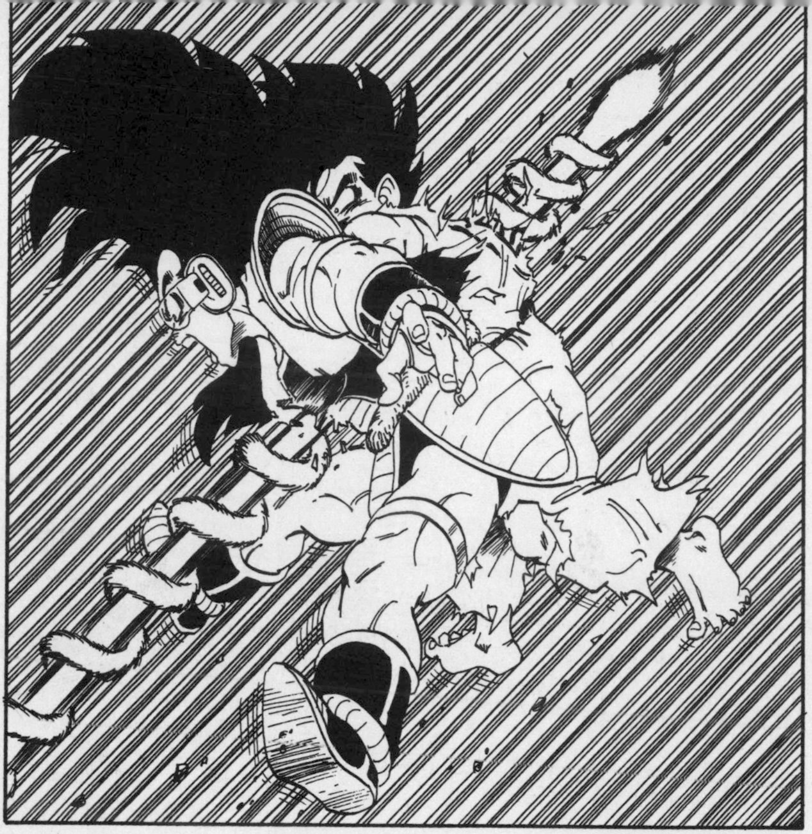

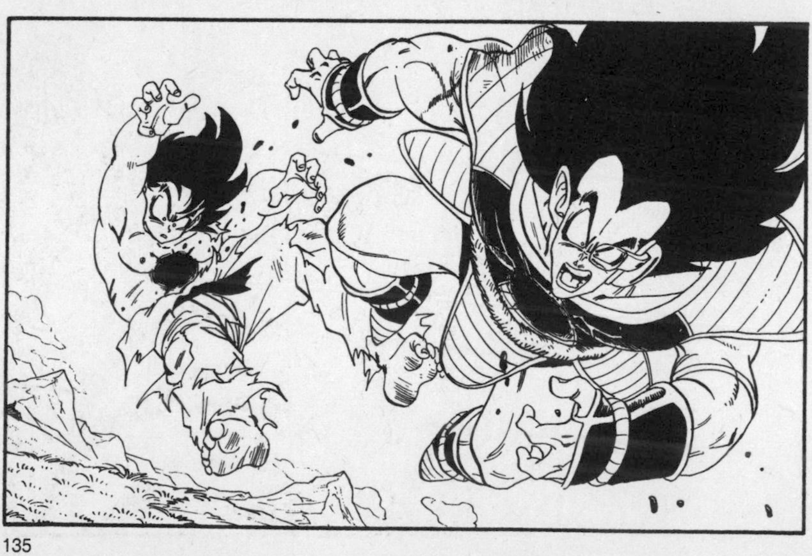

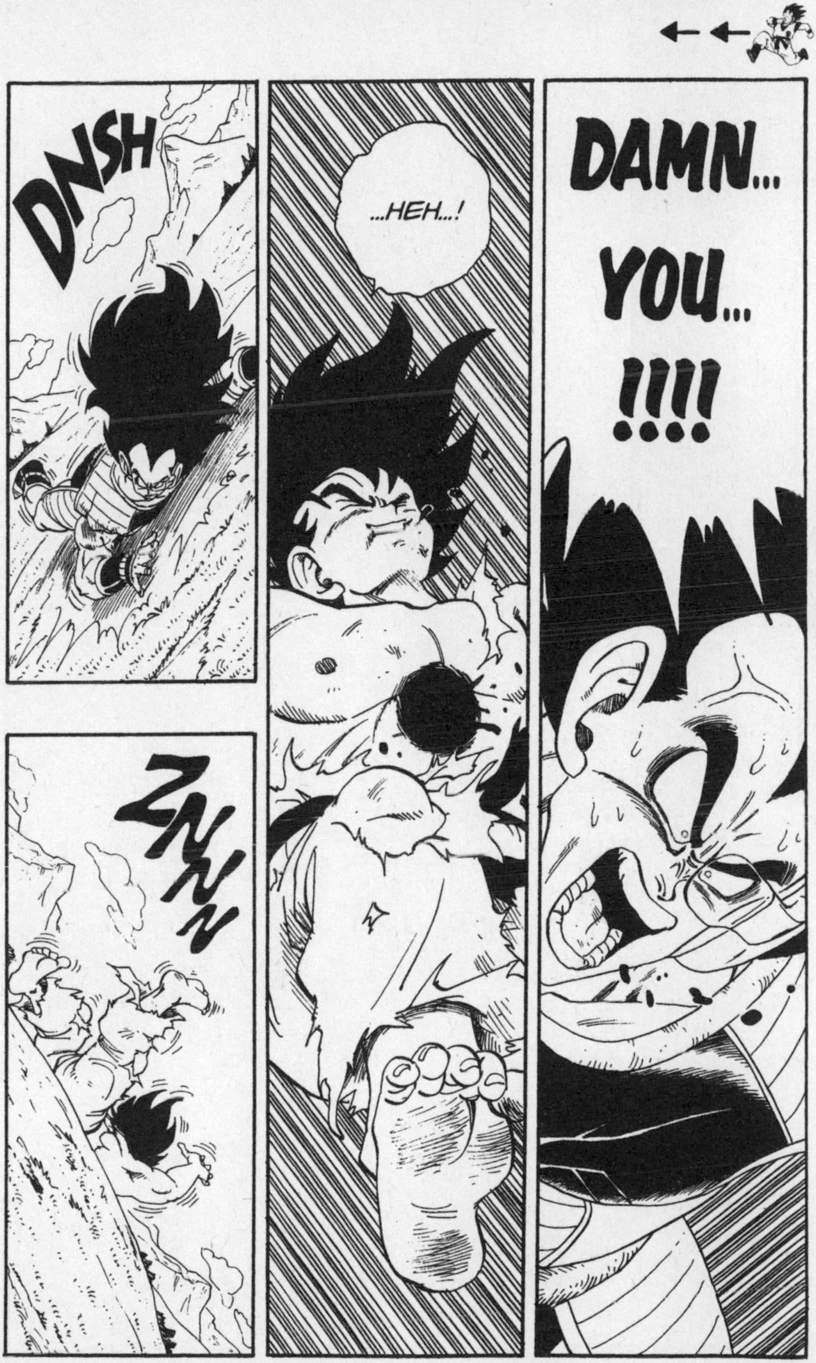
DAMN... YOU... !!!!
...HEH...!
DNSH
ZNNN

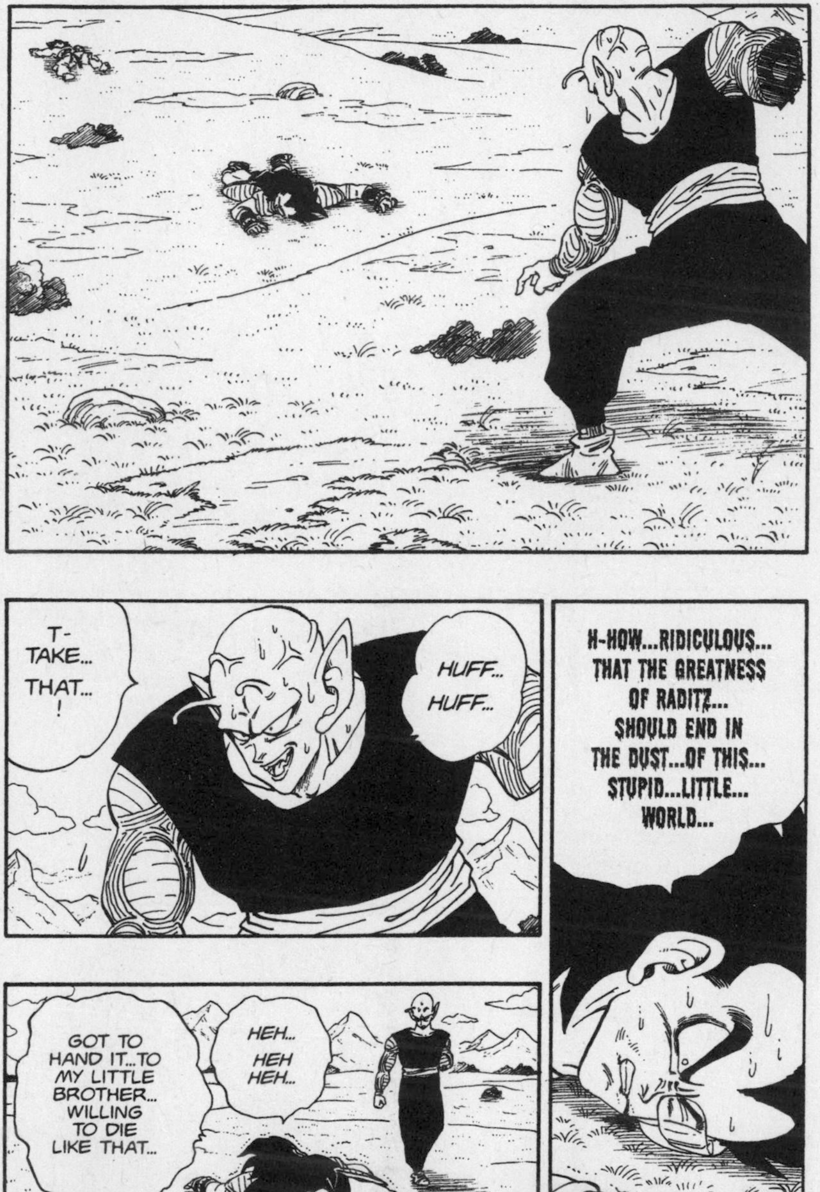
H-HOW...RIDICULOUS... THAT THE GREATNESS OF RADITZ... SHOULD END IN THE DUST...OF THIS... STUPID...LITTLE... WORLD...
HUFF... HUFF...
T- TAKE... THAT... !
HEH... HEH HEH...
GOT TO HAND IT...TO MY LITTLE BROTHER... WILLING TO DIE LIKE THAT...

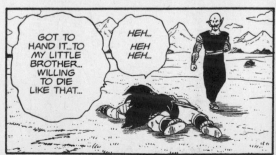

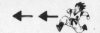

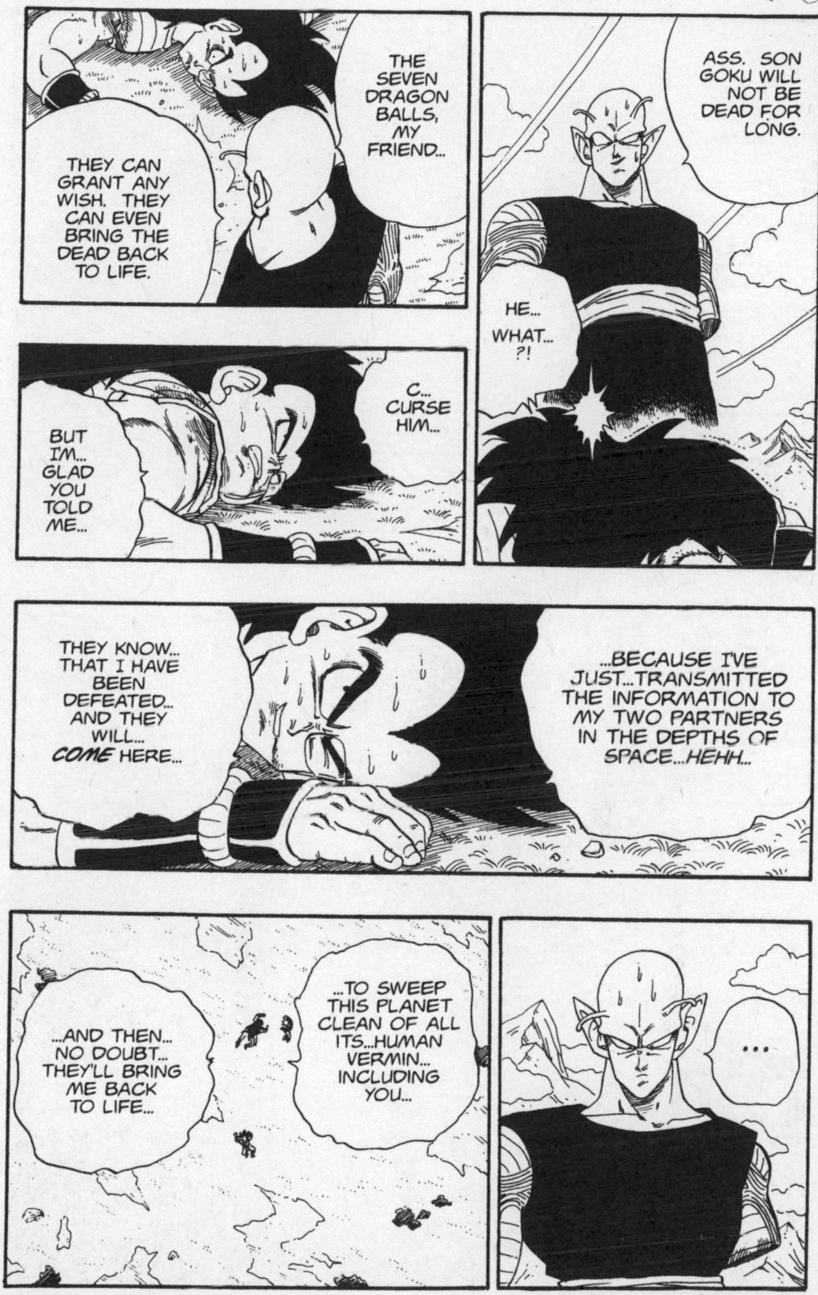
ASS. SON GOKU WILL NOT BE DEAD FOR LONG.
HE... WHAT... ?!
THE SEVEN DRAGON BALLS, MY FRIEND...
THEY CAN GRANT ANY WISH. THEY CAN EVEN BRING THE DEAD BACK TO LIFE.
C... CURSE HIM...
BUT I'M... GLAD YOU TOLD ME...
...BECAUSE I'VE JUST...TRANSMITTED THE INFORMATION TO MY TWO PARTNERS IN THE DEPTHS OF SPACE...HEHH...
THEY KNOW... THAT I HAVE BEEN DEFEATED... AND THEY WILL... COME HERE...
...
...TO SWEEP THIS PLANET CLEAN OF ALL ITS...HUMAN VERMIN... INCLUDING YOU...
...AND THEN... NO DOUBT... THEY'LL BRING ME BACK TO LIFE...

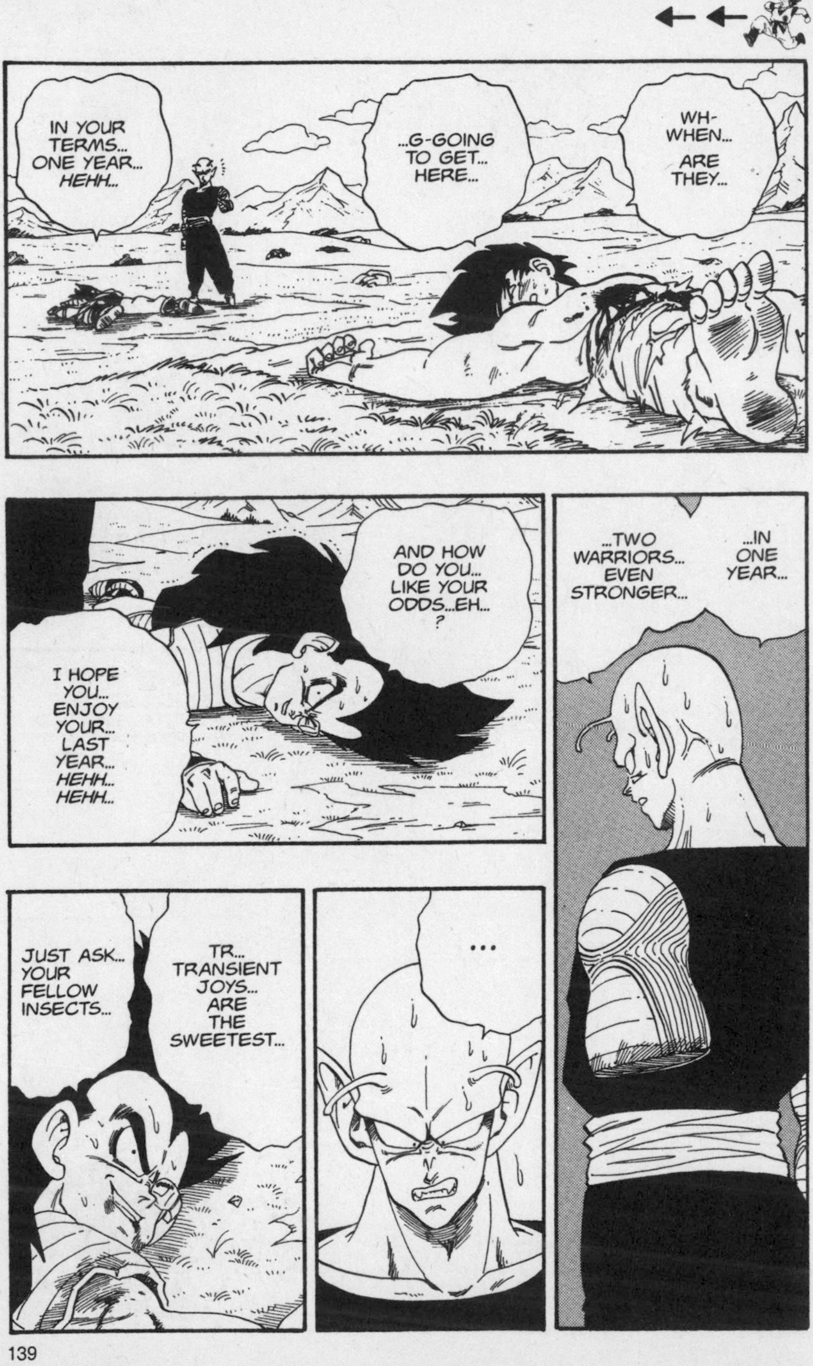
WH- WHEN... ARE THEY...
...G-GOING TO GET... HERE...
IN YOUR TERMS... ONE YEAR... HEHH...
...IN ONE YEAR...
...TWO WARRIORS... EVEN STRONGER...
AND HOW DO YOU... LIKE YOUR ODDS...EH... ?
I HOPE YOU... ENJOY YOUR... LAST YEAR... HEHH... HEHH...
...
TR... TRANSIENT JOYS... ARE THE SWEETEST...
JUST ASK... YOUR FELLOW INSECTS...

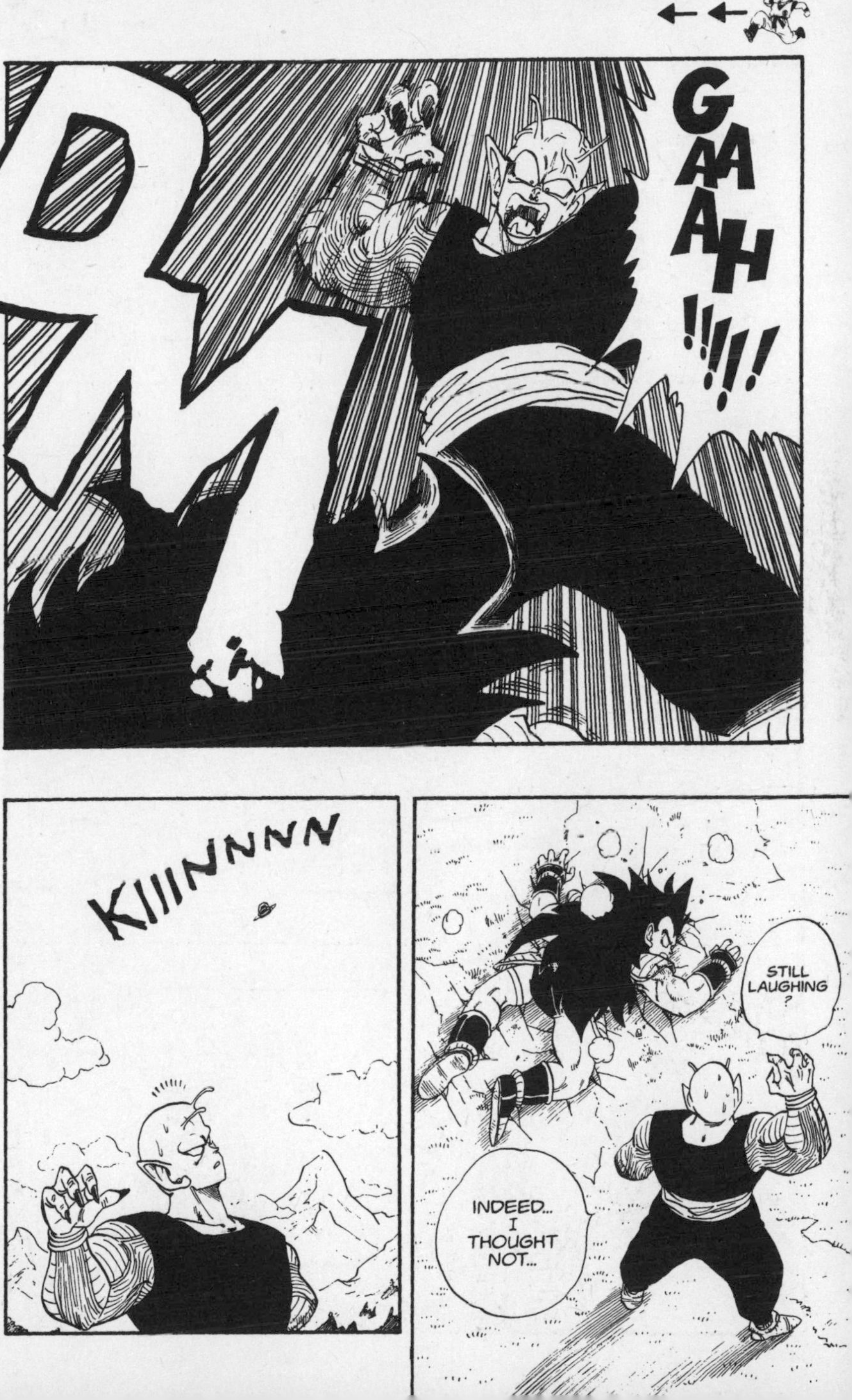
GAAAH!!!!!
STILL LAUGHING?
INDEED... I THOUGHT NOT...
KIIINNNN

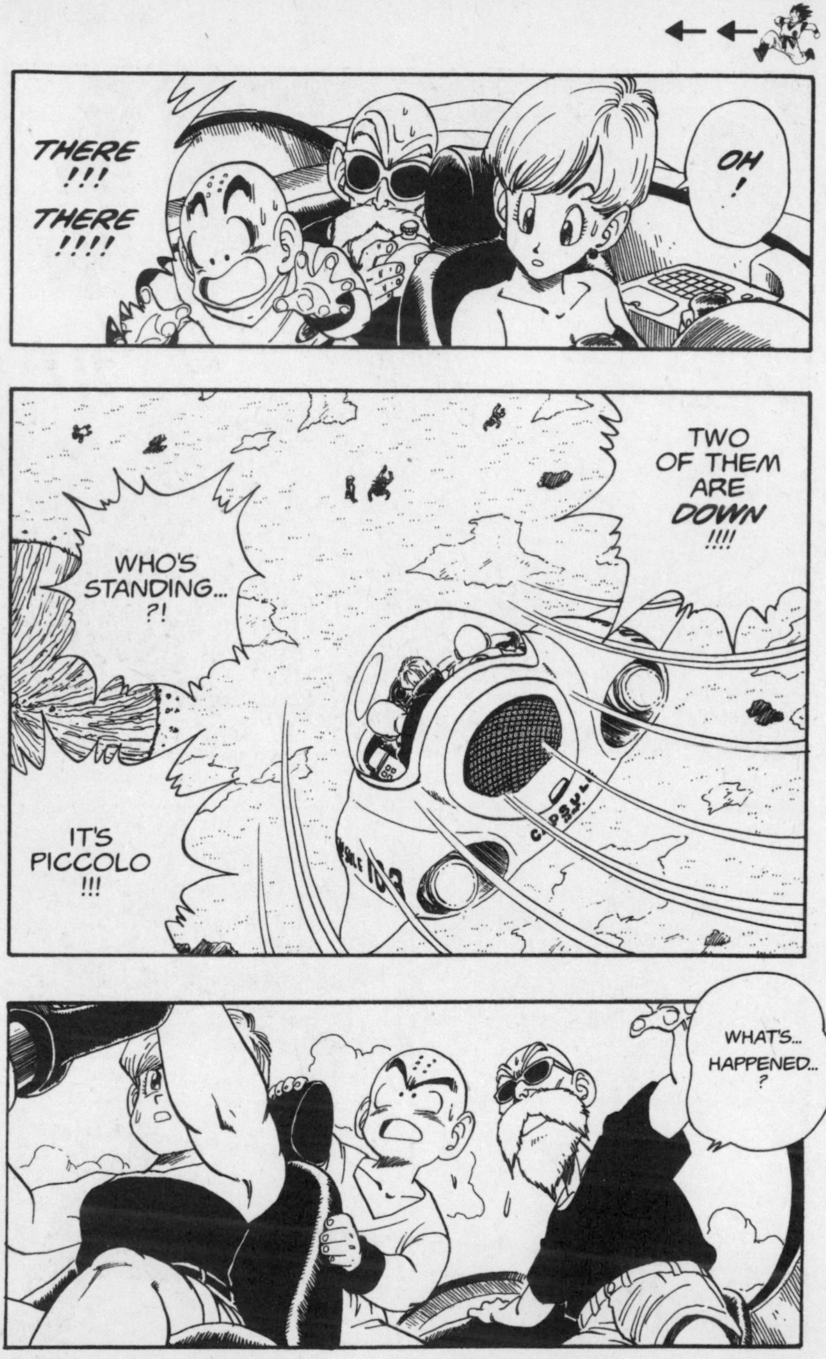
OH!
THERE!!! THERE!!!!
TWO OF THEM ARE DOWN!!!!
WHO'S STANDING...?!
IT'S PICCOLO!!!
WHAT'S... HAPPENED...?

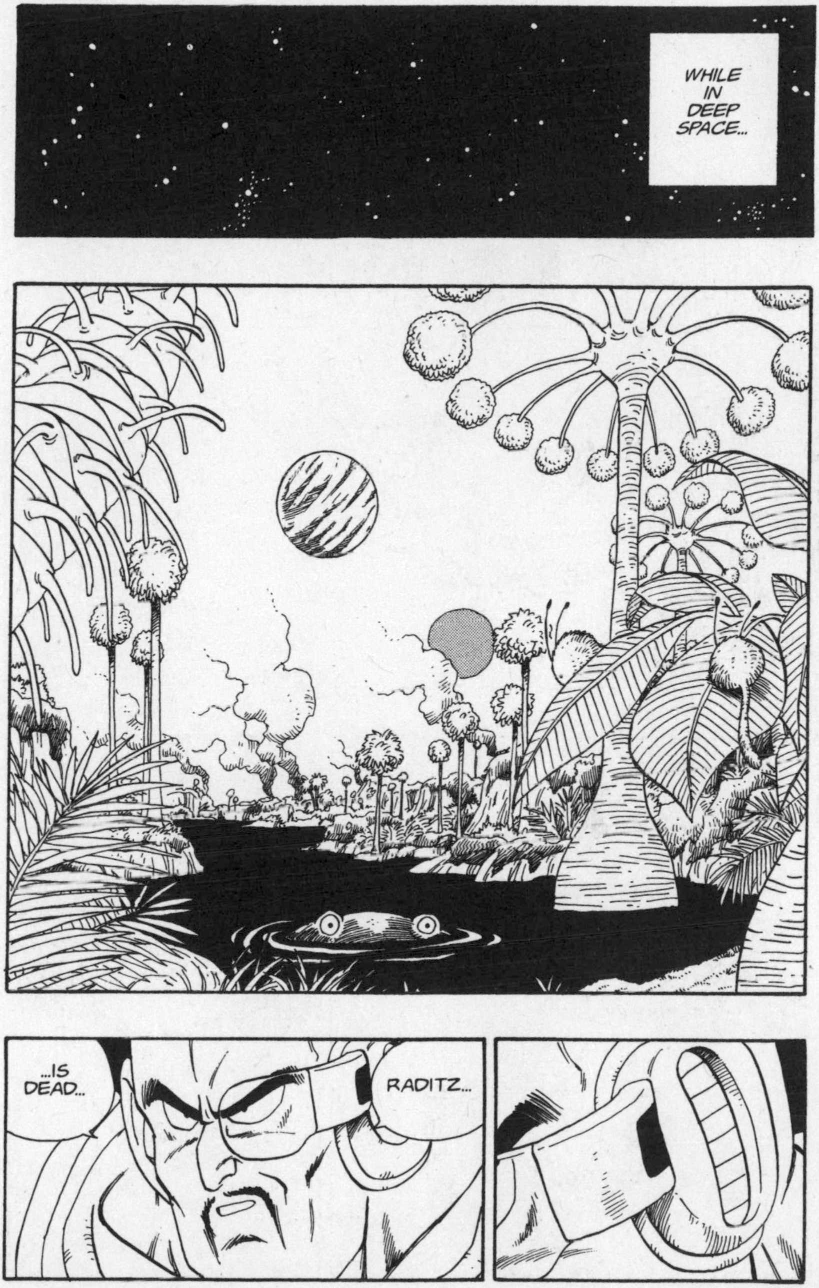
WHILE IN DEEP SPACE...
RADITZ...
...IS DEAD...

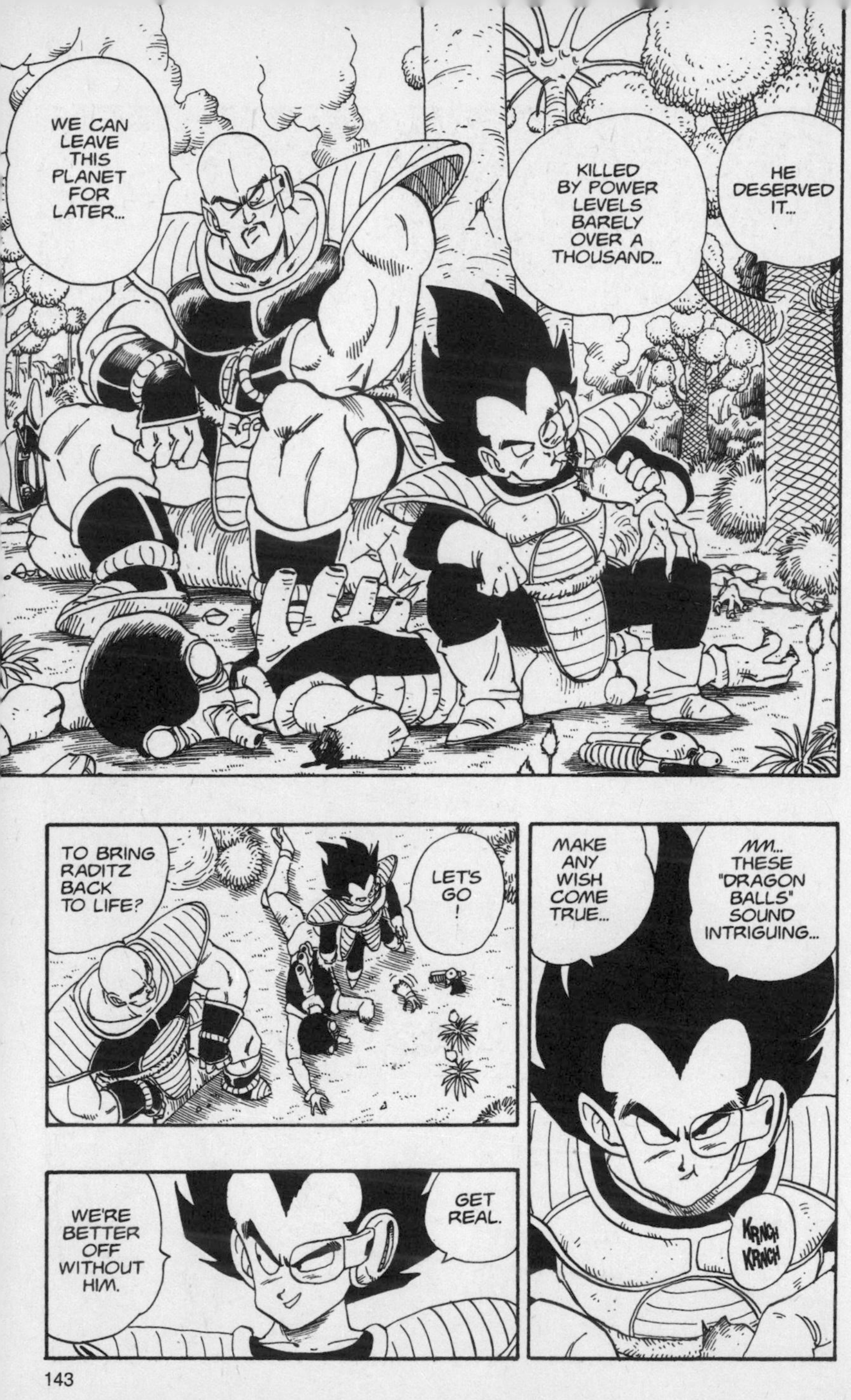
HE DESERVED IT...
KILLED BY POWER LEVELS BARELY OVER A THOUSAND...
WE CAN LEAVE THIS PLANET FOR LATER...
MM... THESE "DRAGON BALLS" SOUND INTRIGUING...
MAKE ANY WISH COME TRUE...
KRANCH KRANCH
LET'S GO!
TO BRING RADITZ BACK TO LIFE?
GET REAL.
WE'RE BETTER OFF WITHOUT HIM.

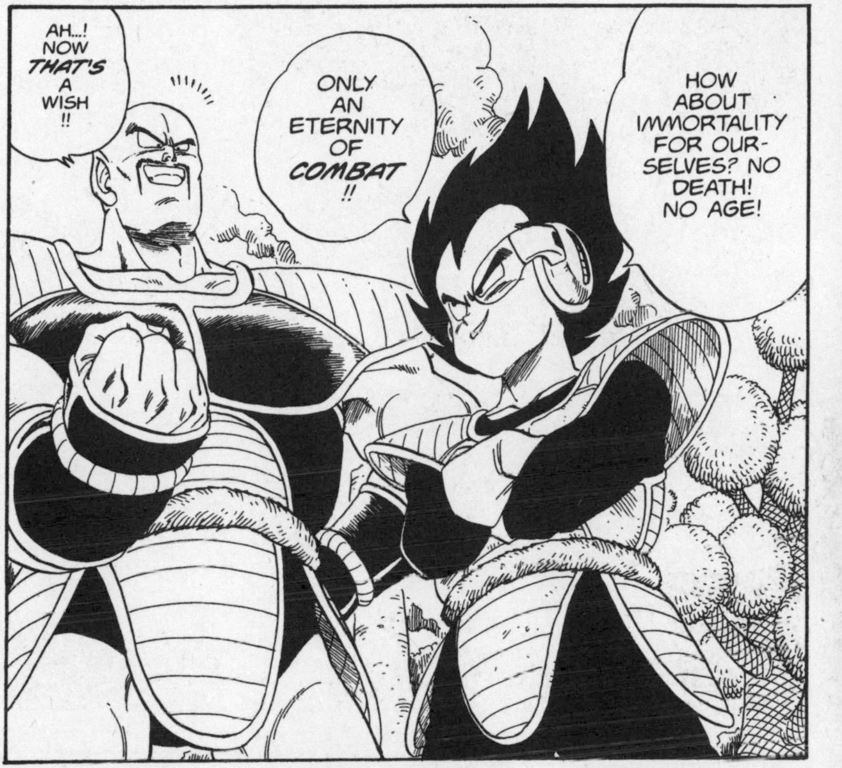
HOW ABOUT IMMORTALITY FOR OUR-SELVES? NO DEATH! NO AGE!
ONLY AN ETERNITY OF *COMBAT* !!
AH...! NOW *THAT'S* A WISH !!

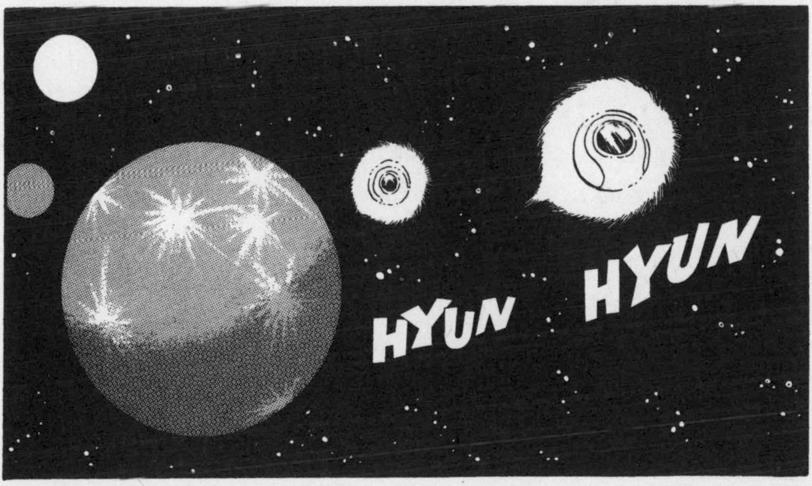
HYUN HYUN

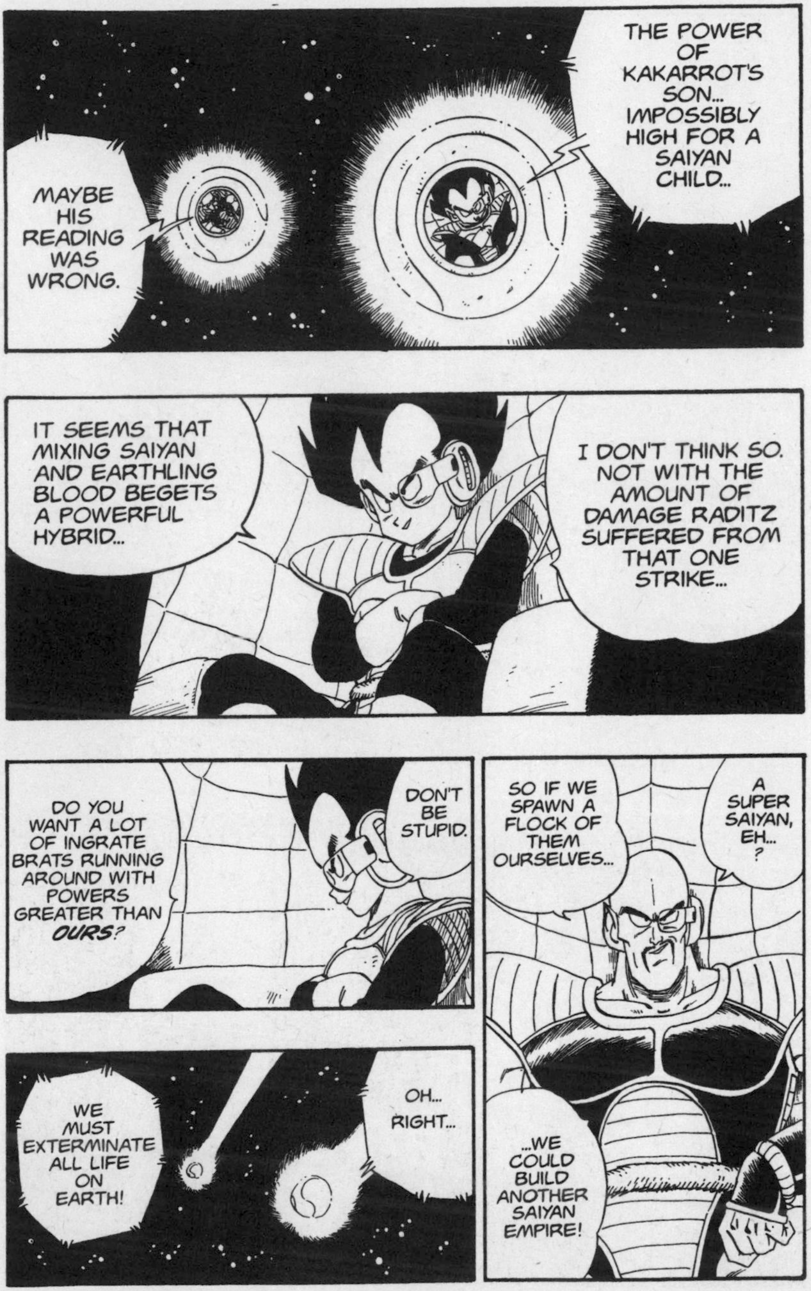
THE POWER OF KAKARROT'S SON... IMPOSSIBLY HIGH FOR A SAIYAN CHILD...
MAYBE HIS READING WAS WRONG.
I DON'T THINK SO. NOT WITH THE AMOUNT OF DAMAGE RADITZ SUFFERED FROM THAT ONE STRIKE...
IT SEEMS THAT MIXING SAIYAN AND EARTHLING BLOOD BEGETS A POWERFUL HYBRID...
A SUPER SAIYAN, EH...?
SO IF WE SPAWN A FLOCK OF THEM OURSELVES...
...WE COULD BUILD ANOTHER SAIYAN EMPIRE!
DON'T BE STUPID.
DO YOU WANT A LOT OF INGRATE BRATS RUNNING AROUND WITH POWERS GREATER THAN *OURS*?
OH... RIGHT...
WE MUST EXTERMINATE ALL LIFE ON EARTH!

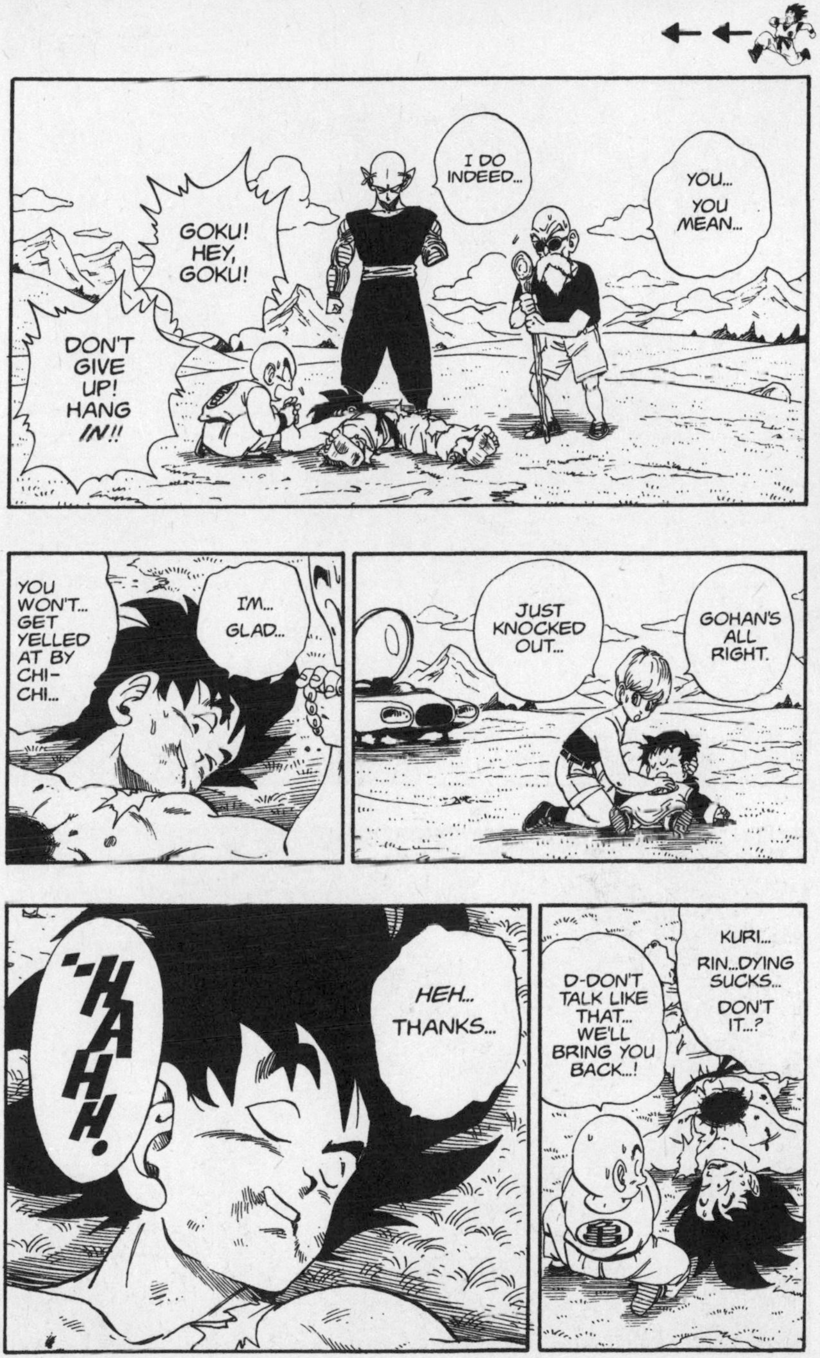
YOU... YOU MEAN...
I DO INDEED...
GOKU! HEY, GOKU!
DON'T GIVE UP! HANG *IN*!!
GOHAN'S ALL RIGHT.
JUST KNOCKED OUT...
I'M... GLAD...
YOU WON'T... GET YELLED AT BY CHI-CHI...
KURI... RIN...DYING SUCKS... DON'T IT...?
D-DON'T TALK LIKE THAT... WE'LL BRING YOU BACK...!
HEH... THANKS...
...HAHHH!

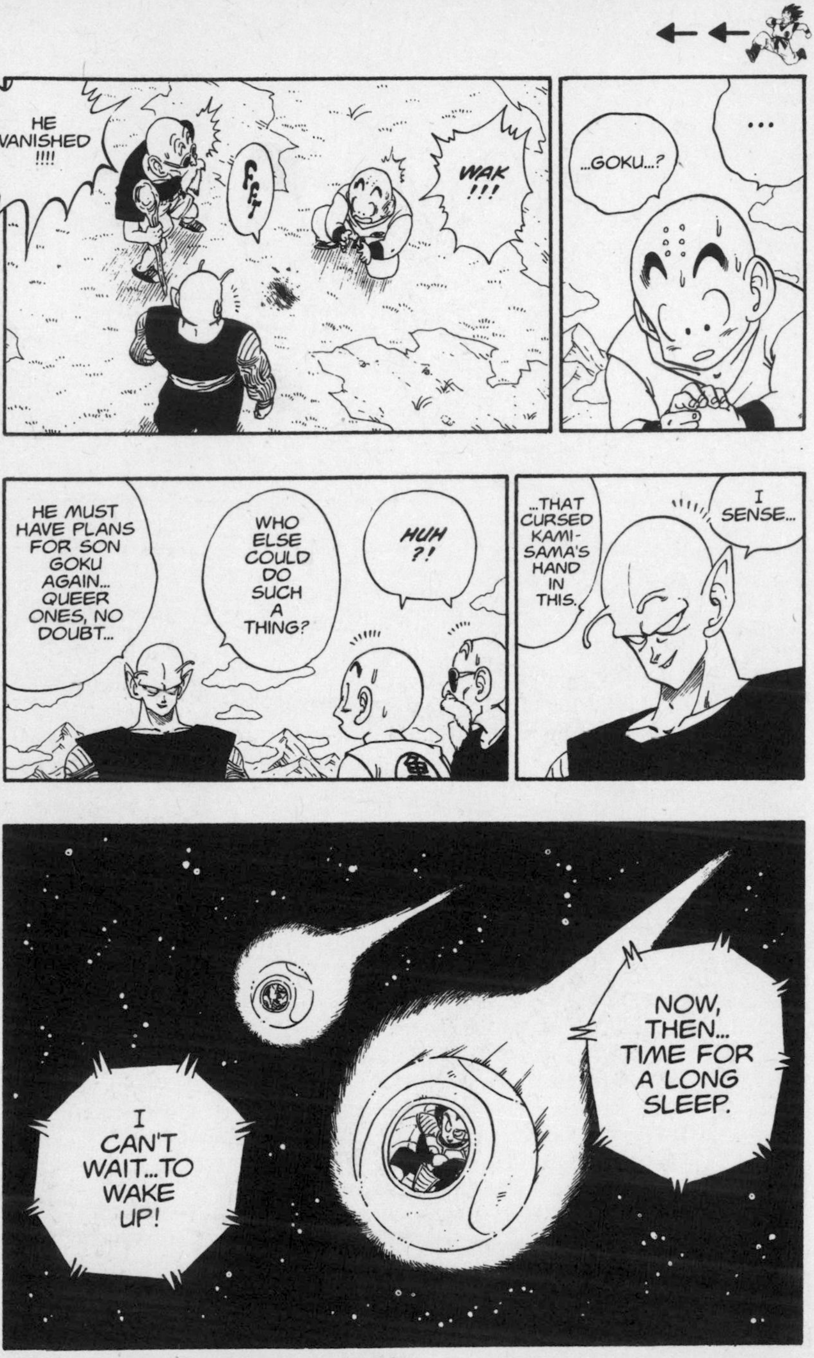
...
...GOKU...?
WAK !!!
HE VANISHED !!!!
FFT
I SENSE...
...THAT CURSED KAMI-SAMA'S HAND IN THIS.
HUH ?!
WHO ELSE COULD DO SUCH A THING?
HE MUST HAVE PLANS FOR SON GOKU AGAIN... QUEER ONES, NO DOUBT...
NOW, THEN... TIME FOR A LONG SLEEP.
I CAN'T WAIT...TO WAKE UP!

NEXT: WELCOME TO HELL!!

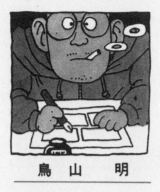

鳥　山　明

Most of the time, when my assistants aren't around, I work in a TV room while sitting at the *kotatsu* (a low table with an electric heater underneath and a comforter around the sides to keep in the warmth). Part of the reason is that I just can't get comfortable at a desk and chair. Also, it's kind of lonely working without the TV or a video on. But it's important not to get distracted by the TV and stop drawing. While I'm working, I always try to act like I'm not paying any attention to it. I'm such a good boy!
    —Akira Toriyama, 1989

Artist/writer Akira Toriyama burst onto the manga scene in 1980 with the wildly popular **Dr. Slump**, a science fiction comedy about the adventures of a mad scientist and his android "daughter." In 1984 he created his hit series **Dragon Ball**, which ran until 1995 in Shueisha's best-selling magazine **Weekly Shonen Jump**, and was translated into foreign languages around the world. Since **Dragon Ball**, he has worked on a variety of short series, including **Cowa!, Kajika, SandLand**, and **Neko Majin**, as well as a children's book, **Toccio the Angel**. He is also known for his design work on video games, particularly the **Dragon Warrior** RPG series. He lives with his family in Japan.

DRAGON BALL Z VOL. 1
SHONEN JUMP Manga Edition

This manga is number 17 in a series of 42.

STORY AND ART BY
AKIRA TORIYAMA

English Adaptation/Gerard Jones
Translation/Lillian Olsen
Touch-Up Art & Lettering/Wayne Truman
Initial Cover Design/Izumi Evers
Final Cover & Graphic Design/Sean Lee
Original Editor/Trish Ledoux
Senior Editor/Jason Thompson

In the original Japanese edition, DRAGON BALL and DRAGON BALL
Z are known collectively as the 42-volume series DRAGON BALL. The
English DRAGON BALL Z was originally volumes 17-42 of the
Japanese DRAGON BALL.

Printed in the U.S.A.

Published by VIZ Media, LLC
P.O. Box 77010
San Francisco, CA 94107

15
First printing, March 2003
Fifteenth printing, March 2016

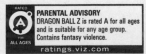
PARENTAL ADVISORY
DRAGON BALL Z is rated A for all ages
and is suitable for any age group.
Contains fantasy violence.
ratings.viz.com

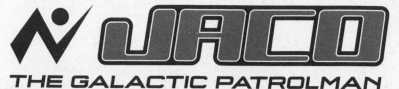
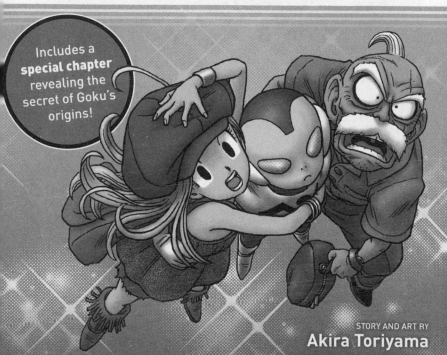
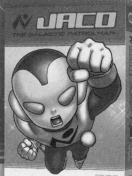

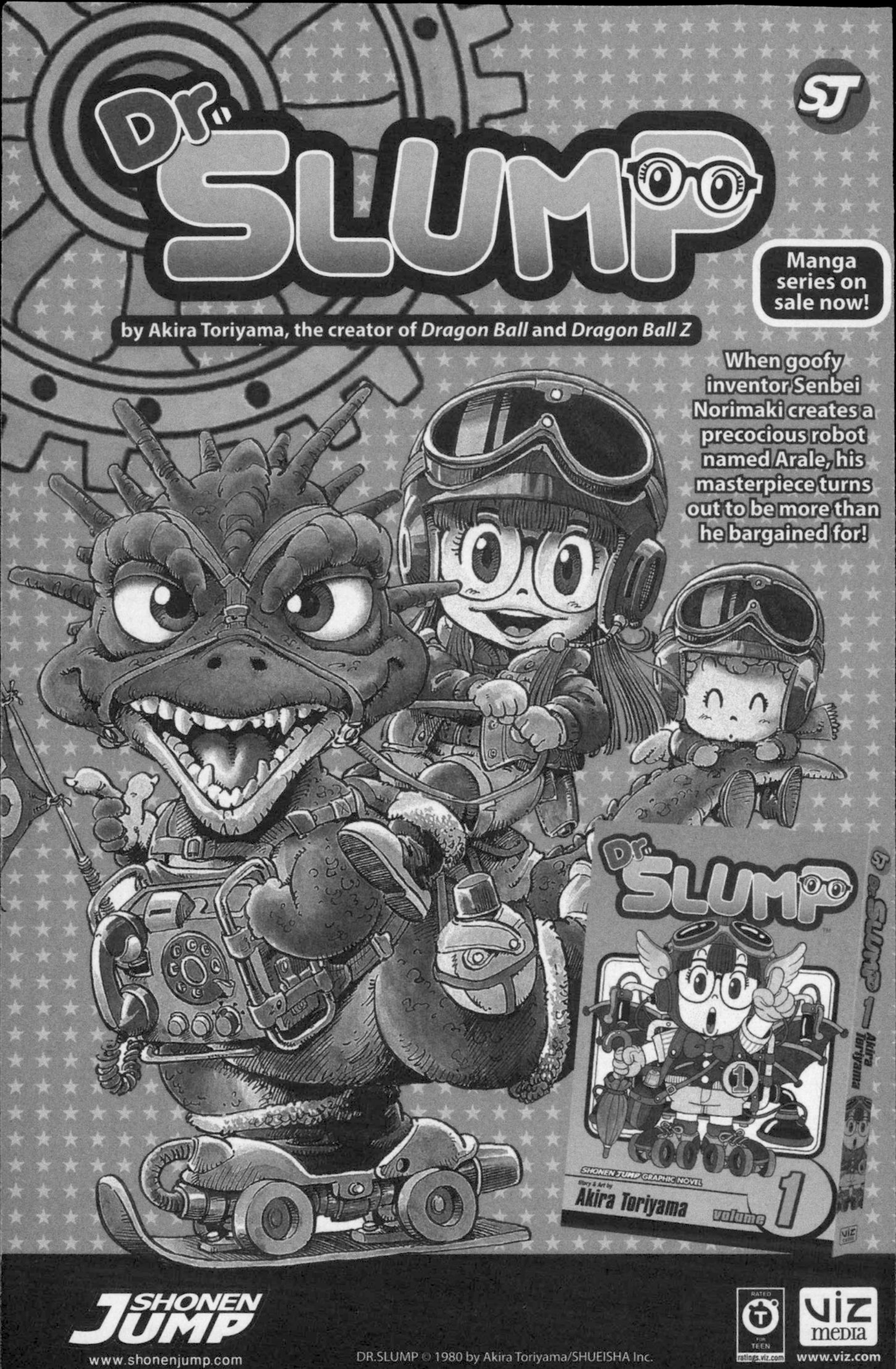
Dr. SLUMP
SJ
Manga series on sale now!
by Akira Toriyama, the creator of *Dragon Ball* and *Dragon Ball Z*
When goofy inventor Senbei Norimaki creates a precocious robot named Arale, his masterpiece turns out to be more than he bargained for!
Dr. SLUMP
SHONEN JUMP GRAPHIC NOVEL
Akira Toriyama
volume 1
SHONEN JUMP
www.shonenjump.com
DR.SLUMP © 1980 by Akira Toriyama/SHUEISHA Inc.
RATED T FOR TEEN
VIZ MEDIA
www.viz.com

You're Reading in the Wrong Direction!!

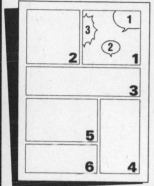

Whoops! Guess what? You're starting at the wrong end of the comic!

…It's true! In keeping with the original Japanese format, Akira Toriyama's world-famous **Dragon Ball Z** series is meant to be read from right to left, starting in the upper-right corner.

Unlike English, which is read from left to right, Japanese is read from right to left, meaning that action, sound effects and word-balloon order are completely reversed…something which can make readers unfamiliar with Japanese feel pretty backwards themselves.

For this reason, manga or Japanese comics published in the U.S. in English have traditionally been published "flopped"—that is, printed in exact reverse order, as though seen from the other side of a mirror.

By flopping pages, U.S. publishers can avoid confusing readers, but the compromise is not without its downside. For one thing, a character in a flopped manga series who once wore in the original Japanese version a T-shirt emblazoned with "M A Y" (as in "the merry month of") now wears one which reads "Y A M"! Additionally, many manga creators in Japan are themselves unhappy with the process, as some feel the mirror-imaging of their art reveals otherwise unnoticeable flaws or skews in perspective.

In recognition of the importance and popularity of **Dragon Ball Z**, we are proud to bring it to you in the original unflopped format.

For now, though, turn to the other side of the book and let the adventure begin…!

—Editor

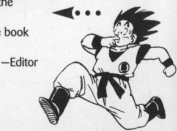